ON MY HONOR

ON MY HONOR

*The Secret History of the
Boy Scouts of America*

KIM CHRISTENSEN

GRAND
CENTRAL

New York Boston

Grand Central Publishing
Hachette Book Group
1290 Avenue of the Americas, New York, NY 10104
grandcentralpublishing.com
@grandcentralpub

First Edition: February 2025

Grand Central Publishing is a division of Hachette Book Group, Inc. The Grand Central Publishing name and logo is a registered trademark of Hachette Book Group, Inc.

The publisher is not responsible for websites (or their content) that are not owned by the publisher.

The Hachette Speakers Bureau provides a wide range of authors for speaking events. To find out more, go to hachettespeakersbureau.com or email HachetteSpeakers@hbgusa.com.

Grand Central Publishing books may be purchased in bulk for business, educational, or promotional use. For information, please contact your local bookseller or the Hachette Book Group Special Markets Department at special.markets@hbgusa.com.

Print book interior design by Marie Mundaca

Library of Congress Cataloging-in-Publication Data has been applied for.

ISBNs: 9781538726730 (hardcover), 9781538726754 (ebook)

Printed in the United States of America

LSC-C

Printing 1, 2024

For Christina

On my honor, I will do my best
To do my duty, to God and my country,
*   and to obey the Scout Law;*
To help other people at all times;
To keep myself physically
*   strong, mentally awake,*
*   and morally straight.*

—Boy Scout Oath

CONTENTS

ON MY HONOR

A KNOCK AT THE DOOR

It's September 12, 2012, and I'm standing on the front porch of a tidy duplex in Newport, Pennsylvania, a small working-class town on the Juniata River about twenty-five miles upstream from Harrisburg. I'm hoping to meet Carl Maxwell, Jr. In 1976, Carl and four of his friends in Troop 222 accused their scoutmaster, Rodger L. Beatty, of sexually assaulting them. I've been trying to reach Carl for a series of stories a *Los Angeles Times* colleague and I are writing about sexual abuse in the Boy Scouts of America (BSA).

When I knock on the door, I'm greeted by a man in a baseball cap who appears to be about the right age and looks a lot like the Newport High School senior photo I saw a couple of hours earlier. The beaming smile is gone, but at five feet five, he still has the compact build of the kid in Gymnastics Club in 1981. I ask if he is Carl Maxwell and tell him I'd like to talk with him about Rodger Beatty. He looks at me a little quizzically, weighing his response.

"I am Carl Maxwell," he says. "And I would like to talk to you about Rodger Beatty." We sit at the kitchen table, and over the next two and a half hours he describes, in chillingly vivid detail, the childhood events that have shaped his adult life. "It is so old," he says, "but it is so fresh."

MY JOURNEY TO CARL Maxwell's front door began more than a year earlier, when fellow reporter Jason Felch and I had set out to write a single story about Canadian scoutmaster Richard Turley, who had molested a dozen boys on both sides of the border. We soon found ourselves peering into a Pandora's box of sexual abuse involving thousands of Boy Scouts victimized by their leaders and betrayed by the nation's preeminent youth group, a tax-exempt organization whose assets in recent years have exceeded $1 billion. Since its founding in 1910, the BSA has spent more than a century espousing self-reliance, honor, and patriotism as it set a course to manhood for more than 100 million boys who pledged to serve God and country and help others along the way.

Over the course of a year, we analyzed 1,900 of the BSA's more than 5,000 Ineligible Volunteer files, a closely held blacklist intended to keep suspected sexual predators out of the ranks. Known within Scouting as the "perversion files," the records detail striking patterns of sexual abuse by troop leaders and volunteers. They also reveal a disturbing history of inaction, complicity, and cover-up by local and national Boy Scouts officials and a long-standing institutional penchant for secrecy.

One particularly egregious case involved Newport's Troop 222 and Scoutmaster Rodger Beatty. For months the Scouts in his troop had been too scared to tell anyone what was happening to them—until Carl, the smallest and youngest of the group at age thirteen, convinced the others to come forward. It was all they could do to summon the courage to tell their parents, who in turn told local Scout leaders, who had the boys come in and spell out the terrible details of their shared secret.

One by one, the five boys sat with pen and paper at a table in a church basement, watched over by a couple of Scouts officials. Carl and the others detailed their experiences with Beatty, who had shuttled them to special events such as the Klondike Derby and taught them how to drive a stick shift, even though they were all just thirteen or fourteen years old. He had taken them camping and invited them to his home, where they had played board games, watched TV, and slept on mattresses spread out on his living room floor. It was what he had done to the boys, at his home and on those campouts, that now spilled onto the pages.

Carl and his pals had been traumatized, but now they had done something about it. They'd given their Scout leaders what they needed to right an awful wrong and hold Beatty to account. Instead, the officials thanked the boys for their candor and sent them home. Then they forwarded their statements to BSA headquarters in North Brunswick, New Jersey, where men at the very top of the organization did what they had done with hundreds of similarly heinous accounts of child sexual abuse for decades: they stuck them into a metal file cabinet and locked it.

This case intrigued me because even a cursory internet search showed that Beatty, who in 1976 was a twenty-nine-year-old social worker, had gone on to enjoy great success and respect in academia and in public health circles after the Boy Scouts had let him resign from Troop 222 and quietly slip out of town right afterward. I wondered if the kids he'd abused had fared as well.

As Carl walks me through the traumatic events of his childhood, reciting nearly verbatim the contents of Beatty's perversion file, which he has not seen, it becomes clear that he has traveled a much rougher road. Horrible as it was, his experience was hardly unique.

Even as the Boy Scouts of America burnished and fiercely protected its finely crafted public image as a beacon of virtue and a maker of men, the youth group trusted by generations of boys and their families failed them by the thousands. Countless men who were abused as Scouts were scarred for life. Many were left feeling ashamed or responsible for what had happened. Too embarrassed or afraid to tell their parents at the time, they suffered in silence into adulthood, fighting to contain the rage and guilt evoked by memories that clash with the Boy Scouts' storied history and its Norman Rockwell imagery of hiking and telling tall tales around campfires.

THIS BOOK AIMS TO disentangle mythology from reality as it traces the rise and fall of the Boy Scouts of America. It connects the dots among key events, including a landmark Supreme Court decision, a pivotal sexual abuse civil trial, the public disclosure of the perversion files, and a protracted and costly bankruptcy with eighty-two thousand sexual abuse survivors filing claims, eight times the number of victims as in the Catholic Church's abuse scandal two decades earlier. It is a sprawling story of the BSA's institutional power, political clout, and religious fervor that spans more than a century, from its roots in British war hero Robert S. S. Baden-Powell's world Scouting movement to its baby boom heyday in the early 1970s to its precarious perch on the brink of financial calamity.

Championed from the start by US presidents and nurtured by the nation's most powerful politicians and religious institutions, wealthy industrialists, civic leaders, and social elites, Scouting has been a cultural force for 114 years, helping to shape the very notions of American boyhood and masculinity. It has also failed, at times spectacularly, to live up to the high standards it set for millions of boys who pointed three fingers skyward, took the Scout Oath, and promised to always help others and keep themselves "physically strong, mentally awake, and morally straight."

Today, the Boy Scouts of America is struggling to clear its name and regain its cultural and financial footing. After being swept into bankruptcy by an avalanche of sexual abuse claims that had taken root in the dark, this American institution, which amassed great power and then greatly abused it, is now on the precipice of losing it forever.

—*Kim Christensen, April 2024*

PART I

—

THE RISE

A Scout is trustworthy, loyal, helpful,
friendly, courteous, kind, obedient, cheerful,
thrifty, brave, clean, and reverent.

—*Boy Scout Law*

CHAPTER I

FEUDING FOUNDERS AND THE BOY PROBLEM

A few weeks after he left the White House in March 1909, Theodore Roosevelt sailed to Africa on a wildlife expedition to collect specimens for the Smithsonian Institution's new Natural History Museum. With the industrialist Andrew Carnegie picking up the tab, the twenty-sixth president of the United States and his nineteen-year-old son, Kermit, bagged thousands of fish, birds, and reptiles. They also shot 512 mammals doomed to be stuffed and displayed, including 29 zebras, 17 lions, 12 elephants, nine giraffes, eight hippos, an assortment of wildebeests and bushbucks, and a jackal or two.[1]

Roosevelt, the swaggering Spanish-American War hero who embodied his era's notions of rugged individualism and American manliness, chronicled the trip in a series of widely read dispatches in *Scribner's Magazine*. Billed not as a big-game killing spree but rather a scientific conservation project, the safari to British East Africa, the Belgian Congo, and Sudan also was a public relations bonanza for Roosevelt, a detail not lost on William Dickson Boyce, the wealthy publisher of the weekly *Saturday Blade* and *Chicago Ledger* newspapers.[2]

Seeking to boost his papers' already robust readership, Boyce made plans for his own African safari but endeavored to one-up the popular ex-president. Instead of shipping home a Noah's Ark of lifeless critters, he would hire someone to shoot his quarry with a camera: a photographer floating above the wilds in a tethered balloon. A multimillionaire former schoolteacher and coal miner with a lifelong love of the outdoors, Boyce would finance and lead the expedition, hiring the photographer George R. Lawrence to capture it on film. Lawrence had sold him on the idea with eye-popping photos of the Rocky Mountains he'd shot from a balloon, convincing Boyce that such a lofty vantage point would allow him to be "as silent as a cloud" while sneaking up on the great beasts of the veldt. Time was of the essence, Lawrence insisted, because Americans' interest in African wildlife was sure to wane once Teddy Roosevelt returned to the United States. Boyce was on board.[3]

On his way to Africa in July 1909, Boyce took up temporary residence at the posh Waldorf-Astoria in New York.[4] Working from the hotel's telegraph office, he fired off daily instructions and promotional ideas to Charles Hughes, a Chicago *Record-Herald* baseball writer he had hired to handle logistics and publicity. Boyce also sent a flurry of cables pitching his "African Balloonograph Expedition" to British newspaper editors, who agreed to buy his photos, sight unseen. "Pictures will live when hides will rot," he said, after landing a contract with the London *Daily Mirror*.[5]

Fifty-one and recently divorced, Boyce mapped out his trip, hired key people, and then headed to London to complete the arrangements. Until then, his interest in America's youth had been confined mostly to the legion of newsboys who peddled his papers throughout the Midwest, pocketing two cents for every copy sold for a nickel.[6] While in London, Boyce stumbled onto the idea for the Boy Scouts of America. As the arguably apocryphal story goes, he left the luxury of the Savoy Hotel one day, wandered into the city's famous fog, and got so deep in the soup that he couldn't find his way across the street.

"A little lad of twelve noticed my futile efforts, and led me with a lantern in the right direction," he recalled. "I thanked him and offered him a penny. But he said: 'Thank you, sir, but I am a Boy Scout, and we never take tips for doing kind acts.'...Then he told me that all Boy Scouts were in honor bound to do one kind act every day."[7]

Boyce's encounter with the unselfish Scout got him thinking about how such a youth group might work in the United States. He visited the London office of Robert Baden-Powell, a British war hero and the founder of the world Scouting movement. He left with a bundle of written materials, including a copy of Baden-Powell's book *Scouting for Boys*, and purportedly digested it all while putting together plans for his American version of the Boy Scouts. But his most immediate concern was his expedition, which continued to grow in size as it took shape.

A train carried Boyce, his hired help, and all of their gear to Nairobi, which would serve as the launching point for what was billed as the largest safari ever to set out from the Kenyan capi-tal. In late September 1909, local residents gathered to watch the American publisher and four hundred members of his party pre-pare to head out for the bush and Lake Victoria, some 235 miles away. Hundreds of Black porters and sixty-four oxen in teams of sixteen would lug twenty-eight thousand pounds of equipment and supplies, including cameras, kites, collapsible towers, and two silk balloons to be carried aloft by hydrogen gas produced by mix-ing sulfuric acid and iron scraps and filings.[8] Before setting out, Lawrence gassed up the balloons and entertained the crowd with demonstrations of their airworthiness. When the expedition got under way a couple of days later, Boyce and the other eight white men on the trip were attended by three servants each, including a gun bearer, a horse handler, and a "tent boy" to draw their morning baths. Tea was served promptly each afternoon at four.[9]

All was going swimmingly, it seemed. Then it all went bust.

Lawrence had forgotten to bring telephoto lenses for his cameras and then ran into a slew of other equipment problems and complications, some apparently of his own making. He would complain that the conditions for his aerial photography were too hot or too windy or not windy enough. Boyce grew ever more irritated and would later grumble that Lawrence "uses up a good deal of time telling what he is going to do, and then about the same amount of time explaining why he failed."[10] In the end, he wound up with almost nothing on film, save for a posed shot of two baby ostriches raised by a local farmer.[11]

Things got so bad that Boyce first took his name off the expedition's stationery and then declared the entire venture a failure and went elephant hunting. He returned to Chicago after bagging two huge pachyderms, including a mammoth bull with seventy-pound tusks. But even that feat was clouded by controversy when his hunting guide claimed to have shot the elephant himself—to save Boyce from being trampled by it.[12] Not all was lost, however. Back home in the Windy City, Boyce found a silver lining to his much publicized if ultimately failed expedition: "We increased the circulation of *The Blade* 300,000 copies per issue."[13]

The details and the timing of Boyce's encounter with the English Scout changed with various newspaper accounts and other retellings of the story, including the publisher's own evolving versions. Skeptics suspected that he had concocted the brief but consequential, fog-shrouded exchange. Handed down for generations as the "Legend of the Unknown Scout," it has been alternately embellished and debunked, its every detail parsed, including whether London was even socked in during Boyce's time there. David C. Scott, who coauthored a 2010 book[14] about the founding of the BSA, initially thought that Boyce had "conjured up the story as a public relations device" to distract from his empty-handed return from the much ballyhooed safari. He later dug deeper, however, studying daily weather logs from 1909 and combing through Baden-Powell's appointment diaries and other records. He concluded that Boyce had likely elaborated on some details but was mostly telling the truth after all.[15]

This much is known: shortly after his return stateside, Boyce incorporated the Boy Scouts of America in the District of Columbia on February 8, 1910, with a vision to "make men" and "teach them patriotism, obedience, courage, courtesy and cheerfulness."[16] At the time, he had no way of predicting the immense cultural influence and political clout his embryonic brotherhood of boys would wield in the coming decades.

EARLY-TWENTIETH-CENTURY AMERICA WAS CHANGING dramatically, as more and more people moved from the farm to the city,[17] and the country shifted from agrarian society to industrial powerhouse. Newly formed corporations devoured or crushed family businesses and smaller manufacturers, while the founders of such commercial giants as U.S. Steel, Standard Oil, and the Ford Motor Company grew wealthy beyond imagination. Railroads linked the coasts and spider-webbed across the heartland, revolutionizing travel and the transportation of goods, hastening the settlement of the Wild West and the end of the frontier expansionism that for decades had fed a culture of rugged individualism. In the East, big cities bustled and strained with a flood of European immigrants and recent arrivals from rural America, all hoping to better their lots in a country that was trading horse-drawn buggies for Model Ts.[18]

From that swirl of events emerged the "boy problem": what to do with a population whose members had once toiled in the fields or worked the mines.[19] Boys were now perceived as going

soft, deprived of the benefits of physical labor and the great outdoors, spoiled by their mothers and schoolteachers. Lacking in
useful skills, they were viewed as bereft of character and manliness, reduced to ineffectual "mollycoddles" and "sissies." This
"manly man" ethos was hardly universal across countries or cultures, but it was decidedly entrenched in Victorian England and
turn-of-the-century America, where no less a force than Teddy
Roosevelt warned that encroaching effeminacy threatened the
nation's future.[20] Such Progressive Era concerns breathed life into
the BSA and the youth groups that preceded it, including Ernest
Thompson Seton's Woodcraft Indians and Daniel Carter Beard's
Sons of Daniel Boone.

Similar worries about misspent youth had launched Robert
Baden-Powell's Scouting movement in Britain. He had returned
triumphant from the Second Boer War, a three-year conflict pit-
ting the British Empire against Dutch-descendant forces in two
South African states, riding a wave of positive press for holding
the besieged town of Mafeking for 217 days beginning in October
1899. Hailed as the "Hero of Mafeking," he had left behind controversy that had marked his time in Africa, including that in 1896 he
was accused but later cleared by a military court of illegally execut-
ing a captured tribal chief who'd been promised safety in exchange
for surrendering.[21] During the Siege of Mafeking, hundreds of the
town's majority-Black residents starved or had to kill and eat dogs
to survive, while Baden-Powell ensured that whites had ample
food supplies.[22] None of that seemed to taint the image of the man
known simply as "B-P" to an enamored British public that had followed his wartime exploits in the newspapers.

Historians have called into question whether Baden-Powell and
the two thousand British soldiers, Cape Police officers, and local
residents he led were truly imperiled, some suggesting that they
faced a greater threat from boredom than from the six thousand
or so Boers who surrounded them. The skeptics include the British

historian Michael Rosenthal, who contended that Baden-Powell had allowed himself to be entrapped in a town that was hardly worth defending. He described Mafeking as a bleak and barren outpost 650 miles north of Cape Town, "one of a host of innocuous trading settlements dotting South Africa." In the Bantu language, Mafeking meant "place of stones," which, Rosenthal said, aptly described its hardscrabble surroundings.[23]

Baden-Powell's biographer Tim Jeal held a more favorable view of Baden-Powell's time in Mafeking, which he cast as an important regional commercial center. He said that the British officer had known that his men were outnumbered and outgunned and "would be wiped out within hours" if they didn't hunker down and play defense in lieu of trying to rout the Boers.[24] B-P's men had dug trenches and otherwise fortified Mafeking, but they had also employed a nineteenth-century version of rope-a-dope to fool the Boers and their spies. Their ruses included planting fake land mines around town and installing dummy gun placements to draw artillery fire away from more vulnerable targets.[25]

While 233 of Baden-Powell's men would eventually be killed or wounded during the siege,[26] the fighting was often less than ferocious. At times, the atmosphere was downright civil: the Boers were strict Sabbatarians, and cease-fires every Sunday allowed the townsfolk to attend church services in the morning and spend the afternoon enjoying cricket matches, concerts, baby shows, and "fooleries of every kind." Baden-Powell himself took part, playing the piano and singing Gilbert and Sullivan tunes or dressing up as a circus ringmaster to run the sporting events.[27]

Then an Army colonel in his early forties, Baden-Powell held Mafeking for seven months until he and his troops were relieved by British forces on May 16, 1900, sparking five days of raucous celebrations in London.[28] He returned from the war as a "kind of demigod," and the youngest major general in the British Empire. "Honored by the Queen, revered by the public, and even enshrined in Madame Tussaud's hall of wax immortals, he left South Africa a fully certified hero, bringing with him a mythic glory that helped guarantee the successful establishment of the Scout movement," Rosenthal wrote.[29]

While in Mafeking, Baden-Powell had put the finishing touches on *Aids to Scouting, for N.-C.O.s and Men*, his 1899 field manual for soldiers. It was geared to making them "all-round players in the game of War" by sharpening their reconnaissance skills, and it imparted his wisdom on tracking, spying, and map reading, all while instilling a sense of self-reliance and adventure. "The very name 'scout' carries with it, even among civilians, the romantic idea of a man of exceptional courage and resource," he wrote.[30]

It was also while in Mafeking that Baden-Powell became interested in scouting activities for boys. His chief staff officer, Lord Edward Cecil, organized the town's youth into a "cadet corps," outfitting them with uniforms and training them as messengers, lookouts, and orderlies—tasks previously performed by soldiers. Some of the boys rode bicycles, delivering mail around town or to neighboring forts, at times coming under enemy fire. "These boys didn't seem to mind the bullets one bit," Baden-Powell said, lauding their bravery and willingness to carry out orders.[31]

Baden-Powell was an artist, actor, and sportsman and the author of a book on hunting hogs, or "pig-sticking," as he called it. Wiry and mustachioed, he was a recognizable figure in his wide-brimmed campaign hat, the kind still worn by US Marine Corps drill instructors and Smokey Bear. Despite his celebrity, B-P was surprised to learn that *Aids to Scouting, for N.-C.O.s and Men* had become a bestseller in England, and not just among his many fans and military aficionados. Teachers and youth leaders used it in outdoor activities based on his personal tales of intrigue from Africa, laid out in chapters titled "Keeping Yourself Hidden and Dodging the Enemy," "Quickness of Eye," "Tracking," and "Spying."

He retooled *Aids to Scouting, for N.-C.O.s and Men* for a youthful audience after meeting in 1906 with Woodcraft Indians founder Seton, the English-born Canadian writer and wildlife artist then living in the States. Seton had given a copy of his book *The Birch Bark Roll of the Woodcraft Indians* to Baden-Powell, who drew liberally from it—too liberally, Seton would later complain, and with too little credit to him—in remaking *Aids to Scouting, for N.-C.O.s and Men.*

IN EARLY AUGUST 1907, Baden-Powell took his youth Scouting ideas for a trial run on Brownsea Island off the southern coast of England. He invited twenty-two boys, ages ten to seventeen, some from the elite public schools Eton and Harrow, others from farms and working-class families, for a week of camping, cooking, chivalry, and storytelling in a remote setting, shielded from the prying eyes of press photographers. He enlisted his longtime friend Kenneth McLaren, whom he'd met in the army and nicknamed "The Boy" for his youthful appearance, to help run the camp.

Baden-Powell was in his glory, decked out in below-the-knee shorts and over-the-calf golf stockings, flannel shirt, and necktie, trading his familiar campaign hat for a dapper, narrow-brimmed trilby. He slept in a tent by himself, with a Union Jack he'd brought back from Mafeking flying from a pig-sticking lance stuck in the ground outside. He was up with the sun each day, rousting the boys with blasts from an African kudu horn, similar to a shofar, then joining them for a cup of hot cocoa and a biscuit before morning calisthenics, followed by a full camp breakfast and a day of scoutcraft and games, including "Deer Stalking," "Spot the Thief," and "Dispatch Running." At night, he held court in the glow of the campfire, regaling the boys with tales of his adventures in India and Africa, capping it all off with a wild dance around the flames to a Zulu chant, something about a lion and a hippopotamus:

"Eengonyama!" he'd cry, to which they would respond, *"Invooboo! Ya-boh! Ya-boh. Invooboo!"*[32]

The Brownsea experiment, in essence the first-ever Boy Scout camp, was deemed a success. The famous "boy man" Baden-Powell, who even at fifty was obsessed with the story of Peter Pan, the never-aging leader of the Lost Boys[33]—and, some would later contend, fixated on the physiques of his young male charges— followed it up the next year with *Scouting for Boys*, a woodcraft guide that also stressed the importance of morality and good deeds. By the end of 1908, his movement was taking off in a big way: Great Britain boasted some sixty thousand Boy Scouts, and troops were springing up in countries around the globe.

Baden-Powell's place in history as the founder of worldwide Scouting was thus cemented, though not uncontested by some of his US counterparts. While Boyce had beaten everyone to incorporating the Boy Scouts of America in 1910, he was at the back of a line of people who'd sought to tackle the boy problem in an organized way, and with decidedly different approaches.

Seton was among the first, founding the Woodcraft Indians in 1902. Born in 1860 in coastal County Durham, England, he was raised in Lindsay, Ontario, Canada, where his family emigrated when he was six, and where his primitive surroundings nurtured his love of nature. In part to get away from his abusive father, Seton moved to New York as a young man to become a wildlife artist and later sharpened his skills in London, Paris, and New Mexico.[34] In the American Southwest, he drew inspiration for his art and writing from the animal world and Native Americans. Unlike Roosevelt and other noted outdoorsmen of his time, who viewed the Indians as "savages," Seton portrayed them as role models for American masculinity: strong, stoic, and resilient, largely basing his idealized views on stereotypes.[35]

By the 1898 publication of his most popular book, *Wild Animals I Have Known*, Seton's acclaim as a writer, artist, and naturalist was well established—and lucrative—and he settled on a 120-acre estate in the Cos Cob section of Greenwich, Connecticut.[36] A group of apparently bored, privileged local boys wreaked mayhem on the community and vandalized Wyndygoul, his sprawling, rustic spread. But instead of punishing them, Seton, by then convinced that city living and modernization were "feminizing" American boys and depriving them of the character-building benefits of outdoor life, chose instead to try to win them over by inviting them to camp out with him on his property in March 1902.

Over several days, he shared his knowledge of Indian lore, taught them woodcraft, and found them to be more than receptive to his message. Originally dubbed "The Seton Indian Program," he later renamed it Woodcraft Indians and opened it up to other boys. Though his group enjoyed a fair degree of success, it did not catch on as an international movement, as he had hoped.

By then another forerunner of the Boy Scouts of America also had taken root. The Sons of Daniel Boone was founded in 1905 by the artist and author Daniel Carter Beard, a crusty, buckskin-wearing character from Cincinnati nicknamed "Uncle Dan." Beard, nearly a decade older than both Seton and Boyce, had trained as a civil engineer and worked for the Ohio River city. But he had made his name as an author and artist, most notably for his illustrations in Mark Twain's 1889 novel *A Connecticut Yankee in King Arthur's Court.*

Beard modeled his notion of American masculinity on frontiersmen the likes of Boone, Davy Crockett, Simon Kenton, Kit Carson, and Johnny Appleseed, men he described as "essentially boyish" and not the product of an "over-refined civilization." As Beard saw them, they were the American "Knights" in buckskin clothes and coonskin caps who sought adventure in the wild, unlike their heavily armored English counterparts of old, who had "dressed like oil-stoves astride of horses covered with gorgeous crazy quilts, and poked each other with long barber poles, or playfully hammered each other's heads with sledge-hammers and broadaxes."[37] By 1909, his Sons of Daniel Boone claimed a membership of some twenty thousand American boys. Like Seton, he viewed his youth group as the foundation of the American Scouting movement and himself as its founder.

CENTRAL TO THE STORIES of all of these men—Baden-Powell, Boyce, Seton, and Beard—was Edgar M. Robinson, a balding, self-effacing, Canadian-born Young Men's Christian Association official who lacked a big public persona but proved to be the glue that held the fledgling Boy Scouts of America together during its first year. Robinson, who was in his early thirties when he was appointed the first boys' work secretary of the YMCA's International Committee in 1900,[38] was also alarmed about the feminization of the American boy, "so carefully wrapped up in the pink cotton wool of an over-indulgent home [that] he is more effeminate than his sister, and his flabby muscles are less flabby than his character."[39]

Robinson had taken an interest in Baden-Powell's Scouting movement but had concerns about various similar efforts springing up in the United States. Some wanted to make Scouts into young soldiers, he feared, while others tried to use them for commercial purposes. His idea was to get the movement into the hands of altruistic men, who would act in boys' best interests and resist attempts to exploit them.[40]

In April 1910, Robinson was in Michigan, meeting with J. A. Van Dis, that state's boys' work secretary. Van Dis showed him a newspaper account of Boyce's encounter with the helpful Scout in London and noted, to Robinson's surprise, that the Illinois publisher had incorporated the Boy Scouts of America. Fearing that the YMCA could be shut out of Scouting, Robinson hurried to Chicago to meet with Boyce and explore his intentions. He was relieved to find out that Boyce was already discouraged by the difficulty and lack of progress in organizing the BSA—and by the amount of money it would take to sustain it.

Robinson told Boyce that the YMCA, with an up-and-running network of state and local organizations and four hundred boys' camps, was in a stronger position to spearhead the effort than he was. The YMCA would do the heavy lifting, he offered, if Boyce would help foot the bill. Boyce agreed and pledged support of $1,000 a month for two years.[41] His only condition was that the organization be open to boys of all races and creeds, a stipulation seemingly at odds with his own expressed belief in white superiority.[42] (In its early decades, the BSA did welcome Black members, but they were mostly confined to segregated "Negro troops.")

Robinson kept his job with the YMCA but became the Boy Scouts' organizing secretary, setting out to eliminate the competition by bringing other youth organizations into the fold. Peter Bomus, a retired US Army officer who headed the US Boy Scouts, saw the light and agreed to merge. So did William Verbeck, the principal of a military school in New York and head of the National Scouts of America, which also dropped its Scouting plans, as did the Leatherstocking Scouts, the Peace Scouts of California, the Salvation Army Scouts, the Polish National Alliance Scouts, and others. Most important, Seton's Woodcraft Indians and Beard's Sons of Daniel Boone consented to be absorbed, despite growing friction between the two men over who had played a bigger role in founding the BSA.

The lone major holdout among leaders of the early competing youth groups was William Randolph Hearst, another rich, powerful newspaper publisher who founded the similar-sounding American Boy Scouts and heavily promoted it with one of his influential dailies, the *New York American*. When Robinson approached Hearst about folding his group into the Boy Scouts of America, the egoistic publishing magnate declined but said that the BSA was welcome to abandon its plans and join *his* Scouting organization.

That June, Robinson opened a temporary national headquarters of the BSA in a room next to his office in the YMCA building on East 28th Street in New York City. A meeting of representatives of more than two dozen organizations involved in boys' work led to the creation of an organizing committee, whose early work was touted in a string of positive stories published by US newspapers, large and small. Word spread. Within three months, 2,500 scoutmasters had signed up and troops were "springing up like mushrooms" across the country, Robinson said. One of the biggest challenges he faced was figuring out how to tap the talents and ideas of Seton and Beard and get Baden-Powell's blessing for the BSA, without alienating any of them.

"They were as different as three men could be, in their background, their experience and ideas," Robinson said. "Baden-Powell could not help thinking in military terms. Seton could not help thinking in terms of the Ideal Indians. Beard thought in terms of the 'Knights of the Buckskin' or the old-time frontiersman who conquered the forests and killed the Indians."[43]

Seton, in particular, was set in his ways, especially his aversion to all things military. He detested uniforms, parades, drills, bugle calls, and flag raisings. He couldn't so much as tolerate tents pitched in a straight line, the way the army did it. In short, his views were bound to clash with the others', and his friend Robinson knew it.

"He simply could not swallow Baden-Powell's evident admiration of the military, nor could he enthuse over Dan Beard's making the pioneer frontiersmen the objects of admiration for American boys," Robinson said. "In his mind they were rough, uncouth, brutal, uncultured men, whose only idea of a good Indian was a dead one."[44]

ON SEPTEMBER 23, 1910, Robinson and Beard met Baden-Powell on his arrival in New York, where he was to be feted at the Boy Scouts of America's inaugural gala. Joined by Seton, they took him to the offices of the *Outlook*, a weekly magazine for which Theodore Roosevelt, then a year and a half out of the White House, served as an associate editor and wrote essays promoting his progressive views. The famous "Rough Rider" dispatched his visitors with regrets that he couldn't attend the gala but gave them a statement of support to be read from the dais: "I believe in the movement with all my heart," it said, while also lamenting "the excessive development of city life in modern industrial civilization" and the "unhealthy atrophying of some of the essential virtues."[45]

That night, Seton was the master of ceremonies and Baden-Powell the guest of honor at the Waldorf-Astoria hotel on Fifth Avenue, a site later occupied by the Empire State Building.[46] An elegantly appointed, bronze-busts-and-Siena-marble favorite of famous Americans, foreign dignitaries, and merely well-to-do New Yorkers, the original Waldorf-Astoria was a combination of two hotels built by feuding descendants of the fur trade magnate and robber baron John Jacob Astor, America's first multimillion-aire. The two structures were linked by a long lobby-level corridor faced in marble and lined with palm trees; it was known as Pea-cock Alley for the upper-crust types who regularly strutted through it in their finest.[47]

On hand that night for the BSA event and a glimpse of the celebrated Baden-Powell were more than two hundred reform-ers, politicians, educators, clergy members, beacons of Ameri-can high society, and moneyed Scouting enthusiasts, including John D. Rockefeller, Jr., the son of the founder of Standard Oil. (Others of America's wealthiest families supporting the Boy Scouts in those early days included the Carnegies, the Vanderbilts, and the Sages.[48]) The guest list also included the likes of Charles "Buf-falo" Jones, a frontiersman and conservationist famous not only for saving the bison population out West but also for lassoing lions in Africa. As Baden-Powell made his way to the head table in the

Astor Gallery, to be seated between Rockefeller and Seton, he was showered with a thunderous welcome, which the *New-York Tribune* described as "a combination of Chautauqua salute and Waldorf warwhoops."[49]

Seton, doing his best to conceal his simmering resentment over Baden-Powell's appropriation of his *Birch Bark Roll* writings, sucked it up and raised a glass to the British war hero, introducing him as the father of the Scouting movement. No one was more surprised than Seton when Baden-Powell demurred. "You are mistaken, Mr. Seton, in your remarks to the effect that I am the father of this idea for scouting for boys," he said. "I may say that you, or Dan Beard, is the father—there are many fathers. I am only one of the uncles, you may say."[50] It's hard to know if Baden-Powell was being sincere or diplomatic or displaying a flair for false modesty. In later writings he also credited other organizations for their contributions to Scouting, among them the Codes of the Zulus, the Red Indians, and the Boys' Brigades. But he was always quick to add that the movement had sprung mainly from *his* experience in training young soldiers and the South African constabulary.

Baden-Powell's speech did little to quell the growing rivalry between Seton and Beard, but it accomplished Robinson's goal of securing the famous Englishman's blessing for the nascent Boy Scouts of America. It also had the bonus benefit of driving a stake through the heart of the holdout American Boy Scouts when Baden-Powell snubbed an invitation to review a parade of Hearst's troops during his New York visit. A few months later, Hearst would resign in scandal from the organization he had founded, complaining that unscrupulous fundraisers had falsely invoked his name while soliciting donations.[51] The American Boy Scouts later changed its name to the United States Boy Scouts and continued operating, but by the end of 1910 it was all but eliminated as a competitive threat to the BSA.

Ex-president Roosevelt, his successor, William Howard Taft,

and Admiral George Dewey, a naval war hero, were all named to the Boy Scouts' first National Council, giving the governing body instant credibility and political heft. Beard was one of the BSA's first national commissioners, and Seton was installed as its first Chief Scout and tasked with putting together an official handbook, drawing from Baden-Powell's *Scouting for Boys* and his own *Birch Bark Roll*. The hastily assembled guide dealt mostly with scoutcraft, woodcraft, and camping but also included chapters on patriotism and citizenship. Those themes would echo in Scouting for generations to come, along with chockablock references to "growing into manhood" and becoming a "good, manly citizen," so many such allusions that some social scientists later dubbed the BSA a "national cult of manliness."

The obsession with "making men" out of American boys was evident in Seton's introduction to the first handbook. A hundred years earlier, he wrote, the American boy could ride, shoot, skate, run, and swim; he was a boy who was handy with tools, self-reliant, and resourceful, a boy who respected his elders and was strong of body, brain, and morals. Now, in Seton's dim view, the American boy had devolved into something else altogether: he was doughy, aimless, and unskilled, forgoing participating in athletics for a place in the crowd at baseball and football games, "content to do nothing but sit on the benches and look on." "*Degeneracy* is the word," he said, and he blamed it for turning "a large proportion of our robust, manly, self-reliant boyhood into a lot of flat-chested cigarette-smokers, with shaky nerves and doubtful vitality."[52]

Although Seton and Beard would feud for decades over their respective contributions to Scouting, they agreed in their assessment of the boy problem. Beard would later echo Seton's sentiments in a book on woodcraft that detailed the safe handling of axes and warned of other perils, including playmates who "play craps and smoke cigarettes" and tempt their friends to forget the Scout Oath. "We must remember that there is nothing in life that is not dangerous, and the greatest danger of all is not firearms, is not edged tools, is not wild beasts, is not tornadoes or earthquakes, avalanches or floods, but it is Luxury; expressed in boy language, it is ice cream, soda water, candy, servants and automobiles; it is everything which tends to make a boy dependent upon others and soft in mind and muscle and to make him a sissy."[53]

CHAPTER 2

AMASSING POWER

Whatever hope that Ernest Thompson Seton or Daniel Carter Beard had for making the Boy Scouts of America in the image and likeness of the Woodcraft Indians or the Sons of Daniel Boone faded on January 1, 1911, with the hiring of James E. West as the new executive secretary. West, a thirty-four-year-old Washington, DC, attorney, took the reins of the BSA from Edgar M. Robinson, who turned down the job to return full-time to the national YMCA. West signed on for six months and stayed for thirty-two years, most of it as chief Scout executive.[1]

West, stocky, bespectacled, and seemingly undaunted by a childhood illness that had left him with only one good leg, dived headlong into his work, moving the BSA offices from the YMCA building to new digs at 200 Fifth Avenue and quickly ramping up staffing. Much more than an administrator, he became the chief architect of an organization and policies that would cultivate strong ties with US presidents and top lawmakers, including Roosevelt, the nation's most powerful business leaders, and its wealthiest philanthropists, among them Andrew Carnegie and

John D. Rockefeller, as well as civic organizations, governmental agencies, and churches that funneled millions of eager, dues-paying boys into its troops. He also injected religion into the BSA's bloodstream and planted the seeds of a controversy that would bear bitter fruit decades later with the exclusion of gay Scouts and adult leaders.

From an early age, West was no stranger to boys' work, children's issues, and personal hardship. He had never known his father, and his widowed mother, stricken by tuberculosis and unable to care for him, had left him at the Washington City Orphan Asylum in Washington, DC, when he was six, three months before she died. Two years later, after the orphanage neglected his complaints of knee and hip pain, little Jimmy was diagnosed with a crippling case of tuberculosis that left one leg shorter than the other. He spent nearly two years in the hospital, much of it strapped to a wooden contraption designed to straighten his leg bones by dangling a ten-pound weight off the end of his bed.[2] It didn't help much, and when he was released from the hospital, the orphanage officials at first refused to take him back, knowing that his disability would make him unfit for indentured labor at a time when one in five American children worked in factories, in mills, or at other jobs that exploited them.[3] When the hospital dropped him off anyway, crutches and all, he was relegated to toil in the girls' sewing room.[4]

Instead of being broken by that experience, West drew strength from it. He went on to become an advocate for himself and his fellow orphans. A family friend helped him enroll at a nearby public school, beginning in the fifth grade, and he thrived. He started a reading program for the orphans and gave them a penny for every book they read, paid from his meager earnings from doing laundry and mending clothes. Despite his disability, he learned to ride a bicycle and organized hikes and other outings. He graduated early from high school and eventually joined the orphanage staff.

After leaving the home at age nineteen, West worked his way

through college and earned a law degree. He became a government lawyer and a prominent children's advocate whose efforts prompted the creation of a juvenile court system and the US Labor Department's Children's Bureau in the Roosevelt administration. His experience made him eminently qualified to run the BSA when Robinson and others recommended him for the job of permanent executive secretary, which led to his becoming the first chief Scout executive.[5]

From the outset, West and Seton clashed both personally and professionally, in part because the new executive favored Baden-Powell's militaristic approach to Scouting. Seton, an avowed pacifist whose naturalist lifestyle translated into infrequent baths and haircuts, identified more with the lone wolf than with the foot soldier, which he demonstrated by signing his letters with a paw print.[6] To say that the straitlaced, autocratic West did not appreciate Seton and his iconoclastic ways would be a profound understatement.

As the BSA's first Chief Scout, Seton gave generously of his time and money, often paying out of pocket for his work-related expenses. After a while, though, he realized that the Boy Scouts of America under West would adopt only selected bits of his Woodcraft Indians, not the entire program, as he'd wished.[7] He became increasingly discouraged and embittered, even as he clung to his contention that he was the true founder of the BSA. In a letter to Beard the day after Thanksgiving 1915, he opened with "My Dear Beard," and then went on the attack, saying he had been "greatly surprised" by recent published interviews in which Uncle Dan had claimed to be the founder. "In this organization the name and about one half of the machinery were contributed by Baden-Powell, practically all of the activities and a considerable part of the machinery, including the manual, were contributed by me," he wrote. "Not one activity, not one principle, not one law was given to it by you."[8]

Seton's harangue took up two and a half typewritten pages and cited pertinent dates and developments to bolster his case and undercut Beard's. He acknowledged Beard's general contributions to Scouting but noted that they were among those of at least a dozen other men; he urged his once friend and now staunch rival to do "the fair and honorable thing" and stop claiming to be *the* founder of the BSA. "In the interest of harmony, I appeal to your manly sense of fair play to drop the unprofitable discussion together with everything that might tend to revive it," he said.

Four days later, Beard brushed off Seton's scalding letter with one of his own. "O, come off, Seton: don't make a fool of yourself," he wrote. "Not interested in the dates. Have no knowledge of the articles to which you refer. Have neither power nor desire to muzzle press. You make me tired. Not guilty!" In fact, he told Seton, if he was still itching for a fight, he should go join the British Army in its war with Germany.[9]

Barely a week after that exchange, Seton's long-festering differences with West culminated in his public resignation from the BSA. It was not surprising: Seton, a British subject, had run afoul of West and other top Scouts officials by not applying for US citizenship at a time when World War I was raging in Europe and patriotic fervor ran high in America. His antiwar sentiments had clashed with Roosevelt's views on American manhood, and his appointment as Chief Scout was not being renewed by the BSA.[10] His friend Edgar Robinson would later describe Seton as heartbroken and disillusioned[11] by that turn of events, but at the time, he was mostly angry. He summoned newspaper reporters to his apartment at 512 Fifth Avenue and unloaded on his nemesis West.[12] "Seton started it. Baden-Powell boomed it. West killed it," he said of the American Scouting movement; the reporters scribbled his words into their notebooks. Seton told them that he'd submitted his resignation months earlier but the BSA had not acted on it, misleading the American public into thinking he was still actively involved in the organization. "My only criticism is that they have allowed all direction and power to centre in the hands of James E. West, a lawyer who is a man of great executive ability but without knowledge of the activities of boys; who has no point of contact with boys, and who, I might almost say, has never seen the blue sky in his life."

The reporters, at once diligent and keenly aware of a hot story in the making, eagerly conveyed Seton's comments to West, who said Seton couldn't have quit because he'd already been fired. He also questioned Seton's patriotism and all but accused him of being in league with "anarchists and radical socialists"[13] for not pursuing US citizenship. "We wanted a whole-hearted, whole-souled American to look after the interests of the Boy Scouts," he said. "That is all there is to this controversy."[14] Whether Seton left Scouting of his own accord or was pushed out by West and others, he was gone by early 1916, and most of his previous contributions would be cut from the next edition of the *Boy Scout Handbook*.

Uncle Dan Beard remained in the BSA hierarchy, but held a similarly unfavorable view of West as chief Scout executive[15] and became more of a figurehead than a guiding light. William D. Boyce, the Chicago newspaperman who had incorporated the BSA and initially supported it financially, withdrew from active participation after West and the national executive board rejected his offer to publish a Scouting magazine in Chicago. Not long after, in 1912, West arranged to buy a Massachusetts magazine, *Boys' Life*, which would grow to have millions of youthful subscribers. A year later, he launched *Scouting* magazine for scoutmasters. Together with the ever-updating versions of the handbook, the periodicals helped BSA headquarters keep in touch with its growing network of local councils, which by 1914 had registered 107,000 boys and 25,800 men to lead them in troops sponsored by churches, civic groups, and other chartered organizations.[16]

While both Seton and Beard had derided West for his lack of

scouting and woodcraft experience, his skills and drive as a hard-working, get-things-done executive were undeniable. Since taking over in 1911, he was almost always in the office by 8:00 a.m. and rarely left before 5:30 or 6:00. He was not averse to putting in eighteen-hour days and expected those working for him to do likewise.[17] A stickler for decorum, seldom smiling and not particularly likable, West quizzed staffers about their efficiency and inspected the office boys every afternoon to make sure the Boy Scout uniforms they'd bought from headquarters for $2.15—75 cents for the shirt, 50 cents each for the hat and shorts, and 40 cents for the belt—were properly worn. West's own workaday uniform was the frock coat and striped pants favored by corporate bigwigs and prominent lawyers.

When *Leslie's Illustrated Weekly* asked West to write a "concise and authoritative statement" of the Boy Scouts movement in America in 1912, he opened his essay with this man's-man definition of youthful masculinity:

> The real Boy Scout is not a "sissy." He is not a hothouse plant, like Little Lord Fauntleroy. There is nothing "milk and water" about him. He is not afraid of the dark.... Instead of being a puny, dull, or bookish lad who dreams and does nothing, he is full of life, energy, enthusiasm, bubbling over with fun, full of ideas as to what he wants to do and he knows how he wants to do it. He has many ideals and many heroes. He is not hitched to his mother's apron strings. While he adores his mother and would do anything to save her from suffering or discomfort, he is self-reliant, sturdy, and full of vim. He is just the sort of boy his father is proud to own as his son.[18]

West immediately put his stamp on the BSA. He admired British Scouting and adopted Baden-Powell's Scout Oath but changed key parts of it: "I will do my duty to God and the King" became "I will do my duty to God and my country." To the end of the oath he appended the phrase "to keep myself physically strong, mentally awake, and *morally straight* [italics added]," a term later widely misinterpreted as a condemnation of homosexuality and invoked to justify excluding gay boys and adult leaders from Scouting.[19]

He also expanded the original nine points of Baden-Powell's Scout Law to an even dozen. To "Trustworthy, Loyal, Helpful, Friendly, Courteous, Kind, Obedient, Cheerful, and Thrifty," he added that a Scout must be "Brave, Clean, and Reverent." The last of those points would signal his unwavering intention to steep Scouting in religious belief. From his point of view, "the real people in America, the people that have made America from the early days," were those with deep religious convictions based on personal religious experiences.[20]

A Sunday school teacher at a Congregational church, West was instrumental in developing a "Declaration of Religious Principle" that was embedded in the Boy Scouts' constitution and remains intact today. It holds that "no member can grow into the best kind of citizen without recognizing an obligation to God" and requires all prospective Scouts and adult leaders to abide by it. The declaration also states that the BSA is absolutely nonsectarian and welcoming of all religions, a proposition that West himself found to be a hard sell to some early-twentieth-century faith leaders.

At a time when Protestants were pushing the progressive tenets of the Social Gospel, which tied salvation to doing good works, Catholicism was rapidly becoming the predominant faith in the United States, thanks largely to an influx of Irish, Italian, and other European immigrants. Many Protestants feared the "Catholic hordes" and undue influence by the Vatican, not to mention the potential impact of more than 2 million Jews immigrating from Eastern Europe.

Catholic leaders in turn were wary of Scouting because of its strong ties to the YMCA, suspecting it of trying to take over the movement as a vehicle for Protestant proselytizing. The *Albany Evening Journal* highlighted the tensions in an article published on September 25, 1911, noting that the pastor of St. Patrick's Church had announced from the pulpit at Sunday Mass that he did not want his youthful parishioners in Scouting: "The movement was a good thing for Protestant boys, he said, but he did not favor the organization seeking recruits among Catholic children."[21]

After lengthy negotiations, West managed to assuage the Catholics.[22] In 1913, the Boy Scouts appointed a national commissioner for Scout work in Catholic churches, whose job was to promote the formation of Catholic troops. Catholic boys were now allowed to join, but with conditions, including that their troops were exclusively Catholic and their scoutmasters were approved by Church leaders.

That same year, West also won over the Mormons when the Church of Jesus Christ of Latter-day Saints voted to affiliate its Young Men's Mutual Improvement Association Scouts with the BSA. Like the Catholics, the Mormons insisted on certain exclusivity provisions, which the Scouts were happy to grant; the move swelled the BSA's rolls by 15,000. The LDS church would go on to become the largest sponsoring organization of troops for more than a century, until cutting ties in 2018 in the wake of the BSA's opening its ranks to gay boys and adult leaders, and girls. Today the Catholic Church remains among Scouting's biggest chartered organizations, just behind the United Methodist Church.

While modern-day Scouting continues to welcome all faiths, it still excludes those who have none. Atheists and agnostics need not apply.[23]

IN LATE MARCH 1913, nearly a foot of rain pounded southwestern Ohio. Coach horses drowned in their stalls, houses were swept off their foundations, and Dayton's Main Street became a navigable waterway as the Great Miami River and its tributaries overflowed their banks, deluging the city and the region. More than 350 people died in the Great Dayton Flood, during which the area was cut off for days; not even the National Guard could get through.[24]

But even in its infancy, the Boy Scouts of America lived up to its motto "Be prepared" and sprang into rescue mode across Ohio. Among the many cases of Scouts pitching in during the devastating floods, the Dayton Daily News noted the generosity of a Pennsylvania troop that had saved $200 for summer camp but instead sent it to Dayton "for the sake of helping their unfortunate brothers and sisters" there.[25] Newspapers around the country trumpeted the lifesaving good turns of other Boy Scouts, none more valorous than one named John Stone, who set out to rescue stranded flood victims and saved a woman who'd been swept away from her husband and twin babies: "He turned a corner on a flooded street just as Mrs. Charles M. Adams was sinking for the third time...and pulled her onto his raft."[26]

The BSA's contributions to Ohio's disaster relief efforts became the foundation of its 1915 bid for a congressional charter, which would raise its public profile and grant it power not shared by similar organizations. A House Judiciary Committee report supporting the bill also cited the services rendered by Boy Scouts to thousands of Union and Confederate veterans at the Fiftieth Anniversary Reunion of the Battle of Gettysburg and their assistance at the inauguration of President Woodrow Wilson. Only one other nonprofit, the American National Red Cross, had received a federal charter, which proved to be much more than an honorific for the BSA.[27]

Unanimously approved by both houses of Congress and signed by Wilson on June 15, 1916, the charter reaffirmed the BSA's character-building mission,[28] while granting it the exclusive right to use "all emblems and badges, descriptive or designating marks, and words or phrases now or heretofore used by the Boy Scouts of America in carrying out its program." In effect, the charter gave the BSA a monopoly on Scouting, down to and including the use of the word *Scout*. The BSA used its newfound power to force more than four hundred companies to either stop producing items that carried a "Scout" label or pony up a royalty to use it. In 1924 alone, the BSA collected nearly $64,000 in such royalties—more than $1 million in today's dollars—comprising 18 percent of its income for that year. It reaped another $65,000 from the sale of BSA-branded supplies, publications, and merchandise, including Boy Scout knives, axes, and tents.[29]

West also used the charter language to sue the American Boy Scouts out of existence in 1917, after it was reconstituted (sans William Randolph Hearst) as the United States Boy Scouts. William Boyce, who had gone on to found the Lone Scouts of America, which focused on boys in rural areas, eventually ran into financial problems and folded its sixty-two thousand members into the Boy Scouts of America. By 1924, the BSA had the field of boys' Scouting all to itself. West's efforts to thwart the use of the term *Girl Scouts* failed, something that gnawed at him for years and would presage acrimonious trademark litigation involving the two youth groups a century later.

While the federal charter required the BSA to report to Congress on its activities every year, it did not grant lawmakers any authority over the organization, nor did it provide for any direct governmental funding of Boy Scouts. But that didn't stop Scouting from benefiting financially in myriad ways from what amounted to Uncle Sam's seal of approval.

From the outset, the BSA leveraged its federal recognition to solicit financial and material support from government agencies and military branches in the form of donated land, transportation, and camping equipment, including US Army tents, cots, and blankets, naval sailing charts, and first aid kits. The BSA also encouraged troop leaders to solicit support from local fire departments, boards of health, playgrounds, museums, conservation groups, and the Red Cross.[30] Mayors, governors, and other state and local elected officials saw the public relations and practical benefits of aligning with the Boy Scouts and were only too happy to hitch their taxpayer-funded wagons to troops' civic-minded activities and special events. Boy Scouts across the country became mayor for a day, or police chief, or city commissioner.

Wealthy philanthropists also jumped in to support the cause. In December 1915, as part of a typical fundraising drive that generated $82,503, John D. Rockefeller, Sr., supplemented his earlier gifts to the BSA with a check for $9,000. His son, John D. Rockefeller, Jr., chipped in $3,000, and other lesser-known but well-heeled benefactors also stepped up. Among them were Charles T. Coutant of Kingston, New York, who told West he appreciated the work he was doing for boys and wanted to be a part of it. He donated a seventy-five-acre campground in the Catskill Mountains, a place with a trout stream and scenery beautiful beyond description. "It is just such a place as would make the heart of the average boy leap for joy, and if you have some delicate members, with weak lungs, they would find health here in every breeze that blows. It will afford us pleasure to place this tract at your disposal, without money and without price."[31]

The Boy Scouts' relationship with ultrawealthy Americans would help it amass an extensive portfolio of donated campgrounds, office buildings, and other valuable real estate now worth billions. Its crown jewels include a 220-square-mile chunk of northeastern New Mexico gifted by the Oklahoma oil magnate Waite Phillips, who threw in a twenty-three-story Tulsa office building to generate rental revenue to support it. The New Mexico property, donated in 1938 and 1941, came with only two conditions: that Phillips's family could continue to use it for recreation and that his favorite horse, Gus, be allowed to roam it at his leisure, never again to be ridden. The expansive plot became Philmont Ranch, now one of BSA's four modern-day High Adventure Bases.

JAMES WEST WAS WELL on his way to establishing the BSA as an American institution when the United States' entry into World War I all but guaranteed it. At the time, the Scouts' 280,000 boys outnumbered the nation's men in military uniforms by about 80,000. The chief Scout executive was a vocal supporter of the war—"There must be no slackers," he said—and, in shades of Baden-Powell's cadet corps in South Africa, he wasted no time offering up thousands of boys to serve as message runners and coast watchers, on the alert for unauthorized radio transmitters and draftees on the lam from active duty.[32]

Among other patriotic pursuits to aid the war effort, Scouts planted gardens to grow food and volunteered to inventory black walnut trees that could be used to make rifle stocks and airplane propellers. They collected a hundred railcars' worth of fruit pits and nut shells to be turned into charcoal filters for more than a half-million gas masks. They worked as hospital orderlies, ambulance assistants, and relief telephone operators and rolled bandages for the Red Cross. They also proved to be adept at hawking war bonds, raising more than $355 million for government coffers[33]— the rough equivalent of $9 billion today.

In May 1919, a month before the Allies and the Germans signed the Treaty of Versailles to formally end World War I, Wilson recognized the BSA's efforts with a presidential proclamation establishing a Boy Scout Week and urging Americans to open their hearts—and their wallets—to the youth group. "The Boy Scout movement should not only be preserved, but strengthened," he said. "It deserves the support of all public-spirited citizens."[34]

By the end of its first decade, the BSA claimed a combined membership of boys and adult leaders of 462,000, up from 60,000 in 1911. Its *Boys' Life* magazine had a national readership, and it boasted the active support of three current and former presidents, Wilson, Taft, and Roosevelt. Two of them, Taft and Wilson, served as honorary presidents of the BSA, as has every US president since. In just ten years, the BSA had become the largest and most influential youth group of its time, but according to the historian Benjamin René Jordan, it was more than that. "It was a big, national, powerful organization," he said.[35]

Even as the BSA's power and numbers grew, so did a secret blacklist that only a select few at the top of the organization knew existed.

CHAPTER 3

A WILD NIGHT IN WEEDSPORT

Murder was in the air on April 26, 1918. Word got around town that a local man had accused Boy Scout leader Lynn C. Townsend of "corrupting the morals" of his son, a popular euphemism for sexual abuse. Townsend, a newspaper reporter and magazine editor from Weedsport, New York, was ordered to appear before Police Justice Frank M. Parsons. A throng of riled-up residents followed him to the police station and was waiting for him when he was released without bail after pleading not guilty. It was pure chaos.

"Weedsport was thrown into a seething mass of angry, howling men and boys," the Rochester *Democrat and Chronicle* reported, noting that Townsend had been attacked by the mob, severely beaten, and nearly killed: "He was ridden upon a rail and when someone yelled 'Lynch him!' a rope was procured and tied about his neck and all that saved him was the failure of the mob to find a pole to string him to."[1]

Rescued "more dead than alive" by a blacksmith named Francisco, Townsend staggered home with the mob at his heels. He barricaded himself inside the little green and white cottage he shared with his wife, Nan, but soon reappeared with a revolver in each hand, threatening to shoot his pursuers. They taunted him, pelted his house with sticks and eggs, and hurled rocks through his windows. They dared him to fire and he did, once into the air and once into the crowd, clipping a nine-year-old boy in the leg. The Weedsport police, who seemed in no hurry to quell the violence, finally showed up and dragged him off to jail for his own protection.

The next day, when the mob reconvened and threatened to bust him out and hang him, Townsend was hustled off to a more secure lockup in nearby Auburn.[2] A Cayuga County grand jury later indicted him on three counts of sexually abusing Boy Scouts.[3] That June, two months after his arrest, he stood trial, proclaiming his innocence and blaming the accusations on "spite over alleged favoritism in the troop." The judge dismissed one sodomy charge after two witnesses corroborated Townsend's alibi that he had been out of town on a reporting assignment when the alleged sex crime had occurred. Two other counts were left standing,[4] but the local papers' coverage fell off. Sometime over the next hundred-plus years the court records were lost or destroyed, so the final disposition of one of the earliest known cases of alleged sexual abuse in Scouting remains unclear.[5]

The criminal charges alone would have made Townsend a candidate for the BSA's fledgling blacklist of ineligible volunteers, established soon after the organization's founding in 1910 (and closely guarded ever since). There had been passing references in the press to a "red flag list" over the years, including a brief mention in the *Iowa City Press-Citizen* in 1923 in a larger story about Boy Scout operations.[6] But its substance and purpose came fully to light only because of a speech by Colonel Theodore Roosevelt, the late former president's eldest son, who chaired the Boy Scouts' personnel committee.

Addressing BSA's policy-setting National Council of volunteers at its Twenty-fifth Annual Meeting in Chicago on May 17, 1935, Roosevelt was touting his committee's achievements when he mentioned that the main office kept a "confidential list of 2,904 men from every state and every large city in the nation who are undesirables." Every man who applied to be a Scout leader was checked against the list, Roosevelt said, boasting that it had served its purpose well.[7] "Through the years—through our twenty-five years of existence—we have tried to safeguard ourselves in every way from men unfit to lead or to influence boys, and we intend to continue to do so," he said. "Our red flag list is in constant use."[8] His comments were the first significant public acknowledgment of what would come to be known within the BSA as the "perversion files," a highly confidential trove of records intended to keep sexual abusers and other miscreants out of Scouting.

Robert Baden-Powell, the British war hero who in 1908 had founded the world Scouting movement in England, two years before the birth of the Boy Scouts of America, had a similar screening known as the "Grey List"[9] to weed out pedophiles and other problem leaders, including those suspected of being homosexual. No matter that Baden-Powell himself was likely a repressed gay man; his admiration of the naked bodies of young boys skinny-dipping and in photographs was well documented and has long been grist for biographers' speculation, although no evidence ever surfaced that he acted upon those tendencies with Boy Scouts or anyone else.[10]

It's not clear if Baden-Powell's US Scouting counterparts modeled their exclusionary list after his, but this much is certain: Roosevelt's red flag list in 1935 caused an uproar, not because it hinted at Scouting's growing child sexual abuse problem but, in the wake of America's first Red scare, many people perceived it to suggest that Communists had infiltrated Scouting and that the organization had kept a lid on that shocking revelation.

Others took it to mean that Boy Scouts officials had politicized the nation's premier youth group and put its members to work as clandestine "Red hunters," a job they considered better left to J. Edgar Hoover's G-men.

In either case, editorial writers and public officials were aghast, including a New York City commissioner who telegraphed Roosevelt demanding an explanation. "As the father of a Boy Scout, I ask you to make this list public, together with the reasons for the presence of each name on the list," Paul Blanshard wrote. "When my son joined the Boy Scouts I was assured that its policies were non-partisan, non-sectarian, non-controversial. Was this assurance true or false?"[11]

The *Chattanooga Daily Times* harrumphed that Roosevelt's disclosure only underscored the importance of "guiding young people aright, and protecting them against un-American, anti-social influences!" The *Capital Times* in Madison, Wisconsin, exhorted Roosevelt to come clean about the red flag list, "lest critics, with some justice, rebaptize that organization as 'The Boy Spies of America.'" Heywood Broun, a New Yorker with a lacerating sense of humor and a widely syndicated newspaper column titled "It Seems to Me," echoed and amplified that notion while taking jabs at Roosevelt, whom he viewed as just one more social elite to be lampooned. "Surely those who have the best interests of the organization at heart can hardly tolerate the suggestion that boy scouts go to the woods, not to hunt wildflowers, but to thumb over a secret list of suspects," he wrote. "In their bright book of outdoor life, the only menaces should be the jaguar and the gnat. These hardy little woodsmen are scouts, not snoopers."[12]

Roosevelt, whom Broun had cast as inexperienced and belittled as "Young Teddy," fired back in a letter to the columnist, accusing him of jumping to conclusions without checking his facts. "The 'Red Flag' list has nothing to do with Communism or any other political doctrine," he wrote. "The list to which you refer is more than 20 years old and is composed of men whose moral character rendered them unfit to associate with the training of boys."[13]

Roosevelt's explanation did little to cool the controversy he'd ignited. In early June 1935, Chief Scout Executive James E. West sought to set the record straight in an interview with the *New York Times*.[14] A lawyer, West had instituted an annually renewable registration system intended to shield the program from incompetents, crooks, and sexual predators. All who applied to be scoutmasters were to be checked against the red flag list and required to subscribe to the Scout Oath, the Scout Law, and a Declaration of Religious Principle recognizing their obligation to God as the supreme power in the universe, whatever their chosen faith.

West explained to the *Times* that the red flag list was not about "Communist or Red doctrines" and said that neither had been a problem for the Boy Scouts. The list had to do only with Scout leaders who had been removed for a variety of causes, including "moral perversion." It had gotten its name from the red stickers attached to the cards of men "we wanted to be careful about," he said. Most of the 2,919 men on that list had been flagged for mishandling Scout funds, for incompetence, or for being "organization misfits." But some 30 percent, or about 875 men, had been deemed "morally unfit," a category that included sexual abuse.

"We have had some very depressing and sad experiences over the years," West said, noting that some morally "unbalanced" men joined Scouting for the sole purpose of abusing boys. "And then again we have those who are soundly balanced, but who...when they get into boys' work, undertake to deal with sex matters and become morbid on the subject and sometimes give way to temptation and develop practices which make them degenerates."

Still, he sought to downplay the problem of sexual abuse in Scouting. He noted that fewer than three thousand of the more than 1.3 million men who had joined the organization since its inception had wound up red flagged—not enough, in his view, to cause alarm. The good news, he assured the *Times*, was that those who had been named to the list were now gone for good, forever banished from Scouting and prevented from moving to a new city to gain readmission.

Time and again, however, the BSA would put the lie to that assertion, as men who were booted from Scouting for molesting boys found ways to get back in and abuse again.[15] But at that moment in 1935 and for several decades to follow, West's explanation of the red flag list sufficed to once again tuck it safely away from public view.

IN ITS EARLIER ITERATIONS, the Boy Scouts' blacklist resembled a Rolodex file, with volunteers' names kept on cards in alphabetical order. Annual registrations were checked against the file to weed out men who'd been previously flagged as ineligible. Over time, the list evolved into a more fully fleshed out tracking system known as the "Confidential file" and then later as the "Ineligible Volunteer file." It was a compilation of men who "through a lack of integrity or loyalty, or by moral or mental weakness, have proven themselves potentially harmful" to Boy Scouts. The IV Files, as they were called, were divided into six categories, according to internal Boy Scouts records: Perversion, Morals, Financial, Leadership, Criminal, and Theft, with the largest group of cases falling into the "P" slot. Instead of index cards with red stickers affixed to the names of excluded scoutmasters, the IV file consisted of paper folders stuffed with varying levels of detail and documentation. Proof of wrongdoing was not required to exclude anyone; all that was needed was enough evidence to support the contention that a man was unfit, for whatever reason, to be around boys.[16]

Each of the folders included a "confidential record sheet" stapled to the inside cover and filled out with a standard set of data points for those rejected: name, age, address, religion, nationality, education, occupation, height, weight, physical characteristics, interests, marital status, children's names and ages, and "Scouting connections," including troop numbers and locations. (In what might have been an attempt at dark humor, Scouts officials who kicked out a Massachusetts leader in 1960 for molesting multiple troop members summed up his "interests" in one word: "Boys."[17]) Most files included correspondence between national and local Scouts officials. Many held newspaper clippings, police reports, court records, statements by victims and witnesses, and letters from prosecutors. All were kept in locked metal filing cabinets at BSA headquarters as it moved from New York City to North Brunswick, New Jersey, to Irving, Texas, where it has been since 1979.

Few at the national office, and far fewer outside it, were even aware of the IV files. The blacklist never left the main office, where only three people had access to it and could check it for the names of suspected abusers. Local Scouts officials could share information with those at the national level but were in turn told only as much as they needed to know—if they were told anything at all. Boy Scouts, their parents, and sponsoring organizations, as well as other youth organizations such as Big Brothers of America, were told nothing about the files. In most cases, those who made the blacklist remained on it until they turned seventy-five or died, when their names were deleted. (The exact number of files has never been disclosed, in large part because in the late 1970s, after a three-year internal review, as many as half were destroyed, ostensibly to purge the names of elderly or deceased abusers.[18])

Although paper recordkeeping and routine destruction of documents gave way decades ago to computerization and a system now known as the Volunteer Screening Database, the perversion files' hallmark secrecy has endured. Boy Scouts officials rankle at the word *secrecy* and instead prefer "confidentiality," insisting for more than a century now that it is necessary to protect the privacy of victims, witnesses, and anyone falsely accused of sexual abuse or other wrongdoing. Largely unstated, at least publicly, have been their deep concerns about the BSA's exposure to civil liability. But as far back as 1922, a top Scouts official, George W. Ehler, touched on it while explaining the red flag list and the need for keeping it secret to those assembled for the Second Biennial Conference of Scout Executives in Blue Ridge, North Carolina.[19] "It has to be kept exceedingly confidential because unless it happens to be backed up positively and definitely by good legal evidence, publicity would be foundation for libel suit," he said.

He also hinted at the scope of the Boy Scouts' abuse problem and its portability by determined sex offenders. "There are all too many cards with those red flags on them in the file," he said. "This, you see, is *the* reason why all men's names come to that office: Time and again, we have had a man's name come from one city that has been red-flagged in another, 2,000 miles away. A man from California had been red-flagged in Denver. One from Florida had been red-flagged in Long Island. Another case in Southern California had been lined up on the red flag list in Buffalo. Hardly a day passes that there does not come to my desk, something concerning this sort of situation."[20]

Decisions about who should be included in the file were left to the same professional Scouters who oversaw the registration system, in consultation with the BSA's top lawyers. In a typical case, the local Scouts council might contact the national registration director about a leader suspected of abusing boys. The registration director would then gather information and available documentation and, without investigating further, decide if the leader should be blacklisted. If the BSA's lawyer agreed, the man's name was added to the files and he was expelled. Sometimes more deference was paid to the accused than to his victims.

In October 1960, Basil F. Starkey was director of registration when he advised a Massachusetts Scouts executive on how to handle a delicate situation: a man discharged from the air force and added to the perversion files eight months earlier for molesting boys in a Scouts troop at a US military base in the Philippines had turned up on the East Coast and applied to a local council to be registered as a neighborhood commissioner. When Starkey checked the name on the application against the confidential file, he got a match and told the local Scouts executive to break the bad news to the former airman that he would not be registered. Just do it quietly and considerately, Starkey advised the executive. "We suggest that you do this in person and through no one else. We also request that you make no mention of the Confidential File, but simply tell him that since he cannot be registered, he cannot have anything to do with Scouting. We have no desire to embarrass him, and this will give him a chance to make up any excuses he may desire in order to withdraw gracefully."[21]

The notion of allowing an admitted child molester to "gracefully" exit a situation in which he'd tried to gain access to even more boys would strike most reasonable people today as outrageous. But in 1960, it wasn't unusual, at least not according to the Boy Scouts' perversion files, which detail many instances when predatory leaders were allowed to concoct cover stories to conceal their wrongdoing. Nor was it unheard of for law enforcement officials to ignore or downplay abuse allegations if it meant shielding the Boy Scouts or its sponsoring organizations from bad publicity.

Seldom were such decisions so clearly spelled out as in the 1961 case of Robert L. Hillard, a Newton, Kansas, scoutmaster accused of molesting ten boys in Troop 150 while on camping trips, at his home, and elsewhere. "Dear Basil," a local Scout executive in Wichita wrote to Starkey, "Here is another one of the ugly situations we have to face from time to time. We have been trying to get something on this man for some time, and finally the right set of circumstances have come into focus."[22]

The Wichita executive attached a letter from Harvey County attorney Richard Hrdlicka, the local prosecutor, whose office had investigated a parent's complaint and substantiated the abuse allegations. "Our information indicated that Mr. Hillard would take one or two of these scouts with him on special trips, and while on such trips engage in acts of perversion, and that during all night parties at his house, he would take one boy at a time into his bedroom for purposes of immoral acts," Hrdlicka wrote to the Scouts executive in Wichita.[23]

Hillard's assistant scoutmaster, Kenneth Welsh, was also accused of abusing boys in the troop. When confronted with the allegations, both men confessed and signed sworn affidavits admitting guilt. Hillard acknowledged that his most recent molestation had occurred just two weeks earlier. But instead of pursuing what should have been a slam-dunk criminal case, Hrdlicka gave both abusers a pass—with the blessing of local and national Boy Scouts officials.

"After the complete admission of these two persons, I came to the decision that to openly prosecute would cause great harm to the reputations of two organizations, which we have involved here—the Boy Scouts of America and the local YMCA, as well as damage the reputations of at least two churches," Hrdlicka wrote, apparently referring to sponsoring groups. "I felt then and do now feel that the price which the community would have to pay for the punishment of these two individuals would be too great, in view of the fact that the damage thusly done to these organizations would be serious and lasting."

Instead of seeking justice for the victims, Hrdlicka cut a deal that let their abusers avoid prosecution—and potentially lengthy prison terms—by promising to get psychiatric help and sever their ties to Scouting, the YMCA, and other youth organizations. Two weeks later, the Scouts executive forwarded the prosecutor's letter to national headquarters, along with the signed confessions and asked Starkey to open perversion files on Hillard and Welsh. Starkey added the pair to the growing blacklist, with no indication that he had weighed in on whether they should have been fully held to account for their sex crimes against children. His letter back to the executive made no mention of them, either. "It is too bad we have to face these situations," he wrote, "but I do appreciate the thorough manner in which you handle them."[24]

Hrdlicka's protection of the BSA's reputation might have had something to do with his own positive, life-changing history with Scouting. As a Czech boy growing up in Prague, he had endured the German occupation during World War II and the Soviet domination that had followed. In 1947, he had traveled to France for the World Scout Jamboree and a year later, at age sixteen, he had defected in Paris while serving as an interpreter for the Czech national hockey team.[25] Stranded in France, he had written to the American Scouts he'd met a year earlier at the Jamboree. They had raised the money to bring him to the United States, where he'd landed in Kansas and gone on to become a lawyer and then the prosecuting attorney in Harvey County.[26] His American success story, launched by the help he received from his fellow Scouts, would include a lengthy stint as senior vice president and general counsel of Fiat USA in New York.[27]

Reached by telephone in early 2023, Hrdlicka, then ninety years old, said he had no recollection of the 1961 case and no desire to discuss something that occurred "a hundred years ago." He abruptly ended the call.[28]

NO ONE IN THE Boy Scouts' national office knew more about the perversion files than one of Basil Starkey's successors, Paul I. Ernst. He was a career Scouter and director of registration, subscription, and statistical services who oversaw them for twenty-two years. As his title suggests, Ernst's job involved such mundane tasks as compiling registration figures for the organization's annual reports and tracking subscribers to *Boys' Life* magazine. But from 1971 to 1993, a peak generation of sexual abuse in Scouting, Ernst was also the chief keeper of the files and the secrets they held, requesting and compiling evidence to support the allegations and, in concert with the BSA's top lawyer, deciding who would be added to the blacklist and who would be left off.

Born in August 1926 to Chester and Olive Ernst on their farm in Caldwell, Ohio, Paul joined Scouting as a youngster and never really left it.[29] After graduating from high school in Brewster, in northeastern Ohio, he attended a two-year business college in Canton and studied accounting. Afterward, he worked a couple of years for the Wheeling and Lake Erie Railway and then spent the next four years as a bank teller and cashier and at a job with a savings and loan. In 1952, while in his midtwenties, Ernst landed a paid position with the Boy Scouts as the assistant to the Scouts executive of the Buckeye Council in Massillon, Ohio. Following a brief detour to work as the office manager for a company that made leather harnesses for racehorses, he returned to Scouting in 1956 as assistant director of statistical services at the national headquarters in New Jersey. Ernst, who also volunteered as an assistant scoutmaster, moved up the BSA corporate ladder over the next decade and a half and in 1971 was named director of registration, the job that put him in charge of the perversion files.[30]

Like his predecessors in that position, Ernst placed a premium on confidentiality. Early on in his tenure, in 1972, he sent out a "personal and confidential" memo titled "Maintaining Standards of Leadership" to all Scout executives. The five-page memo, drafted by Boy Scout lawyers, laid out the organization's "carefully developed" guidelines for determining who should, or shouldn't, be accepted as a Scout leader. Among other things, the memo advised local Scouts officials to tread lightly when dealing with men they decided to exclude: "Make no accusations," it advised, but instead "say we have evidence to convince us that your (financial affairs) (moral life) (lack of leadership ability) do not meet the standards for leadership in the BSA."[31]

Attached to Ernst's memo was a boilerplate rejection letter to be customized and hand delivered to those men deemed undesirable, with suggested wording to placate their negative reactions by assuring them that "we are making no accusations and will not release this information to anyone, so our action in no way will affect your standing in the community." Ernst also told the local Scout executives not to circulate the memo. "This is the first time such information has been printed, and because of the misunderstandings which could develop if it were widely distributed, we suggest that after you have read it, you file it with other policy statements without making photocopies or sharing it beyond the top management of the council."

Among many letters Ernst would write stressing the need for secrecy of the files was one in October 1981 to a local council executive from Peoria, Illinois, who had compiled evidence on a leader accused of molesting at least five Scouts. "Please send me the details which you have in your files," Ernst wrote, noting the potential detriment to the BSA. "We have always asked that all the records in this type of situation be kept in the national office and not in the local council office because of the embarrassment that could be incurred if the wrong individuals would read the file."[32]

It is easy to question Ernst's motives for the nearly total lack of transparency of the perversion files, especially when viewing his actions through a contemporary lens. There is some truth to the Boy Scouts' oft-stated argument that it was "a different time" then and child sexual abuse was treated differently than it is now. It's also true that some parents whose sons were molested went along with Scouts officials' decisions to take no punitive action against the abusers, a form of neglect wrapped in good intentions, ostensibly to protect the boys' reputations and spare them from whisper campaigns and the mockery of their adolescent peers.

All too often, however, the overriding objective was simply to preserve the Boy Scouts' image. The BSA was a nonprofit, but it was also a business, a company with a brand—and negative publicity was bad for the brand. It also jeopardized the support of religious groups and the general public, not to mention the millions of dues-paying parents who might become too afraid to entrust their children's safety to the Boy Scouts.

Ernst, by all accounts, was not a sinister figure. Trim and bespectacled, he was well spoken and genial, always meticulously groomed and businesslike in his customary jacket and tie. He was nothing if not a company man, a good soldier for Scouting. A frequent and sometimes vague witness for the BSA in sexual abuse litigation, even long after his retirement in 1993, he made it clear that he believed it was his job to keep sexual predators out of the Boy Scouts—and that it was not his job to concern himself with what became of them afterward. "We were not trying to ruin this person's reputation or cause them to lose their job," he testified in deposition in a lawsuit in 2013. "We were just getting them out of Scouting. And if some other people wanted to report them to the police, that was their responsibility."[33] He said he had always tried to be honest and have boys' best interests at heart.

Ernst's recommendations had to be approved by the BSA's chief legal counsel, David Park, and were rubber-stamped by Joseph Anglim, its director of administration, who claimed to never have read any of the files.[34] As would become clear when the perversion files came to light near the end of Ernst's career and long afterward, many of their decisions had dire consequences for Boy Scouts who had depended on those men and the BSA to protect them.

At times, the top officials seemed to go out of their way to make life easier for alleged abusers. For example, Oregon Cub Scout leader Carleton "Tim" Coffey, who was convicted in 1985 of sexually abusing a young girl, was placed on probation by a judge and ordered to stay away from anyone younger than sixteen. Ernst and Park could have immediately ejected Coffey and permanently banned him from Scouting but instead allowed him to stay on. "My recommendation would be that we try to phase the individual out in a kind manner and place him on the confidential file at least in a probationary situation," Ernst wrote to the local Scout executive,[35] referring to its policy of allowing some accused molesters to continue in Scouting.[36]

Coffey remained on probationary status until he was charged in 1988 with molesting boys at a Scout camp. Only then was his registration permanently pulled.[37] The BSA scrapped its formal probation policy the same year.

CHAPTER 4

HALCYON DAYS

For more than half a century, Fashion Island has been Orange County, California's, primo open-air shopping mall. A mostly upscale collection of retailers and restaurants perched above the Pacific, it's a favorite destination for southern California's conspicuous consumers. Home to Neiman Marcus and Louis Vuitton, among other luxe outlets, Fashion Island sits on seventy-five acres of prime coastal real estate and is owned by the behemoth Irvine Company, which unabashedly bills it as the place "where life meets style in Newport Beach."[1]

It's also where some fifty thousand Boy Scouts flocked in 1953 for the BSA's Third National Jamboree, on what was then little more than a scrubby hillside expanse with a shimmering ocean view. The first of the quadrennial gatherings to be held on the West Coast, the '53 Jamboree was more than just a massive "kumbaya campout." It was a seven-day celebration of the best of American boyhood and patriotism, underscoring Scouting's prominence in post–World War II popular culture and its clout with Big Money, Hollywood, and the highest echelons of the federal government.

In *Jamboree*, an hourlong documentary film commissioned by the BSA and produced with the help of Hollywood luminaries Cecil B. DeMille and Howard Hughes, no lesser actor than Oscar winner Jimmy Stewart rides into the frame on horseback, looking like a dude ranch cowboy and waxing loquacious as he and his sidekick, the veteran character actor William Demarest, survey the wide-open ranchland before them.[2]

"It's kind of like a gold rush, only the gold these boys are going to be seeking is health and fun, friendship, cooperation," the laconic movie star says in his distinctive drawl. "They'll just camp outside, right next to nature. It's very historic ground on the Irvine Ranch, right down there. These three thousand acres once belonged to a Spanish don. The old padres walked here and brought the word of God, the King's Highway. Kit Carson came, too, and men looking for wealth from the ground. But none thought to find the greatest treasure of all: youth! In 1953, there's to be a gathering here of youngsters from every corner of the globe, and it'll be called the Boy Scout Jamboree."[3]

Cue the patriotic music and invisible narrator Del Sharbutt, who sounds like the same mellifluous voice-over guy in every mid-century newsreel: "Yes, on this naked ground a great city will be built, which will hold *fifty thousand boys!*" he intones. "It will last for only one week. *But what a memorable week that will be!*"

A year before the Jamboree, Boy Scouts officials approached Myford Irvine, the president of the company that bears his family's name, to seek his support for the event and the massive infrastructure project it would require.[4] Irvine, the great-grandson of company founder James Irvine, an Irish immigrant who made his first fortune in California selling food and supplies to Forty-niners pouring into the state for the Gold Rush,[5] readily agreed to provide the three-thousand-acre site and kicked in $250,000 to improve it. Magnanimous, yes, but pocket change for a man whose family owned the Irvine Ranch, a 185-square-mile amalgam of three former Mexican and Spanish land grants that sprawled along the coast for nine miles and stretched inland for twenty-two.

Over the coming months, workers filled in ravines, cut and graded roads through the burnt-brown hills, laid more than eighty miles of water and sewer lines, plotted some 1,200 troop camp-sites, strung miles of electrical and phone lines, and dug 4,500 pit latrines, many of them later planted with eucalyptus trees that flourished in the organically enriched soil. One of the dirt access roads was paved and became Jamboree Road, now a main artery linking Newport Beach with inland Orange County and the San Diego Freeway. Big chunks of the Irvine Ranch have since been developed into the city of Irvine, the University of Califor-nia, Irvine, campus, and high-end housing; some ninety thou-sand acres are still held by the Irvine Company's current owner, the reclusive billionaire Donald Bren, America's richest real estate baron.[6]

In 1953, two years before Disneyland would open in Anaheim, the Jamboree site was "nothing less than a temporary city" with a population about the size of Santa Ana, the late local historian Phil Brigandi, whose father attended as a Boy Scout, wrote in a 2019 ret-rospective.[7] "There were commissaries, and trading posts, and hos-pitals, and post offices, and fire crews, and about 30,000 tents," he wrote. The First National Bank of Santa Ana even opened a branch office there.[8]

Scouts came from across the United States and Canada and from more than a dozen other countries including Japan and England. Most arrived by rail on special "Scout trains" at stations in Santa Ana, Fullerton, East Los Angeles, and La Puente, then boarded buses to the Jamboree, which opened on July 17 to much hoopla and positive press. "The once drab hills of Irvine Ranch are blossoming with the color of bright green tents, gigantic camp entry ways, troop flags and thousands of eager youngsters in Scout khaki or Explorer green," the *Newport Balboa News-Times* wrote in one of many boosterish newspaper stories published across the country.[9]

Freshly minted Eagle Scout Richard "Skip" Leifer was thirteen when he arrived with his troop from Wisconsin after traveling by train to Los Angeles by way of Yellowstone National Park, Salt Lake City, and Las Vegas, where one Scout leader's attempt to demonstrate the futility of gambling backfired when he dropped a silver dollar into a slot machine and hit a $100 jackpot. A future aerospace industry manager, Skip would remember the Jamboree for many things, not least of which was meeting Jimmy Stewart, who'd been intrigued by his troop's flag, adorned with an image of a cow udder to honor his home state of Wisconsin, America's Dairyland. It was but one of many encounters that would etch the Jamboree in Skip's memory as "just a fantastic thing" that would help shape his life for the better, and for years to come.[10]

While most of the Jamboree would be spent on traditional Scout activities—cooking over open charcoal fires, swapping souvenirs, hiking in the hills, catching lizards and field mice, and taking field trips to Huntington Beach and Mission San Juan Capistrano—the week of fellowship and skills training was infused with a heavy dose of star power, glamor, and patriotic schtick.

Opening ceremonies featured "The Building of a Nation," a historical pageant staged at a huge amphitheater carved into the hillside, with seating for seventy-five thousand. It began with a lone Boy Scout onstage talking about his cross-country trip to get there, then moved on to "an old-timer" portrayed by the actor Chill Wills, who traced the country's history from General George Washington's winter at Valley Forge to the Gold Rush and beyond. The high-gloss, professional-grade production was replete with covered wagons, mock Indian battles (and mock Indians), and two authentic steam locomotives that chugged across the stage on specially laid rails.

The next day, Vice President Richard M. Nixon showed up, a

characteristically starched-shirt fish out of water in suit and tie, hardly the picture of the rugged outdoorsman. He spent the night with a California troop from his hometown of Whittier, then helped the boys whip up breakfast and set out with them for a walking tour of the grounds, trading his DC business duds for a pair of rarely worn shorts and stopping every now and then to sign autographs. Later that Sunday, Nixon addressed another campwide gathering, themed "My Duty to God," reminding the lads of the BSA's deep religious roots. Top leaders of the Catholic, Protestant, Jewish, and Mormon faiths were honored guests and participants.

It's fair to assume, however, that even among the most devout Jamboree attendees, religion finished a distant second to showbiz. The comedian and box-office star Bob Hope emceed a Tuesday-night gala, "Hollywood's Salute to Scouting," treating the audience to a drive-by brush with fame, a procession of celebrities in Chevy convertibles. It was the same model of car made famous by the quintessentially all-American singer Dinah Shore, who closed her popular TV show each week with her trademark ads for the auto-maker, which featured her belting out the jingle "See the U.S.A. in your Chevrolet."[11]

Most of their names carry little weight today, but several dozen Hollywood A-listers took bows on the 1953 Jamboree stage. The cowboy star Roy Rogers was there with his famed palomino, Trigger, and his wife, Dale Evans, whom he introduced in that order. Dorothy Lamour, Hope's costar in a series of popular "On the Road" movies with the crooner Bing Crosby, wore a sleeveless sundress and pearl choker, much to the delight of the mostly adolescent male audience. "Miss Lamour made a big hit, with a hula dance and songs," the Associated Press noted in a nationally circulated story.[12] "After the show, swarms of boys followed her, trying to shake her hand. At one point, the harassed actress cried, 'Help! Help!—Girl Scouts!'" Jane Powell was on hand, too—more naked arms, more pearls, more deliriously cheering pubescent boys.

Other stars of stage and screen present included Eddie Bracken, Mitzi Gaynor, Jerry Colonna, Johnny Mack Brown, Lash LaRue, George Montgomery, Tex Ritter, June Allyson, Anne Francis, Rory Calhoun, Jeff Chandler, Dick Powell, Debbie Reynolds, Will Rogers, Jr., Danny Kaye, and the one and only Francis the Talking Mule, who had starred in a series of popular comedy films.

President Dwight D. Eisenhower drew enthusiastic cheers and applause from the crowd that week with a filmed speech that endorsed an appreciation for "the vastness and complexities of this nation" and struck themes of unity, of "working together in our country and in the world."[13] His nemesis Joseph McCarthy, the Red-baiting Republican senator from Wisconsin famous for stoking fears of Communist infiltration of the government, was nowhere to be seen at the Jamboree. But the Scouts' documentary managed to inject a bit of his spirit just the same.

"Here is a visitor who has lived in East Germany under Communist rule," the narrator says over footage of a foreign Scout chatting with his American counterparts. "And these Scouts are listening intently as he tells how the Communists not only put an iron curtain around the countries but also around each individual. He tells of all the restrictions, rules, regulations, and hardships under the Communists and that he is happy to be at the Jamboree. And his newfound American friends are happy to have him."[14]

The film's anti-Communist subtext was no coincidence: the pro-democracy production in which the East German Scout and his newfound American friends were unwitting extras was underwritten in part by Uncle Sam. In 1954, when the film was screened for an audience at MGM Studios, the *Hollywood Reporter* revealed that the documentary had been conceived and pitched by the actor George Murphy, who later served as a Republican US senator from California. Two-thirds of the film's cost was financed by the tire industry magnates Leonard K. Firestone, who also was a

Los Angeles Scouting executive, and Edwin Thomas, a top hon-
cho with Goodyear. The remaining third of the cost was borne by
the US State Department, at the urging of famed director DeMille,
and with the understanding that its Overseas Information Service would distribute the film internationally "as a testimonial on
behalf of democracy and against Communism."[15]

Major newspapers also were eager to boost the American ideals on full display at the Jamboree. In addition to the obligatory
gee-whiz reports on the gallons of water drunk that week (18
million), number of eggs eaten (500,000), and number of loaves
of bread (169,595) washed down by quarts of milk (623,656),
some reporters covering the event happily jumped onto the
anti-Communist bandwagon.

"This is democracy in the working. And it works well," one
Los Angeles Times story gushed. "Here at Jamboree City—freedom
city—there is no regimentation. Participation is entirely voluntary.
This is the contrast to the pro-communist protests such as the Reds
staged recently in East Germany following revolts against tyranny
there."[16]

THE PATRIOTIC, RAH-RAH TENOR of the 1953 Jamboree was befitting
its time, a postwar era of white middle-class prosperity and opti-
mism when 8 million military veterans went to college or received
job training through the G.I. Bill.[17] Suburban housing tracts and
shopping centers sprouted from midwestern cornfields, and the
burgeoning Interstate Highway System was opening up the country. Young families were growing and settling into houses financed
by VA loans. Their television sets, still mostly black and white, were
tuned in to *Father Knows Best, Leave It to Beaver,* and *The Adventures
of Ozzie and Harriet,* with the Andersons, the Cleavers, and the Nel-
sons ruling the airwaves as the quintessential American families,
white bread as could be and headed by worldly wise dads who

wore neckties to the dinner table and were always there to help their sons navigate the pitfalls of becoming a man.

The country was experiencing a postwar baby boom that would add an average of 4 million newborns to the population every year, many of whom would become Boy Scouts. The BSA, born a half century earlier, had come to symbolize the idealized patriotic American boy in an era when parents enrolled their sons in Scouting as a matter of course. By the 1950s, more than 3 million boys were in Scouting, as its membership rolls continued to swell—as did those of most major civic organizations, during what the Harvard political scientist Robert D. Putnam described as a "massive outpouring of patriotism and collective solidarity" in "one of the most vital periods of community involvement in American history."[18]

Those were halcyon days for the Boy Scouts and for the country at large—most of it, anyway. Americans in the 1950s found themselves with more discretionary income and more consumer goods to spend it on: cars, televisions, the latest household appliances. The '50s were hailed as the decade of "the affluent society," a term derived from the title of economist John Kenneth Galbraith's celebrated book that explored the causes and effects of the postwar economic boom. The gross domestic product, a key economic indicator that measures the total annual output of goods and services, rose significantly, as did personal income and the consumption of consumer goods. But as Galbraith stressed, much that seemingly underpinned the affluent society was illusory. It was an era of "ever-increasing opulence in privately produced goods," an accumulation of private wealth that overshadowed serious deficits in spending on public services, education, the environment, and infrastructure. Galbraith wrote:

The family which takes its mauve and cerise, air-conditioned, power-steered and power-braked automobile out for a tour passes through cities that are badly paved, made hideous by litter, blighted buildings, billboards, and posts for wires that should long since have been put underground. They pass on into a countryside that has been rendered largely invisible by commercial art....They picnic on exquisitely packaged food from a portable icebox by a polluted stream and go on to spend the night at a park which is a menace to public health and morals. Just before dozing off on an air mattress, beneath a nylon tent, amid the stench of decaying refuse, they may reflect vaguely on the curious unevenness of their blessings.[19]

Indeed, 1950s affluence belied a serious wealth gap between the haves and the have-nots. It concealed the fact that the general decline in poverty had not extended to poorer, mostly rural whites and most African Americans, who also continued to struggle for civil rights taken for granted by the majority of US citizens. The Boy Scouts from early on had accepted Black members, but mostly in segregated troops. It was just beginning to broadly integrate its units, a process that would drag on well into the 1970s as some parts of the country clung to the vestiges of the Jim Crow era that denied African Americans the right to vote and deprived them of employment and educational opportunities.[20]

By 1960, the BSA's golden jubilee year, youth rolls had swelled to 3.8 million and, with the roster of adult leaders added in, total membership topped 5 million. President John F. Kennedy, the first former Boy Scout to hold that office, noted the membership milestone two years later in remarks to the Boy Scouts' "family of the year," the Harry G. Fairs from Bartlesville, Oklahoma, in a ceremony at the White House. Like every president since William Howard Taft, who had served from 1909 to 1913, Kennedy, once a member of Troop 2 in Bronxville, New York, held the title of honorary president of the BSA, highlighting its ties to the Oval Office.

"I think we've got a great American family and I think they have typified what Scouting means to this country," Kennedy said of the Fairs in a gathering in the Fish Room. "I strongly believe in Scouting. I think it's a source of great strength to us. I'm very appreciative to all the adults who give leadership. I would recommend it to the sons and daughters of every American family....I congratulate you all and tell you that we are grateful to you and the millions of families you represent today."[21]

It seemed as though William D. Boyce's mission to make men of America's boys had been passed on to the next generation and was well under way, judging from a snippet from the 1967 edition of the *Boy Scout Handbook*, which sang the praises of troop leaders' contributions to the effort: "First, there's your Scoutmaster. What a wonderful man he is! He spends hours figuring out how to give you fun and adventure in your troop....He is the friend to whom you can always turn for advice. He coaches the patrol leaders. Why does he do all this? Because he believes in Scouting, because he likes boys and wants to help them become real men."[22]

But the definition of "real men" in the 1960s was far different from that of just the previous decade. Men of the 1950s had been the recently returned winners of a righteous world war and veterans of the less clear-cut but honorably resolved Korean War. They were seen as hard workers, often stoic, good providers to their young families, and possessed of a clear sense of right and wrong. Being a man in the 1960s was far more complicated, as the Vietnam War ripped apart the country, the civil rights movement gained momentum marked by spasms of racial strife that boiled over into deadly riots in Los Angeles and Detroit, and more women left the household to enter the workforce.

Traditional roles at home and at work were evolving and, in the view of some segments of the population, threatening the definition of American manhood. Just as concerns about the "feminization" of the American boy had boosted early Scouting's membership numbers, similar fears of and disdain for the growing counterculture appeared to help drive up the Boy Scouts' membership, as did the surging popularity of Cub Scouts. The BSA's youth membership peaked at 4.9 million in 1972,[23] when one of three American boys between the ages of ten and nineteen wore the familiar uniform: navy blue for Cub Scouts, khaki green for their older counterparts in Boy Scouts.

Those heady days were not to last, as the 1950s and early '60s would prove to be the calm before the storms of social and political upheaval that would follow. Those fed a backlash against organizations such as the Boy Scouts that were seen to toe the lines of tradition and authority. The BSA would find itself competing for the attention of baby boom kids with Little League baseball and other increasingly popular organized youth sports.

The coming years would also present the Boy Scouts with threats from within, including a cheating scandal spawned by intense internal pressure to keep membership numbers from slipping.

CHAPTER 5

UPHEAVAL AND BACKLASH

Hundreds of millions of people around the world tuned in to astronaut Neil Armstrong's historic walk on the moon, none more engrossed on that Sunday night in July 1969 than thirty-four thousand Boy Scouts camped out in the Coeur d'Alene Mountains of northern Idaho, craning to hear transistor radios or huddled in front of a few flickering portable black-and-white TVs.

Armstrong, the commander of the Apollo 11 mission, was an Eagle Scout from Wapakoneta, Ohio, and one of their own.[1] He'd made that clear two days earlier in a message broadcast by Mission Control as he hurtled through space with crewmates Michael Collins and Edwin "Buzz" Aldrin, another former Boy Scout. "I'd like to say hello to all my fellow scouts and scouters at Farragut State Park in Idaho having a National Jamboree there this week," he said; "and Apollo 11 would like to send them best wishes."[2]

Armstrong's Space Age shout-out was more than a mere highlight of the Jamboree, Scouting's massing of troops from around the country every four years; it would be among the few bright spots in a particularly dismal stretch for the BSA during a time of national political and social upheaval. The country was convulsed with anti–Vietnam War protests and racial strife and reeling from the assassinations of Martin Luther King, Jr., and Robert F. Kennedy, the Kent State shooting, stagflation, gas shortages, and Watergate. For the BSA, the decade beginning in the late 1960s would be marked by decline, fueled in part by a well-intended but ultimately disastrous shift in programming away from traditional scoutcraft.

Four months before Armstrong's immortal utterance "One small step for man, one giant leap for mankind," the BSA issued its *59th Annual Report to Congress*.[3] In sharp contrast to the sunny dispatches sent out during Scouting's heyday years following World War II, its opening section was more apocalyptic than optimistic, arguably the Boy Scouts' darkest portrayal of the United States and its youth since Congress had chartered the BSA in 1916. The words under the heading of "The Concerns" read like an advertisement for Camp Dystopia: "America is a disturbed land. Problems mount and frustrations surround us. Young people are deeply involved, whether it be discontent with our foreign policy, demonstrations and riots in our cities, or our escalating crime rate…and most of the Nation's crimes are being committed by young people." It went on to lament "the mushrooming drug market, the impractical flower world of the Hippie, the something-for-nothing attitude of many young people, the 'God is dead' illusion, moral decline [and] the shadow of international communism."

The gloom-and-doom report came on the heels of a yearlong research project commissioned by the BSA that asked "Is Scouting in Tune with the Times?" The report concluded that it wasn't. While the researchers found that Scouting was well regarded by boys and their parents and an "unqualifiedly accepted part of the American scene," they also discovered a high dropout rate and a variety of underlying negatives: It was too regimented, too childish, and too boring.[4]

The BSA's response to all of that was something it called

"Boypower 76," as in "America's manpower begins with Boypower." The eight-year initiative grew out of an earlier effort that had met with mixed results: 1965's Inner-City Rural Program, which had focused on boosting membership in eighteen urban and rural areas and, among other things, featured a roving "Scoutmobile" to help generate interest that never quite materialized.[5]

Boypower launched on New Year's Day 1969 and was planned to culminate with the nation's Bicentennial celebration in 1976.[6] Its goal was to involve one-third of all American boys in Scouting by increasing combined youth and adult membership from 4.6 million in 1968 to 6.5 million eight years later. It would target impoverished boys in cities and rural areas that the BSA had largely ignored for decades, especially since the postwar baby boom that had fueled "white flight" from the cities. A key component of the $65 million recruitment campaign was increasing the paid Scouting staff at the local and district levels by about 50 percent, to more than six thousand. Filling out Scouting's ranks with 30 percent more African American boys was also essential but posed a steep challenge for the traditionally white, middle-class, suburban BSA.

Scouting's history regarding racial inclusiveness had more or less kept pace with that of the rest of the country,[7] which is to say that it had not moved very fast and certainly not boldly, ever since William D. Boyce, one of the BSA's founders, had insisted on making Scouting open to all boys, regardless of race or religion—despite his own belief in white superiority.[8] From the outset, the Boy Scouts welcomed Black members, but mostly in separate and supposedly equal "Negro troops." Early on, in response to questions about integrating a white troop in New Orleans, Chief Scout Executive James E. West said that that would not be necessary because "the Negro interests in the Boy Scout movement could be handled in the same way as you handle the public schools in the South, that is, providing separate schools, teachers and administration."[9] And so it went for decades, as the BSA was slow to integrate, especially in the South, where some leaders and chartering organizations threatened to pull their support if white units accepted Black Scouts.

While most troops in the North were integrated by the early 1950s, only one in the Deep South had achieved that status by the middle of the decade. The Supreme Court's 1954 decision in *Brown v. Board of Education* had outlawed racial segregation in schools, reversing the "separate but equal" doctrine that had been in place since 1896. That had helped prod the BSA to integrate, as had the growing civil rights movement led by King and the passage of the Civil Rights Act in 1964 and the Voting Rights Act a year later. But not until 1968 did the Boy Scouts of America stop chartering segregated troops, and full integration wouldn't occur for several years after that.[10]

In 1972, in a bid to make Scouting more relevant to the urban kids whom its Boypower campaign aimed to recruit, the BSA revamped its program and rewrote its handbook, jettisoning many of the outdoor skills that previous generations had learned and loved. It translated the handbook into Spanish to appeal to Latino prospects, and it dropped "Boy" from the title to blunt any negative racial connotation that word might convey to the African American community.

Under the "Improved Scouting Program," as it was dubbed, tutorials on swimming, camping, canoeing, and cooking over an open fire gave way to subjects such as child care, mitigating safety hazards at home, household finance, and drug abuse, including the hallucinogenic peril of LSD. Mapping techniques now had more to do with bus and subway routes than using a compass in the backcountry to find true north. Knowing how to use pay toilets and disinfect rat bites became more important than tying a bowline knot or making fire by friction, and learning self-defense took the place of recognizing which berries to eat to survive in the wild.[11] Other big changes included loosening requirements for merit badges and advancement from one Scouting level to the next: it was now possible to become an Eagle Scout without setting foot in the countryside, much less mastering previously mandatory skills related to camping, cooking, and the great outdoors.[12]

The result, traditionalists complained, was that the BSA had lost its way. It had taken "the outing out of Scouting," along with much of the fun, and had mostly gutted its own program. Legions of longtime Scouts and their adult leaders abandoned the Boy Scouts, and Boypower 76 did not drum up nearly enough recruits to replace them.

Some new urban Scouting units did spring up, notably in inner-city Cincinnati, Philadelphia, and south Brooklyn, where members of Troop 503 dubbed themselves "Black and Puerto Rican Stoners," hard as the concrete all around them. In homage to the Black Power movement, the Stoners were decked out not in traditional uniforms but in military fatigues, combat boots, and berets. They said the Pledge of Allegiance with clenched fists over their hearts, and to the twelve-tenet Scout Law they added a new one: "Have ethnic pride." They tweaked the law to include their brothers and sisters and community, and they came up with their own chant: "Stoners, Stoners, hard as we can be. Stoners, Stoners, for real. Dig on me. Never victims of a needle high. Hard work, cleaning up dirt and a forward strive, no jive. That's our high."[13]

Such scattered urban success stories notwithstanding, the BSA's full-throttle push to add 2 million to its ranks over eight years did not go well. In 1969, the Boy Scouts lost sixty-five thousand members, the first decline in many years. The dip was partly due to the baby boom fizzling out and shrinking the pool of eligible boys. But the rise of the antimilitary, antiestablishment counterculture also cut into the appeal of the BSA's patriotic messaging and square, conformist image. The backlash was so strong that some on the left derided Boy Scouts in uniform as "little fascists,"[14] a harshly unfair comparison to the Hitler Youth movement of a previous generation.

The pressure to meet membership quotas did not subside, however, and some Scout leaders in local councils around the country succumbed to it. Larry John O'Connor, a Boy Scouts district executive in Kansas City, Kansas, from 1967 to 1969, remembers being drilled, along with other professional Scouters at a forty-five-day training program in New Jersey, on the importance of "the three M's": membership, money, and manpower. Translation: without membership there is no money, and without money there is no manpower.[15]

At the time, the local council where O'Connor worked was receiving United Way funds and needed to keep its membership numbers up to justify requests for additional support. He and other local Scouts officials were under heavy pressure to make sure that all of the units in their districts were reregistered on time, so when the troop in the "little bitty town" of Fontana, Kansas, missed the deadline, he made the sixty-five-mile trip to find out why. The scoutmaster there told him that the unit no longer existed, a fact O'Connor relayed to his boss. O'Connor was surprised and dismayed when his supervisor, a BSA field director, directed him to dig out the former Fontana Scouts' names and reregister them anyway. He refused and almost lost his job over it, but the defunct troop was resurrected and reregistered when someone else with a more pliable spine went along with the scam.

It was but one of several personal encounters O'Connor had with BSA "ghost units" that existed only on paper. During his time as a professional Scouter and again after quitting his paying job in disgust and continuing in Scouting as a volunteer, he witnessed quota-driven fraud in Kansas, Iowa, and Texas, from the late 1960s to the early '80s, all by men who'd promised to obey the Scout Law, to be trustworthy. "It was a known factor among professional Scouters," O'Connor said. "I was shocked at what was being done and I continuously refused to do it, and it cost me my job. It was prevalent throughout the entire Boy Scouts organization."[16]

In June 1974, the *Chicago Tribune* blew the lid off Boypower 76 with a series of stories exposing widespread schemes by local Scouts officials who had cooked the books to pad their rosters and secure federal funding and charitable donations to pay the dues of inner-city recruits. The *Tribune* reported that up to half of Chicago's eighty-seven thousand registered Boy Scouts existed only on paper, many of them signed up for troops that had never been formed. Others were Scouts who had long since left the program but hadn't been purged from the rosters. Still others had been recruited for one-month cut-rate memberships at 10 cents each—anything to boost the numbers.[17]

The fraud, which included one den mother who purportedly oversaw thirty phantom Cub Scout packs, extended to Chicago's suburbs and well beyond, involving at least ten councils in Illinois, Michigan, Georgia, Texas, Tennessee, Oklahoma, and California. BSA Chief Scout Executive Alden G. Barber, who had pushed the Boypower concept, was compelled to admit that "some of our people cheat, quite frankly," and in an epic way. "If we were in the business of covering it up, it could be the Watergate of the Boy Scouts," he said just months before that political scandal came to a head when President Richard Nixon resigned and was replaced by Vice President Gerald Ford, the first Eagle Scout to occupy the Oval Office.[18]

By then Boyhood 76 was two years behind schedule and headed for the rocks. Membership would never hit the lofty goals the organization had set and instead continued to drop. Boy Scout historian David Scott, who has written several books on the BSA, said that the organization has never fully recovered from the misguided program that drove off thousands of middle-class white kids while trying to attract poor Black and Hispanic Scouts. "Boypower had great altruistic intentions, but the follow-through was bumbled.

The messaging was bumbled. And the execution was bumbled," he said. "Therefore, you had a collapse of membership."[19]

Boypower 76 was put out of its misery two years early, in 1974, its goals deemed out of reach. The BSA did not entirely abandon its efforts to attract and retain urban Scouts and leaders, but it reversed course on many of the Improved Scouting Program changes, including those made to the *Boy Scout Handbook*. Lifelong Scouter Bill Hillcourt, who had written a dozen Scouting books, including a biography of Robert Baden-Powell and earlier editions of the manual, came out of retirement at age seventy-eight to redo the one that had been gutted of traditional content. Hillcourt, a native of Denmark who joined the BSA's professional staff in 1926 and penned a long-running column in *Boys' Life* magazine as "Green Bar Bill," a nickname derived from the uniform emblem worn by patrol leaders,[20] produced a ninth edition of the handbook in 1979 that reinstituted such traditional skills as tracking, signaling, and mapmaking—and sold more than four million copies.[21] He also scoffed at the BSA research study that had prompted all of the changes a decade earlier. "Scouting had never been in tune with the times!" he said. "Even in 1908, it was idiotic to suggest that you should go out and do camping because everybody knew that the night air was bad for you—you might get malaria, for heaven's sake....It was exactly because [of the facts that] it was idiotic and out of tune with the times that made Scouting appealing."[22]

Along with the remade handbook came a revival of programming that had been dropped. Advancement requirements reverted to making outdoor skills mandatory, and Scouts would once again have to earn hiking, first aid, cooking, and camping awards to achieve First Class status. By the end of the 1970s, BSA membership had sunk to 4.27 million,[23] some 200,000 less than when Boypower 76 had been launched in 1969—and far off its target of 6.5 million.

The upside for Scouting was that it had survived a tumultuous decade and the national Zeitgeist pendulum was beginning to swing back in its direction. The Vietnam War was, at long last, mostly in the rearview mirror, having ended ignominiously for US forces when North Vietnamese army tanks had rolled onto the grounds of the Presidential Palace in Saigon on April 30, 1975.[24] With a resurgence of political conservatism on the horizon in the Ronald Reagan presidency, the BSA's future seemed to brighten once again. Membership began to rebound, bolstered by the support of Scouting's most powerful religious partners, the Mormon, Methodist, and Catholic churches.

But the next decade would prove to be no less fraught for the BSA than the one just ended. Its allegiance to organized religion would help draw it into the gathering culture wars, most notably over gay rights, and a sexual abuse scandal that had been germinating for years was soon to shed the veil of secrecy that had kept it from public view for the better part of a century.

CARL MAXWELL, JR., HAD no inkling of any of that when he signed up for Scouting in his seemingly all-American hometown, Newport, Pennsylvania, in the early 1970s.

Newport had the look and feel of a place that had changed little since long before Carl became a Boy Scout. The streets in and around downtown were lined with two- and three-story homes and commercial buildings, some dating to the early 1800s, a mix of brick structures and frame houses whose original clapboard siding had been replaced by vinyl or aluminum. Built on the banks of the Juniata River, the town had gotten its start as a shipping center for grain and other goods headed downriver to Harrisburg and Baltimore.[25] It had enjoyed its greatest prosperity between the Civil War and World War II, and many of the buildings from that era were still intact, part of a designated historic district, with some structures now listed on the National Register of Historic Places.[26]

As well preserved as it was, Newport wasn't trying to be Colonial Williamsburg. It mostly felt like a pleasant old town, well worn and a little tired.

The Maxwell family's roots ran at least three generations deep in Newport and surrounding Perry County in south central Pennsylvania, a woodsy area of Appalachian Mountain ridges and valleys drained by the Juniata and a veining of creeks. Carl's grandparents had raised his dad and his uncles in the same neighborhood where Carl romped in the woods as a kid, on foot or on his minibike, the same area where he swam in the "cricks" and fished in the river.

Carl's mother, Dorothy, had grown up not far away in the even smaller town of Blain and quit high school to help support her family as a seamstress. She had "worked her fingers to the bone" at her union sewing job, Carl said, making garments for the J. C. Penney Company until she had retired with a $109-a-month pension.[27] His late father, Carl Sr., had worked for the Pennsylvania Department of Transportation as a manager in the motor vehicles division. To ease the confusion of there being too many Carls under one roof, Carl Jr. was given the nickname "George" in honor of one of his dad's friends, a man with seven daughters but no sons.

His mom played bingo in her spare time, and his dad was a member of the Newport Social Order of Owls, in those days a men-only club. Carl and his parents and his older sister, Cindy, were just a normal, happy, tight-knit middle-class family enjoying life in small-town America. "I didn't get in any trouble," Carl said. "My sister didn't, either. We were good kids, so my parents had no reason to be strict. But we knew right from wrong, and when we needed punished, we got punished."[28]

Carl got into Scouting more on a whim than by design. His best friend, Scott, was a member of the Protestant church that sponsored Troop 222. Scott wanted to join Scouts, so Carl did, too, along with their friends Mike Kunkel and his stepbrother, J. P. Culhane.

Their scoutmaster was Rodger Beatty, a tall, fit US Army veteran just shy of thirty who worked as a counselor for a Columbia-Perry counties substance abuse program. He seemed like a great guy at first, Carl and others recalled, and he took a keen interest in boys from broken homes or troubled families, some of whose parents he'd met through his job as a counselor.[29]

As Carl and his friends would soon find out, though, Beatty's interest in them was anything but altruistic.

CHAPTER 6

DOWNPLAY, DENY, DEFLECT

L awrence F. Potts, the BSA director of administration, was in Washington to testify before the House Judiciary Subcommittee on Civil and Constitutional Rights, which had convened to consider a new law that would allow states to require FBI fingerprint checks for employees and volunteers of youth-serving nonprofits.

The July 16, 1993, hearing came on the heels of a decade in which Scouting's declining membership had rebounded, ticking up to the drumbeat of "traditional family values" during a Reagan-era comeback of political conservatism. What should have been cause for celebration by Scouting was overshadowed by negative publicity surrounding two high-profile lawsuits that had exposed a sexual abuse problem the BSA had managed to keep largely hidden. The unwavering trust that generations of American parents had placed in their children's scoutmasters, and in the venerated institution they represented, would be shaken as never before, years before a similar betrayal by sexually predatory Catholic priests drew widespread outrage.

In 1987, a jury in Corvallis, Oregon, awarded $4.3 million to a former Boy Scout who was repeatedly abused by William Tobiassen, a longtime scoutmaster, life insurance agent, father of three Eagle Scouts, and recipient of the Silver Beaver Award, the BSA's top honor for local volunteers.[1] The boy's mother had reported his abuse to local Scouts officials and police in 1982, but neither had taken action until 1984, when Tobiassen was arrested and his name was added to the BSA's Ineligible Volunteer files.[2]

In a deal with prosecutors to avoid additional charges for molesting other Scouts, Tobiassen pleaded guilty to second-degree sexual abuse and contributing to the delinquency of a minor and was sentenced to thirty days in jail and five years' probation. The civil lawsuit that followed was among the first BSA sexual abuse cases to go to trial, generating widespread publicity, unlike so many others that had been resolved quietly and sealed with confidential settlements. Tobiassen's case resulted in what was then the largest judgment in BSA history—at least until a state appellate court slashed $2 million from the jury award in 1989.[3]

Just a year earlier, in 1988, lawyers for a Virginia abuse survivor had forced the Boy Scouts to turn over 231 of its perversion files as part of a lawsuit that also wound up in court. The *Washington Post*, the Associated Press, and local news outlets covered the trial of Carlton L. Bittenbender, a scoutmaster who'd been convicted in 1981 of abusing boys in a troop in Rhode Island before he moved to Virginia.[4] At the time of the trial in Reston, an upscale community twenty-two miles west of Washington, he was already serving a thirty-year sentence for abusing three Scouts there, including the plaintiff in the civil suit. Dismissed as a defendant but called as an adverse witness by the former Scout he had molested, Bittenbender used his time on the stand to tout his preincarceration achievement of helping eighteen boys become Eagle Scouts while casting himself as the helpless victim of a sickness beyond his control.[5]

In a gloves-off defense, the BSA's lawyer contended that the national organization was not responsible for Bittenbender's abuse, since he'd been selected by local Scouts officials, in keeping with the organization's decentralized command structure: the BSA issues charters to geographically distinct local councils made up of volunteers, who hire their own staffs and raise their own funds to promote the program through churches, civic organizations, and other troop sponsors. Troop committees pick scoutmasters.

The BSA lawyer told jurors that the victim, who had been twelve when Bittenbender had abused him more than sixty times over the course of a year or more, had willingly submitted to the scoutmaster's advances—never mind that any adult sexual contact with a child that age was a crime. The BSA attorney also blamed the boy's severe psychological damage on his alcoholic father and his chaotic home life, not the sexual abuse inflicted by Bittenbender. On its sixth day of deliberations, the jury found the BSA blameless and ordered the local Boy Scout council to pay a relatively meager $45,000 to a state compensation fund for crime victims. Most of that money went to the court-appointed lawyer who had represented Bittenbender.[6]

Although the BSA had prevailed in the Bittenbender case, it would serve to amplify the emerging story of sexual abuse in Scouting. Patrick Boyle, a *Washington Times* reporter, had followed the trial coverage and talked his editors into letting him delve into the perversion files. His work had resulted in a multipart investigative series for the newspaper in 1991 and later his nonfiction book *Scout's Honor: Sexual Abuse in America's Most Trusted Institution.*

The publicity from the Tobiassen and Bittenbender trials also helped raise public awareness of child sexual abuse in America in the 1980s and fueled a push for stronger vetting of volunteers and better incident reporting—hence the National Child Protection Act of 1993 and the congressional hearing featuring the BSA's Larry Potts. Joining him at the witness table that day was Lynn Swann, the former Pittsburgh Steelers star wide receiver and future Hall of Famer, who was then president of the national board of Big Brothers Big Sisters of America.

Swann told the bipartisan panel of lawmakers that his organization was solidly behind the proposed law, which would enhance states' reporting of child abuse and expand access to the FBI's criminal fingerprint database, with an eye toward making such checks mandatory for nonprofits. These are dangerous times, Swann testified, when young people are exposed to random gun violence, drugs, and sexual abuse. While the Big Brothers' primary mission was to mentor boys and girls and provide them a "productive and positive outlook" on life, he said, its chief responsibility was to protect them, which was why the group had been conducting criminal background checks of its volunteers for nearly a decade. "This sometimes has been costly. This sometimes has met with great obstacles," he said, "but we have endured the cost and the burden of getting this done." If the rigorous screening meant that only one of six men who volunteered to be a Big Brother made the cut, so be it: that was the cost of protecting kids.[7]

In 1993, many states required criminal background checks for licensed day care workers, schoolteachers, and the staffs of juvenile detention centers, but charities and nonprofits were largely exempt.[8] The Boy Scouts had no such background checks and, as Potts was about to make clear, strongly opposed them. After telling the panel that the BSA "has been deeply concerned about the welfare of youth since 1910," Potts recounted the BSA's efforts. He lauded former Chief Scout Executive Ben Love for naming child abuse as one of five "unacceptables" in Scouting in 1986, along with drug abuse, hunger, illiteracy, and youth unemployment. He extolled the benefits of the BSA's special five-point plan to combat child abuse, including educating parents and volunteers, strengthening leader selection procedures, and encouraging prompt reporting of and action on sexual abuse incidents.[9] By "prompt reporting," he meant to Scouts officials; the BSA at that time did not require child sexual abuse to be reported to police.

Along with his testimony and a written statement, Potts submitted a copy of a five-page article that carried his byline and detailed the formal "Youth Protection Program" that BSA had put into place in 1988.[10] The article, which Potts later acknowledged had been ghostwritten by a public relations consultant with no substantive input from Potts himself,[11] detailed policies designed to prevent child sexual abuse, including "two-deep leadership" that required more than one adult to be on all trips and outings and prohibited all one-on-one meetings between Scouts and adult leaders. Skinny-dipping was banned, as were physical hazing, secret cliques, and initiation rituals. The BSA also established a five-member task force of psychologists, psychiatrists, and other child sexual abuse experts to develop the program and keep it on track.

But when it came to checking prospective volunteers' fingerprints against the FBI database—the gold standard of background screening at the time—Potts said that that was out of the question: it would be too expensive and might produce a false sense of security because such checks wouldn't catch all sexual predators, only those who'd been convicted of crimes. He did not address whether the BSA, which that year took in $10 million more in revenue than it paid out in expenses,[12] might be able to afford the checks itself, at a cost of about $18 each. But he was adamant that local chartering groups—PTAs, churches, and others that sponsored troops and were responsible for choosing their leaders—did not have the funds to do it. Nor did volunteers, who were already stretched in terms of time and the costs of participating, he said, and might be put off by background checks. "It is undoubtedly true that many worthy volunteers would simply not wish to subject themselves to being fingerprinted," he said. "The cost in the loss of volunteers will be significant....And the loss of volunteers will translate directly into a loss of programs for youth."[13]

Not only would the proposed federal law be financially burdensome, Potts said, but it could also adversely affect the BSA's already rising insurance rates by setting a standard of care that might result in "massive civil justice damages" against youth groups that chose not to perform the checks and were hit later with sexual abuse allegations and lawsuits.

In the end, the lawmakers sided with the Boy Scouts of America. The National Child Protection Act of 1993 was ultimately signed into law, but with the limits on liability and costs that the BSA wanted—and without the required background checks that it opposed. The BSA went on to successfully lobby against mandatory fingerprint checks in states including Pennsylvania and Florida.[14] Once again, the Boy Scouts of America had flexed its political muscle and gotten its way.

While it is true that fingerprinting would not have kept all abusers out of Scouting, it is also likely that the existence of the checks would have discouraged some sexual predators from applying in the first place. It's also true that the BSA's refusal to institute the checks cleared the way for hundreds of men with criminal histories of molestation to slip into the ranks, including many who became repeat offenders.[15] Without background checks and with little guidance from BSA headquarters, local Scout leaders were left to their own devices and gut instincts to determine the suitability of prospective volunteers. It was anything but fail-safe: in a six-year period beginning in 1985, when national background checks became widely available, the BSA registered some 230 men with prior arrests or convictions for sex crimes against children, reporters for the *Los Angeles Times* found.[16] Those men were accused of abusing nearly four hundred Scouts during that time span.

Had Scouts officials checked the criminal record of William S. Schilling, for example, they would have learned that the Las Vegas scoutmaster and elementary school teacher had been charged in 1979 with six counts of indecent exposure involving children, though he managed to avoid most of the charges. A decade later, Schilling had been kicked out of Scouting after he had sexually abused a twelve-year-old boy on a camping trip to California. Schilling, who had pleaded guilty to a reduced charge in that case, had also allegedly exposed himself to three other children at his home, where he had hosted swimming parties for them and walked around in the nude.

An irate parent from Schilling's troop castigated local Scouts officials in a letter pointing out that Las Vegas casino workers were more heavily vetted than men who were trusted to take young boys into the woods on overnight camping trips. "The black eye which scouting has suffered in this community could easily have been avoided if the council had taken the simple expedient of doing a background investigation on Schilling," he wrote.[17]

The Boy Scouts of America did institute fingerprint checks for employees in 1994 and began screening new volunteers in 2003. But even then, the program had a glaring flaw: it did not require checks for volunteers already involved in Scouting. That loophole wasn't closed until 2008, some fifteen years after the BSA first swatted down the idea of fingerprint checks at the congressional hearing. Mandated reporting of sexual abuse to law enforcement was finally instituted two years later, in 2010.

The unduly belated background checks were but one in a series of missed opportunities for the BSA to do a better job of protecting the children in its care, and it reflected the organization's long-standing tendency to downplay, deny, or deflect from its sexual abuse problem.

At the 1993 hearing, Potts stressed that most molestations involved family members. His ghostwritten article on child protection noted that the BSA had "no accurate statistics" on child sexual abuse in Scouting while also asserting that "all the available indicators suggest that the problem is far less than in the population at large." Potts would later concede, while testifying under oath in civil litigation, that the "indicators" had been gleaned mostly from articles he'd read in periodicals and that he had no data to back up his contention that kids were safer in Scouting than anywhere else.[18]

In fact, the big reason the BSA lacked statistics on sexual abuse was that it had never analyzed its own confidential files and had rebuffed others' attempts to do it.

St. Louis attorney Donald L. Wolff served as legal counsel to Big Brothers Big Sisters of America and had joined its national board of directors in 1980. It was around that time that he had become alarmed by the threat of child sexual abuse after reading a report by a Big Brothers social worker recommending better screening and training of volunteers and employees. He'd also seen an excerpt of an article published by the North American Man/Boy Love Association, which advocates for "consensual" sexual relationships between adults and male children. He said it sent pedophiles a chilling message, which he interpreted as "The place to go to get your boys is to the Boy Scouts of America and to Big Brothers and Big Sisters."[19]

Wolff called FBI director William Webster, an old friend and former federal judge, who put him in touch with Special Agent Kenneth Lanning, the recently named head of a bureau task force on child sexual abuse. By then he had reached out to Big Brothers' board with a "very difficult proposition" to meet the problem head-on. "I felt that we, as a national organization, could no longer hide our heads in the sand," he said. "National Big Brothers and Big Sisters had to take a position, had to come out in the open and admit that there was a potential for a problem in our organization, and that we needed to do something about it."

Who better to team with on that effort than the BSA, the other organization named in the NAMBLA article? Wolff thought. He'd heard that the Boy Scouts kept some sort of blacklist of alleged abusers and reckoned that by joining forces and sharing information, they could create a "clearinghouse" for volunteers that would prevent predators from jumping from one organization to the other. At Wolff's urging, Big Brothers' executive director reached out to top BSA officials to pitch the idea. They turned him down.

Not only were the Boy Scouts not interested in cooperating with Big Brothers, Wolff said, they also denied keeping files on alleged abusers—files the BSA had maintained and continually updated since shortly after its founding in 1910. BSA officials refused to even acknowledge the existence of sexual abuse in Scouting, according to Wolff, who died in 2015. "They tried to hide it and that was a bigger part of the problem," he said in 1993. "They didn't recognize it was a problem and they didn't seek to be part of the solution."[20]

Undaunted by the Boy Scouts' rejection, Wolff pressed on with his own investigation of sexual abuse in Big Brothers Big Sisters. He collected information on all allegations of abuse, not just those involving the men who served as Big Brothers. He was also interested in accusations involving staff and Little Brothers, teachers and Little Brothers, stepfathers and mothers' boyfriends and Little Brothers. Over several years beginning in 1981, he rounded up about a hundred such allegations, compiled a comprehensive report, and used it to develop training programs and stringent screening, including the criminal background checks that Lynn Swann touted at the congressional hearing.

Big Brothers' thirst for knowledge on child sexual abuse in the 1980s stands in sharp contrast to the Boy Scouts' approach during that period. While Wolff sought to analyze every allegation and share his findings with the FBI and other youth groups, the BSA chose to sit silently on its extraordinary cache of information: thousands of Ineligible Volunteer files. Members of its vaunted expert advisory panel on child sexual abuse were not shown the files, much less asked to read and analyze them.

In 1986, the BSA published a pamphlet titled "Child Abuse: Let's Talk About It," which advised Scouts' parents on how to warn their sons about potential molesters: "Tell your children that an adult whom they know and trust, perhaps someone in a position of authority (like a babysitter, an uncle, a teacher, or even a police-man), might try to do something like this." Conspicuously missing from the BSA's list of potential child molesters were scoutmasters.

Other BSA publications and subsequent articles in *Boys' Life* and *Scouting* magazines ignored the same elephant in the room, as illustrated by this nugget from an April 1989 article: "Usually, child molesters are known by their victims. Often, they are fam-ily members—a stepparent, older brother or sister, uncle, or some-times a grandparent." The closest it came to raising the prospect of Scout leader as abuser was a reminder that "a child molester can be anyone."

In 1989, the BSA also produced *A Time to Tell*, a thirty-minute video for boys ages eleven to fourteen, warning them of the dan-gers of sexual abuse and offering tips on how to respond to it. The video showcased three abuse situations: a man trying to seduce his stepson, an adult family friend making sexual advances on an ado-lescent boy, and a "secret club" led by an older teenage boy who took videos of the younger ones wrestling in the nude. The video, which was widely distributed to Scout leaders and made available to other youth organizations, made no mention of the Boy Scouts.

The BSA's tendency to look the other way on its sexual abuse problem wasn't due to the inability or unwillingness to conduct deep-dive, data-driven research; it had done so on a variety of other topics. As early as 1916, it had polled all scoutmasters across the country before making changes to *Boys' Life* magazine.[21] In 1960, it had published a 418-page study, *Boy Scouts and Their Scoutmasters*, conducted by the University of Michigan's Institute for Social Research. Eight years later, it had commissioned a social science and public opinion research firm to produce the 162-page report *Is Scouting Out of Touch with the Times?* that had led to the failed Boypower experiment. And for more than a century, its annual reports have been packed with statistical data, much of it laid out clearly in charts and tables.

For some reason, however, the BSA drew the line on its inquisitiveness at sexual abuse, according to the historian Benjamin Rene Jordan. "They did all of these studies on social science stuff, budgetary stuff, economic analysis. It's very unfortunate they didn't do that with their abuse problem much earlier and much better," he said. "They had the evidence and the know-how to study their program and make it better, but they did not turn a critical eye on themselves—and they do not have a good excuse for that."[22]

CHAPTER 7

THE THREE G'S: GAYS, GIRLS, AND GOD

James Dale climbed the marble steps to the US Supreme Court Building, headed for a hearing that would cap his decade-long legal fight with the Boy Scouts. It was April 26, 2000, and a buzzing gaggle of lawyers, legal observers, reporters, supporters, and protesters had gathered ahead of the much-anticipated arguments in *Boy Scouts of America v. Dale*, a landmark case that would decide whether Scouting had a constitutional right to exclude homosexuals.

Dale, then twenty-nine, was an Eagle Scout and former assistant troop leader from Middletown, New Jersey, who had been booted from Scouting in 1990 after a Newark newspaper story had identified him as openly gay.[1] With his parents at his side, he was heartened to see the "overwhelming" support for him on display that Wednesday morning in front of the nation's highest court. He also encountered a smaller, much more rabid group of detractors, including a Tennessee street preacher and culture warrior named

Dan Martino who often graced the Supreme Court steps, where he'd demonstrated against right-to-die laws and once told a *Los Angeles Times* reporter that abortion "tears the heads off of babies."[2] On that chilly spring morning three days after Easter, Martino carried a wooden cross made of one-by-fours splashed with red paint and a hand-lettered sign that read "A HOMOSEXUAL BOY SCOUT LEADER IS LIKE ASKING A FOX TO GUARD THE CHICKENS! IT IS STUPID AND A SIN!"[3]

Martino and his sign caught Dale's eye, but what really got his attention were two other demonstrators who zeroed in on him as he waited in line to go through the security check. One of the men literally thumped a Bible as he screamed antigay epithets at Dale, while the other never stopped glaring at him, even while being repeatedly turned away for setting off the metal detectors. *Is this guy carrying a weapon?* Dale wondered. *Is one of these "laughably anti-gay people" going to try to kill me, right here and now, right in front of my mom and dad and the US Park Police?* He felt more than a little vulnerable.[4]

Dale's journey to that uneasy moment had begun more than twenty years earlier, when he had joined Monmouth Council's Cub Scout Pack 242 at the age of eight. The second son of middle-class suburban New Jersey parents, he had played soccer and practiced karate moves but never really found his niche until he landed in Scouting. It was only then, for the first time in his young life, that he sensed he belonged. He felt he was "a unique and necessary part of a larger whole" and it didn't matter how many home runs he could hit.[5] When he was ten, Dale had moved up from Cub Scouts to Boy Scouts, and with each passing year he had sharpened his skills. His sense of achievement and self-worth had grown along with his collection of merit badges, and even as he began to consider that he might be gay, he had never felt anything but welcome in Scouting. He was happy to just be himself.

Dale won his Eagle Scout badge in June 1988, the year he entered Rutgers University to major in communications and sociology. It was there that he embraced his homosexuality, while also remaining active in Scouting. By his junior year, he was copresident of Rutgers' Lesbian/Gay Alliance and assistant scoutmaster of Troop 73 in Matawan, New Jersey. In July 1990, a reporter for the *Newark Star-Ledger* interviewed him for a story about a Rutgers conference that focused on the health and psychological needs of gay and lesbian teenagers. The three sentences about Dale, who spoke at the conference, amounted to little more than an anecdotal nugget, but they would change his life:

James Dale, 19, co-president of the Rutgers University Lesbian Gay Alliance with Sharice Richardson, also 19, said he lived a double life while in high school, pretending to be straight while attending a military academy.

He remembers dating girls and even laughing at homophobic jokes while at school, only admitting his homosexuality during his second year at Rutgers.

"I was looking for a role model, someone who was gay and accepting of me," Dale said, adding he wasn't just seeking sexual experiences, but a community that would take him in and provide him with a support network and friends.[6]

Neither Dale nor the story mentioned his Boy Scouts affiliation, nor had he ever broached the subject of homosexuality with his troop, much less advocated for it. Less than a month later, however, he received a letter from Monmouth Council executive James Kay informing him that the Boy Scouts were revoking his adult registration because he did not meet the BSA's "high standards of membership." When Dale pressed for a fuller explanation, he was told he was being expelled because of "the standards for leadership established by the Boy Scouts of America, which specifically forbid membership to homosexuals."[7]

Dale, who had spent more than half his life dedicated to Scouting and the all-American ideals it promoted, had never heard of such a policy, and for good reason: the Boy Scouts had never publicly articulated one.[8] He was hurt and saddened, and angry. "To have them say 'You're not good enough. You're not welcome' was very, very upsetting," he said. "It definitely was like a gut punch."[9]

Unknown to Dale at the time, the BSA's contention that membership is "a privilege, not a right" was the same language it used to exclude men accused of sexually molesting Scouts, men added to the blacklist known as the perversion files. As stated, Boy Scouts officials in hundreds of those cases chose not to pursue criminal prosecutions, at times covering up for sexual predators by allowing them to quietly resign under false pretenses or, worse yet, letting them back into Scouting only to abuse again. But they were more than willing to spend a decade and hundreds of thousands of dollars in legal fees to banish Dale, a tall, clean-cut, articulate Eagle Scout with a spotless record, Vigil Honor status in the prestigious Order of the Arrow, dozens of merit badges, and a promising future. The BSA could not have designed a better prototype for an Eagle Scout.

Faced with an overwhelming preponderance of research that had found no correlation between pedophilia and homosexuality and concluded that gay men were no more likely than heterosexuals to be child molesters,[10] the BSA clung to its contention that Dale's sexual orientation alone should disqualify him.

Without so much as a hearing, the Boy Scouts rejected Dale's internal appeal of the decision to kick him out, leaving him with two options: he could take his lumps and move on, or he could fight the BSA in court. He believed everything that Scouting had taught him about standing up for himself and doing the right thing. It left him no choice but to sue, an expensive and iffy proposition at best.

Other gay Scouts had pursued similar legal action without success, including one whose case paralleled Dale's. In 1980, eighteen-year-old Eagle Scout Tim Curran had applied to be an assistant scoutmaster in Berkeley, California, where he had grown up. Curran had been in Scouting for years and loved everything about it: the camaraderie, the merit badges, the weekly meetings, the standing alone "in a still, silent pine grove at summer camp" in the Sierras.[11] Like Dale, he had been an exemplary Scout. Also like Dale, he'd been featured in a newspaper article in the *Oakland Tribune* that had identified him as gay and included a photo of him with his male date at his high school's senior prom.

Curran said nothing in the story about the Boy Scouts but described himself as someone "who was proud of being gay— someone who didn't just say it, but who acted on it." Clippings of the story quickly found their way to the Mount Diablo Council, the local governing body for the BSA, which promptly denied Curran's application for a volunteer leadership post, citing his sexual orientation.

As he weighed his options, Curran remembered the adage "Once an Eagle Scout, always an Eagle Scout" and a passage from his *Boy Scout Handbook* that said if a Scout thinks "rules and laws are unfair, he seeks to have them changed in an orderly manner."[12] He enlisted the help of the American Civil Liberties Union and filed a lawsuit accusing the BSA of unlawful discrimination under California's Unruh Civil Rights Act, which required "full and equal accommodations, advantages, facilities, privileges, or services in all business establishments of every kind whatsoever." California's statute, and similar state laws elsewhere, were most commonly applied to restaurants, theaters, libraries, hotels, retail outlets, transportation systems, and other businesses that are open to the public. The courts would now have to decide if Scouting belonged in the same public accommodations category.

Curran's case trudged through California's civil court system for seventeen years, culminating in a March 23, 1998, California Supreme Court decision for the BSA. The court held that the Boy Scouts of America is a social organization, not a business subject to the state civil rights law. The BSA's constitutional right to freedom of expressive association allowed it to exclude homosexuals, the court ruled.

The same decision sided with the BSA in a discrimination case brought by nine-year-old twins William and Michael Randall, of Anaheim Hills, California, who sued in 1991 after being excluded from Cub Scouts for refusing to accept the BSA's Declaration of Religious Principle, which requires Scouts and leaders to recognize "an obligation to God." A Studio City, California, den leader was also ejected for his lack of religious faith after writing a letter of support for the Randall brothers, prompting him to lament that "a devious and clever child molester has a better chance of remaining a Scout leader than an honest atheist."[13]

When all was said and done, the Curran and Randall decision had favored the Boy Scouts in two of the oft-referenced "Three G's" at the center of long-standing membership disputes: Gays, Girls, and God(less).

SHORTLY BEFORE DALE'S LAWSUIT was filed in New Jersey Superior Court, the BSA did something it had not done before in its eighty years of existence: it directly linked the Boy Scout Oath to the unacceptability of homosexuality, contending that that was what the phrase "morally straight" had meant all along. In fact, since the first chief Scout executive, James E. West, had appended those words to the oath in 1911, the *Boy Scout Handbook* had never defined them in terms of sexual orientation. Dale had studied his own handbooks and remembered the morally straight part as having to do with "respecting and defending the rights of all people," not anything sexual.

A year after his expulsion from Scouting in 1990 but before he filed his lawsuit, the BSA issued a carefully crafted "Position Statement: Homosexuality and the BSA" that, probably not coincidentally, justified its exclusion of Dale and other gay Scouts and leaders.[14] "We believe that homosexual conduct is inconsistent with the requirements in the Scout Oath that a Scout be morally straight and in the Scout Law that a Scout be clean in word and deed, and that homosexuals do not provide a desirable role model for Scouts," it said in what would become a familiar, if somewhat ironic, refrain by an organization founded on the principle that it welcomed all boys.

Dale filed his lawsuit in 1992, alleging that the BSA violated the New Jersey statute prohibiting discrimination in places of public accommodation on the basis of sexual orientation. The first round played out in the state court's Chancery Division, a venue where judges typically settle disputes by issuing injunctions and restraining orders to stop harmful practices or by enforcing actions that are legally required. Dale's case likely landed there because in addition to demanding monetary damages, it sought an order reinstating him as an assistant Scout leader.

Round one did not go Dale's way. Judge Patrick McGann ruled that the Boy Scouts was not a place of public accommodation and thus was not subject to New Jersey's law against discrimination. But in granting a summary judgment for the BSA, he took it a step further, issuing a written decision that at least bordered on homophobia, if not jumped across the line with both feet. In it, he called Dale "an active sodomist" and quoted from the Bible to underscore his contention that someone of that description is "simply incompatible" with Scouting. "To suggest that the BSA had no policy against active homosexuality is nonsense," the judge wrote. "It was an organization which from its inception had a God-acknowledged, moral foundation. It required its members, youth and adult, to take the Scout Oath that they would be 'morally straight.' It is unthinkable that in a society where there was universal governmental condemnation of the act of sodomy as a crime, that the BSA could or would tolerate active homosexuality if discovered in any of its members."[15]

McGann's decision was a setback for Dale, to be sure, but it would not stand. A New Jersey appeals court reversed it, and the case eventually wound up before the state Supreme Court. In a unanimous 7–0 decision, that court, on August 4, 1999, affirmed the appellate ruling, finding that the Boy Scouts of America had indeed violated New Jersey's antidiscrimination law. It rejected the BSA's arguments that it was not a public organization and that its expulsion of Dale was protected by its First Amendment right to freedom of expressive association. In batting down the BSA's argument that keeping "morally straight" translated to banning homosexuals, the justices noted that the *Boy Scout Handbook* drew no such conclusion: "The words 'morally straight' and 'clean' do not, on their face, express anything about sexuality, much less that homosexuality, in particular, is immoral," the decision noted. "We doubt that young boys would ascribe any meaning to these terms other than a commitment to be good."[16] Which was how Dale had always interpreted them.

The court also blasted the judge's contention that homosexuality is immoral, likening McGann's views to earlier discrimination against women and African Americans. Dale's expulsion "was based on little more than prejudice," according to Chief Justice Deborah T. Poritz, who wrote the unanimous opinion. "The sad truth is that excluded groups and individuals have been prevented from full participation in the social, economic and political life of our country. The human price of this bigotry has been enormous. At a most fundamental level, adherence to the principle of equality demands that our legal system protect the victim of invidious discrimination."[17]

At a press conference after the decision was announced, Dale said it underscored what Scouting had always taught him: to believe in the system and goodness will prevail.

His victory celebration would be short-lived: The Boy Scouts' lawyer immediately decried the decision, saying it marked "a sad day when the state dictates to parents what role models they must provide for their children,"[18] and vowed to appeal it to the US Supreme Court. That seemed a bit of a long shot, since the nation's highest court accepts only a small fraction of cases submitted to it. But on January 14, 2000, the conservative-majority Court agreed to hear the Dale case, signaling that at least four of the nine justices—the minimum necessary to grant a writ of certiorari allowing it to move forward—were open to the idea of overturning the New Jersey decision.

JAMES DALE HAD MADE it through security without being attacked by the two antigay protestors who had hectored him while he stood in line that Wednesday in late April 2000. He took a seat in the stately courtroom gallery behind his lawyers and those for the BSA, who sat at tables facing the long, elevated wooden bench occupied by the nine black-robed justices looming over them.

Boy Scouts attorney George Davidson opened the arguments at 10:10 a.m. by saying that the case was about "the freedom of a voluntary association to choose its own leaders" and decide for itself who should wear the scoutmaster uniform and serve as a role model for boys.[19] Both sides had filed extensive briefs, and dozens of "friends of the court" had also outlined their positions for and against reinstating Dale in amicus curiae submissions. So there was little need for a full recitation of the case—and not much time for it, anyway, since each side would have just thirty minutes for argument.

Davidson got no further than a couple of paragraphs into his presentation when the justices began to pepper him with questions about Boy Scout policies on homosexual members and how the organization would respond to various hypothetical situations involving gay leaders. Davidson reminded the Court that the BSA had issued several position statements since 1978[20] that had clearly spelled out its prohibition on gay members and leaders, seeking to establish its ban on homosexuals as a core belief of the organization. He also noted that since its founding, every boy and adult in the program had promised to be "morally straight and clean in thought, word, and deed."

"May I ask right there," Justice John Paul Stevens chimed in, "is it the [BSA's] position that a person who is a homosexual, engages in homosexual conduct, cannot fit that definition?"

"That's correct, Your Honor," Davidson replied.[21]

Dale's attorney, Evan Wolfson, was up next and ran into the same gantlet of questioning shortly after commencing his argument. He spent much of his time parrying with the justices over whether having a gay troop leader would undermine the Boy Scouts' values or its "expressive message" by forcing it to associate with people whose lifestyles it found objectionable. The justices also quizzed him on the broader implications of admitting gays: Wouldn't that also open the door to girls? Justice Sandra Day O'Connor asked. Not necessarily, Wolfson said, trying to move on quickly. Justice Stephen Breyer, an Eagle Scout, posed a similar query about potential impacts on other organizations.

"Then in your view a Catholic organization has to admit Jews, [and] a Jewish organization has to admit Catholics?" Breyer asked. "...That's your view of the constitutional law?"

"No, Your Honor," Wolfson said, explaining that he did not think that public accommodations laws should or would be applied to such clearly religious groups.[22]

In a case that had taken ten years to reach the highest court in America, oral arguments wrapped up in one hour, with no clear winner. Afterward, Dale, lawyers for both sides, and representatives of religious groups and other organizations that had weighed in took turns shagging reporters' questions at a bank of microphones set up next to a gurgling fountain near the steps of the Supreme Court Building.

Among those who made that day's C-SPAN highlights were the Reverend Robert Schenck, the general secretary of the National Clergy Council, who said the case was "all about the government telling private organizations what they may believe and what they may practice," warning that a decision in Dale's favor would spell calamity for religious freedom. David Adams, a representative of the Lutheran Church Missouri Synod, stepped up to echo Justice Breyer's earlier line of questioning, cautioning that a pro-Dale decision could force the Boy Scouts to accept girls and require Catholic organizations to take on Jewish members, and vice versa.[23]

Dale took a few questions, including one from a reporter who asked why he had chosen to go through such a long legal ordeal, considering that he had achieved so much in Scouting already. "I have always loved the Boy Scouts of America. It is a program that I hold dear to my heart, and I hope to one day be able to be back in the program," Dale replied. "I've always believed in Scouting, and the reason why I did this is because I care about the Scouting program."[24]

What Dale didn't share with the press that day was that the publicity surrounding the case had not only worried his mother for his safety but also caused him to take precautions. When he moved to New York City after graduating from college, he did his best to keep a low profile. His home phone number was unpublished, and he kept his name off the buzzer directory in the lobby of his apartment building. It had all become pretty overwhelming. He didn't regret any of it, but it was stressful, and he realized he was just a part of something much bigger than himself when his lawyer told him one day, "If you get hit by a bus, this case will go on without you."[25]

*   *   *

Two MONTHS AFTER HEARING arguments, the Supreme Court rendered its decision on June 28, 2000. It was 5–4 in favor of the Boy Scouts of America, and it was announced by Chief Justice William Rehnquist, who was joined in the majority by Justices Anthony M. Kennedy, Sandra Day O'Connor, Antonin Scalia, and Clarence Thomas.[26]

"We reverse the judgment of the New Jersey Supreme Court and hold that the application of New Jersey's public accommodations law in this case violates the Boy Scouts' First Amendment rights," said Rehnquist, who spelled out the majority's reasoning in a twenty-one-page written decision. In sum, it said that the BSA's right to freedom of expressive association—i.e., to choose to associate or *not* associate with anyone—allowed it to exclude those, including Dale, whose viewpoints would undermine its shared goals and values.

Rehnquist said that the Court was neither endorsing nor condemning homosexuality or the BSA's stance on it. He acknowledged that neither the Scout Oath nor the Scout Law expressly mentions sexuality or sexual orientation and that the terms "morally straight" and "clean" are open to interpretation. But, he said, the Court accepted the BSA's assertions—based largely on its position statements—that it teaches "that homosexual conduct is not morally straight" and that it did "not want to promote homosexual conduct as a legitimate form of behavior." Allowing homosexuals into Scouting would contradict those core beliefs, he wrote. "Dale's presence in the Boy Scouts would, at the very least, force the organization to send a message, both to the youth members and the world, that the Boy Scouts accepts homosexual conduct as a legitimate form of behavior."

The decision was not out of character for the conservative-majority Rehnquist Court, which had moved to the right of its previous two predecessors, the Warren E. Burger and Earl War-ren Courts, and had rendered decisions that favored conservative issues, including the expenditure of tax funds for individual tuition at religious schools.[27] The Rehnquist Court's most controversial decision would come several months after *Dale* when it stopped the recount of votes in the 2000 presidential election, sealing George W. Bush's victory over Al Gore.

The decision in *Dale* was nowhere near as contentious, but it was not without fierce criticism. Justice Stevens wrote the main dissent, a forty-one-page excoriation of the majority's reasoning. He quoted passages from the Boy Scout and scoutmaster handbooks, demonstrating that neither spoke to the issue of sexual orientation. He said that the BSA had never made the "clear, unequivocal statement necessary to prevail" on its claim that homosexuality was fundamentally incompatible with its mission. He and the other dissenting justices, including Stephen G. Breyer, Ruth Bader Ginsburg, and David H. Souter, said that the majority had done little more than take the Boy Scouts' word for it.

"This is an astounding view of the law," Stevens wrote. "...It is plain as the light of day that neither one of these principles—'morally straight' and 'clean'—says the slightest thing about homosexuality. Indeed, neither term in the Boy Scouts' Law and Oath expresses any position whatsoever on sexual matters."[28]

As has routinely been its practice with major news developments in recent decades, the Boy Scouts responded to the decision with a statement. It hailed the ruling as an affirmation of its right to set its own membership standards and continue to instill in boys the values of the Scout Oath and Law. It also doubled down on its no-gays policy, saying that "an avowed homosexual is not a role model" for Scouts.

Dale's takeaway was that the Boy Scouts of America had just won the right to embed bigotry in the Scout Oath and Law and had adopted discrimination as its brand. It was all very deflating, and it sent him into something of a funk. As time went on, however, he began to appreciate how much had changed in the world of gay rights between his expulsion from Scouting in 1990 and a decade later when the Supreme Court issued its landmark decision. When his case had started, there was no *Will and Grace* on television and Ellen DeGeneres was still in the closet. There was little or no public discussion of gays in the military, and marriage equality was not even on the table.

By 2000, Americans' attitudes toward gay rights were changing, and for the better as Dale saw it: America was moving in the right direction, while the BSA was stuck in the past, clinging to last century's views on homosexuality and its own out-of-step ban on gays. The silver lining, if there was one, was that the decision had made people confront the issue and take sides.

"It happened in PTA meetings. It happened in local churches. It happened in troops. It happened at the United Way," Dale later recalled. "All of those organizations had to discuss the issue of gay youth, and did they want to be an organization that discriminates against gay kids. And I think that's kind of the beautiful thing of losing at the Supreme Court…it really forced Americans to struggle with these issues, for a decade or more."[29]

A MONTH AFTER THE Dale decision, US Representative Lynn C. Woolsey, a California Democrat, introduced the Scouting for All bill,[30] which sought to revoke the BSA's federal charter on the grounds that it "sets an example of intolerance" with its bar on gay members and leaders. The bill, which was largely symbolic and would not have affected Boy Scout operations or membership policies, was killed in the House Judiciary Committee by a procedural vote—but not before the BSA flexed its political muscles with a show of support and impassioned speeches by a parade of members from both parties, including at least three Eagle Scouts.

Most of the speeches were variations on themes that the bill was an attack on the Boy Scouts, the First Amendment, the fundamental values of America, or all of the above.[31]

Republican Stephen Buyer from Indiana, who reminded his House colleagues that 50 percent of them had been Boy Scouts, lamented the "onslaught of criticism, intimidation and extortion" that Scouting had endured since the *Dale* decision.[32] He said that anti–Boy Scout protests had been staged in twenty-one states, including in his own district, urging businesses and organizations to withdraw their support, while the Interior Department had attempted to "bully and harass" the BSA over the use of public parklands.[33] Some delegates to the Democratic National Convention had gone so far as to boo a group of Scouts during opening ceremonies at the Staples Center in Los Angeles, he said; never mind that it had been a handful of delegates and the leader of the troop onstage had said that the Scouts couldn't hear the jeering above the din of the crowd, anyway. "Our youth today face a daily onslaught from some parts of our culture that promote self-gratification and alternative lifestyles," Buyer said. "…I believe we should commend, not punish, an organization that attempts to foster a sense of personal responsibility and strong character in our boys and young men."[34]

Republican congressman J. D. Hayworth of Arizona noted that he didn't see the Baptists or the Buddhists trying to crash the membership rolls of the Jewish War Veterans, another federally chartered organization, so if gay people wanted to join such a group, they should just go start one of their own: "My suggestions to those who place such an emphasis on sexual identity is to have another freely formed association, the sexual identity seekers of America."[35]

At least two prominent Democrats, Sheila Jackson Lee from the BSA's headquarters state of Texas and John Dingell of Michigan, also spoke in support of the Boy Scouts and against the bill, which was dead on arrival and never got a formal hearing.[36] For her part,

Woolsey, the bill's sponsor, said she was not trying to override the Supreme Court but wanted to send the message that "the civil rights movement is alive and well in the United States of America" and that Congress does not condone discrimination: "We are not saying that the Boy Scouts are bad. We are saying that intolerance is bad."[37]

The BSA easily survived Woolsey's bid to cancel its charter. But it would continue to face widespread criticism, lose financial support from businesses and civic organizations, and struggle with the issue of gay members and leaders, and for years it seemed destined to land on the wrong side of public opinion, if not history.

More than a decade would pass before it openly sought to change its course in 2013. By then, most of the rest of the country had already moved forward on gay rights. The military's discriminatory "Don't ask, don't tell" ban on gay and lesbian service members was a thing of the past, and same-sex marriage was being embraced by states from coast to coast. Once again, the BSA was left behind the times.

PART II

—

THE TURNING POINT

CHAPTER 8

FRENCH FRIES FOR BREAKFAST

Construction of the Multnomah County Courthouse began in 1909, a year before the founding of the Boy Scouts of America. By 2010, both the eight-story courthouse and the venerable youth group were showing signs of decay. The Neoclassical building in downtown Portland, Oregon, had been deteriorating for decades: The electrical system and plumbing were shot, and the unreinforced masonry structure was seismically unsafe.[1] The last century had also taken a toll on the BSA, whose once sterling reputation as a patriotic, civic-minded, character-building maker of men had been corroded by allegations of child sexual abuse. Now the organization was headed for a legal showdown that would bring its murky history of abuse into sharp relief—and set the BSA on a decidedly downward trajectory.

The case of *Jack Doe v. the Boy Scouts of America et al.* attracted national attention, but with little of the hoopla that routinely surrounded proceedings involving celebrities or notorious criminals. On trial in the old courthouse in Portland was not a famous person but one of the nation's most trusted institutions. The star witness would be 1,247 of the Boy Scouts' own perversion files.

Six men, former members of a Portland troop sponsored by a Mormon congregation, had sued the BSA, its Cascade Pacific Council, and the Church of Jesus Christ of Latter-day Saints. They alleged that all had failed to act after assistant scoutmaster Timur Dykes had confessed to molesting seventeen boys, including some of the plaintiffs. In the run-up to the trial in March 2010, the men, then in their late thirties to early forties, reached a confidential settlement with the LDS Church, which was dropped as a defendant. Multnomah County Circuit Judge John A. Wittmayer ordered their remaining claims against the BSA and the local council to be tried one at a time.

He picked Kerry Lewis to go first, essentially drawing his name out of a hat.

Kerry was the first of five children born to Helen and Jimmy Lewis, two army brats who had fallen in love and married in El Paso, Texas, in 1969, three years before he came along. When Kerry was about five, the family moved to southern California, where Technical Sergeant Jimmy Lewis worked as a jet mechanic at George Air Force Base, a training post for fighter pilots in the high desert northeast of Los Angeles. Jimmy's job was to help keep F-4 Phantoms at the ready, and he often took his rambunctious young son, who dreamed of being a pilot one day, with him to the flight line to admire the jets.[2] "It was the coolest thing in the world," Kerry would later say of his dad's work.[3]

When Kerry was nine, his family moved to Portland for Jimmy's new job with the Oregon Air National Guard. They settled into a house in a working-class neighborhood in southeast Portland, about eight miles from the National Guard base at Portland International Airport. They also joined a local ward of the LDS Church. Kerry, who'd been a Cub Scout in California, signed on with a pack there, and his mom, a nurse, served as den mother, holding the meetings at their home.

Timur Dykes, a seemingly solid member of the congregation in his twenties, served as a home teacher to the newcomers. He dropped by occasionally to see how they were doing and to offer spiritual "blessings" and help with their material needs as they settled into the community. An avid outdoorsman and rock climber who was involved in Scouting at the church, Dykes immediately hit it off with the family. "He was a very clean-cut young man," Helen recalled. "He was very vibrant. He was good-looking. He was healthy. He was involved in things. He was part of our church. He was part of the Scouts. He was everything we wanted in somebody to mentor our son."[4]

As time went on, Dykes's role as a home teacher diminished, but his involvement with Kerry grew, especially when the boy advanced from Cub Scouts to the next stage, Webelos, which held its meetings at the church. Kerry idolized Dykes, an assistant troop leader who literally showed him the ropes of rock climbing and took him on several outings, including to Rocky Butte, an extinct volcanic cone just off of I-205, the freeway to the airport. When Kerry and his mom drove out to pick up Jimmy, he'd always point out Rocky Butte, whose sheer walls made it popular with local climbers. "That's where we climbed, Mom!" he'd blurt out. On the way back, he'd show it off to his dad.

Kerry's parents were so trusting of Dykes, who often stopped by for dinner, that when they had to drive the 275 miles downstate to Klamath Falls to scope out a job prospect for Jimmy, they accepted his offer to stay with the kids that weekend. Even though Helen thought the world of Dykes, she wasn't taking any chances when the assistant scoutmaster asked if Kerry could spend the night at his apartment to work on a merit badge project with other boys from Troop 719. She did what she had done whenever one of the kids went to someone's house for the first time: she checked the place out. She drove Kerry over to Dykes's apartment, not far from the Lewis home, and found it to be clean and sparsely decorated, a typical "bachelor pad." Dykes had at least two pet ferrets, Kodo and Podo, named for characters in the sword-and-sorcery movie *The Beastmaster*, which Helen thought were kind of cute, and a couple of snakes, constrictors, which caused her some concern. She quizzed some of the other boys who were there, and they told her not to worry; the reptiles were no problem. The cages were clean and the animals looked healthy and well cared for, Helen said, "So I just had another one of those 'get-over-it' moments, and 'this is what boys do,' and it was, it was okay."[5]

Dykes's apartment was every twelve-year-old's delight: He let the boys stay up as late as they wanted, allowed them to play Dungeons & Dragons—taboo for Mormon kids in the 1980s—and cheerfully served them meals that would make their mothers cringe, including French fries for breakfast.[6]

The Pacific Northwest is a place of breathtaking beauty, especially in summer when the rains subside and the skies go from gunmetal gray to blue. It's the perfect time to visit the coast, a couple of hours west of Portland. In July 1984, Dykes drove a vanload of boys, including Kerry, there on a camping trip. It wasn't an official Boy Scout outing, although Kerry and some of the others were Scouts. In the coastal town of Tillamook, the local police pulled over Dykes's van for a minor traffic violation. When they ran his name, the computer flagged him as a convicted child molester, who was on probation and had an active arrest warrant after failing to pay a $90 fine in that case.[7] The cops put him in handcuffs and took him to jail. They took the boys there, too, and called their parents.

Helen Lewis's stomach dropped when she got the news. Kerry was fine, the caller told her, but worst-case images of Dykes and her oldest son suddenly flooded her thoughts.[8] Were they sure they had the right man? Timur Dykes? she asked. Yep, we're sure, ma'am, come get your boy.

Helen and Jimmy found someone to watch the other kids and made a beeline for Tillamook. At the jail they found a scared twelve-year-old waiting alone in a room and decided not to pepper him with all the questions they were dying to ask. Instead, Helen gave him a big hug and the three of them shared a long, quiet ride back to Portland.

The next morning, Kerry was the first one up. His mother found him on the couch in the living room, sat down next to him, and wrapped her arms around him.

"Well, that was pretty scary, huh?" she said. "Yeah, that was," he replied. She told him that the police said they thought nothing had happened between him and Dykes, but she wanted to be sure. "That's true, Mom," Kerry said, "he didn't do anything."[9] Whatever relief she felt was short lived. Jimmy Lewis went to see Bishop Gordon McEwen, who headed the local LDS congregation and also served as troop representative to the BSA, to find out what he knew about Dykes's history. Kerry's dad didn't like what he heard; months earlier, Dykes had confessed to molesting boys in the troop, but no one in the youth organization had warned the Lewises or the parents of a dozen other Scouts.

Helen and Jimmy were dumbfounded and furious. They decided that Dykes would never get near their son again. Kerry was about to lose his mentor[10] and, arguably, his closest friend. "I don't remember the exact words or anything," he recalled. "But she basically reiterated to me very strongly that Timur Dykes never will see me again, ever. She was not going to allow it." The boy stood there for a moment to let that sink in, then went outside with his dog, Nicky. "I sat down on the cold pavement with my back up against the house. And Nicky came up and sat down next to me....And I put my arm around him and sat there and cried. He didn't move.

He didn't bark. He just sat there the whole time with me....I think it was a couple of hours. At least that's what it felt like."[11]

A YEAR AFTER DYKES's arrest in Tillamook, the Lewis family moved to Klamath Falls, just north of the California state line. Kerry was thirteen, and his grades began to slide. He was losing interest in all of the things that had used to excite him: scouting, baseball, wrestling. He grew more and more withdrawn and stopped bringing friends over to the house. He even quit talking about becoming a fighter pilot. As his frequent heart-to-heart talks with his mother became fewer and farther apart, she feared she was losing her close connection with him.[12]

The increasingly troubled teenager started drinking and was arrested on a minor-in-possession-of-alcohol charge when he was about sixteen. He gave up on his plan to join the air force when it rejected him after he admitted to having tried LSD and instead enlisted in the navy right out of high school. He served on the USS *Abraham Lincoln*, an aircraft carrier in the Pacific Fleet, and saw duty in Iraq, the Indian Ocean, Asia, and Australia. His four-year tour was cut short by a drug investigation involving him and others on board, and he came home early with an other-than-honorable discharge and a methamphetamine habit.[13]

Lewis stayed for a while with his mother, who by then was divorced from his father. Kerry's behavior became increasingly erratic: He'd throw parties at her house when she was away and steal things from her to sell to feed his addiction. It was a rough time, and it got no smoother until he moved to New York and lived with his sister, Misty, and her husband. He eventually married and had a daughter there, and he worked his way into a supervisory job with a heating and air-conditioning company. But the marriage fell apart, he and his wife divorced, and about ten years after he had left Oregon he was back, landing in Corvallis, where his sister had resettled.

One night in 2007, Helen was watching the late local news when Timur Dykes's picture flashed onto the screen with a story about some former Boy Scouts filing a lawsuit accusing him of sexual abuse. It rocked her, and not just because it dredged up bad memories and reignited her fears about Dykes and her son. "Part of what was said was that the Mormon Church and the Boy Scouts denied knowing that Timur Dykes was a pedophile," she recalled. "And I just couldn't believe that statement. And I was so upset about it and so angry, because I knew better. I was up all night. I couldn't go to sleep. I had to do something to help these boys, because I knew that the Boy Scouts and the Mormon Church knew better."[14]

Helen called Kelly Clark, the Portland lawyer representing the accusers, to make sure he knew about Dykes's history, including his arrest in Tillamook. She also called Kerry, then in his midthirties, with a question she had not asked him in more than twenty years. "I told him what I had seen, and that these boys were needing the information that I had. And I was going to ask him one more time if what he had told me was true...that Timur Dykes had never touched him....It took him a while. And he said, 'Yes, Timur did.' And he said he was lying to me, that he didn't tell me the truth. He was afraid to tell me."

After talking it over with his mother and Clark, Kerry joined the lawsuit against the Boy Scouts and the Mormon Church. Three years would pass before it came to trial in Portland. During the pretrial discovery phase, the plaintiffs' lawyers asked the BSA to turn over its perversion files, suspecting that they would yield evidence of the organization's long-standing, systemic failure to protect kids such as Kerry Lewis. When the Boy Scouts denied the request, the attorneys won a court order to compel the files' production. Judge Wittmayer, a veteran jurist, former prosecutor, and criminal defense attorney, ordered the Boy Scouts to hand over unredacted Ineligible Volunteer files from 1965 to 1985, a period spanning the twenty years before and just after Dykes's alleged abuse of Lewis. Wittmayer also placed the files under a protective order: the parties were not allowed to share them publicly, and all copies had to be returned to the BSA when the trial concluded, whatever its outcome.

"They fought tooth and nail that we didn't get those files, and they dumped them on us a week before trial," recalled Portland attorney Gilion Dumas, a member of Lewis's legal team. With the help of three assistants, she scrambled to sort through the stacks of folders, picking out files to highlight at trial, and sending the entire batch to the plaintiff's expert witnesses, a former Los Angeles police sex crimes investigator and a licensed psychologist and sexual abuse consultant, for their analyses. But even from her first-glance reading, Dumas said, clear patterns of child sexual abuse—and the organization's responses to it—leaped out.[15]

"What is unbelievable is not the abuse, really, because you know that there are perverts who molest kids and, yeah, that's terrible; it's reading it over and over and over and over," she said. "The Boy Scouts' response to it is like, 'Well, good thing they don't know the Scouts are involved,' or 'So far, we've kept it out of the press' or 'Well, we got him to agree to resign and we haven't told anybody.' I mean, it was the cover-up—over and over and over. And that was shocking."[16]

It was the first time that such a large tranche of the perversion files—1,247 in all—would be viewed and weighed by a jury. If Lewis's legal team, led by the seasoned sex abuse attorneys Clark and Paul Mones, could be shocked by their contents, what would twelve everyday Oregonians sitting in the jury box make of them? Dumas said it was easy to see why the Boy Scouts had fought so hard to keep them under wraps.

On March 17, 2012, six banker's boxes holding the files were lugged into the courtroom and stacked in full view of the jurors. While Dykes was the one who had actually abused Lewis and the others, he was just part of the grotesque picture of abuse that Lewis's attorneys would seek to paint at trial. In his opening statement, Lewis's attorney Clark told the jury that Dykes was but one more in a long line of single male Scout leaders who had lured boys to their homes under the guise of Scouting projects, only to abuse them. It was but one more instance of the BSA failing to warn boys and their parents of a predator in their midst, he said, one more time the Boy Scouts had sandbagged the police; one more of a thousand terrible stories sitting in those boxes, right over there.

Charles T. "Chuck" Smith, a prominent Portland attorney hired to defend the BSA, told jurors in his opening statement that there was nothing to be seen there, at least nothing nefarious. Keeping the Ineligible Volunteer files confidential was a long-standing policy and practice, he said, and it was justified. It was key to protecting everyone's privacy and safeguarding boys in Scouting. "We do not produce them willingly or voluntarily unless it is under court order for a very good reason, because they are full of confidential information, which should not be disseminated in our opinion throughout the world," he said. "They are designed for a reason, one reason only. To do our very level best, the evidence will be, to keep out repeat offenders."

OF THE SIX JACK Does, Kerry Lewis was not the ideal plaintiff. He wasn't particularly introspective or articulate, and the sexual abuse he had suffered, while serious, had not been as egregious as what Dykes had inflicted on some of his other victims. A boyish thirty-seven when the trial began, Lewis also had anger issues and was still dealing with his meth habit.[17] He readily acknowledged and took responsibility for his problems, but his lawyers wrestled with how best to present that information to the jury. Rather than lead off with his testimony, they built up to it with other witnesses.

First up when testimony began on the afternoon of March 17, 2010, was another former Scout from Troop 719, also a John Doe plaintiff in the lawsuit. A couple of years older than Lewis and admittedly nervous to be telling his story publicly, he testified that he had been raised by a single mom, had first gotten to know Dykes as his Sunday school teacher, and ultimately had come to regard him as a trusted father figure in Scouting. Dykes had taught him how to rappel in the church gym and helped him become an Eagle Scout at a younger-than-average age. The stocky assistant scoutmaster had had swagger, had worn a big Bowie knife on his belt during campouts, and kept a menagerie of lizards and other fascinating creatures in his apartment, which featured a large aquarium in the middle of the living room and a community pool outside.

The former Scout said he and the other boys had loved hanging out there—except when things had gotten weird with Timur, as they all called him.

Dykes had kept a pet snake in the bathroom, and he cranked up the baseboard heater to full blast to keep it comfy. Or at least that's what he told his adolescent overnight guests, whom he had required to strip down to their underwear if they wanted to go in and handle the reptile. Dykes had sometimes joined him in that hot box of a bathroom, the former Scout testified, recalling that the leader would doff his own clothes and drape the snake around the boy—and then proceed to molest him. Dykes had also assaulted him in the apartment complex pool, he said, and on rock-climbing outings and while he was sleeping. "When that happened, he would wake me up or I would come to and he would tell me that I was dreaming, that I was having a wet dream and that I had made a mess and that I needed to go clean myself up," he said. "I thought it was a normal thing. I didn't understand. I was embarrassed."[18]

Like Kerry Lewis, the former Scout had met Dykes through the LDS Church, then the largest sponsor of Boy Scout troops in the country. The church deemed the organization's values and mission to be so closely aligned with its own that it had adopted Scouting as its official youth program. Mormon boys, who were expected to participate, made up 20 percent of Scouting's membership nationwide, and church officials served as leaders of the troops their wards sponsored. Bishop Gordon McEwen headed Troop 719.

McEwen, a former Portland Public Schools phys ed and math teacher, had retired and moved to Utah, so his videotaped deposition was played for the jury. His testimony revealed that in January 1983, months before Kerry Lewis was abused, the mother of another Scout had told him that Dykes had molested her son and she was going to the police. McEwen testified that he had reacted "pretty fast" to that allegation, summoning Dykes to a face-to-face meeting. The young assistant scoutmaster had admitted abusing the boy, McEwen said, and confessed that he had also molested sixteen others in the troop. Dykes wrote down seventeen names and gave the list to the bishop, who said he had reached out to the parents of all of those boys and asked them to find out if their sons had been molested. None of the parents had reported any problems, or at least none they wanted his help with, McEwen said, noting that he had not been surprised because the prevailing practice at the time was to keep child sexual abuse under wraps.[19]

In all, there were thirty boys in Troop 719, and McEwen conceded during his deposition that he had not contacted the rest of their parents, including Kerry Lewis's mom and dad, to warn them about Dykes. Why not? "Because Timur didn't list them. He was really outright honest about everything he said," McEwen said. Nor had he notified the Boy Scouts of America or told a Multnomah County Sheriff's detective investigating Dykes that he had fessed up to abusing seventeen boys.[20]

Detective Charles Shipley, then retired, told jurors that he had believed at the time that there were just four victims: two that the outwardly remorseful Dykes had admitted to molesting when he had questioned him and two others whose parents had said they did not want the Scout leader prosecuted. If McEwen had mentioned seventeen victims, Shipley said, he surely would have expanded his investigation.[21] As it was, the report he had filed before learning of the full magnitude of Dykes's abuse had cast the Scout leader as seemingly less dangerous than the admitted predator he was. "It is quite apparent from all the people that I have talked to that Mr. Dykes is extremely well thought of," the detective noted in his report. "This includes the bishop, the families and the victims themselves. The consensus of everyone seems to be that while he caused harm in this situation, he has done a tremendous amount of good for the Mormon Church and its members."[22]

Dykes was charged with a misdemeanor sex offense and placed on probation by a judge, who ordered him to stay away from children, specifically the identified victims in the case. He also was "disfellowshipped" by McEwen, a sanction short of excommunication that restricted some of his church activities, including praying and teaching in public settings. The bishop claimed in his deposition that Dykes had also been suspended from Scouting, but by all other accounts he continued his involvement with the boys of Troop 719, including hosting sleepovers.

As the first week of trial drew to a close, Lewis's attorney Paul Mones called to the stand Nathaniel Marshall, the BSA's senior membership administrator. Marshall was attending the trial as the youth group's designated representative and was now questioned about his duties at national headquarters in Irving, Texas, where he oversaw the Ineligible Volunteer files. Like his predecessor, Paul Ernst, he was one of a very few there who had access to them.

It wasn't the first time that Mones had sparred with Marshall, who'd been a professional Scouter since 1977 and assumed his national post in 2005. Two months earlier, Mones had deposed him at Chuck Smith's office in Portland, producing this bit of semantic gymnastics:

"Child sexual abuse of Scouts, is that a problem today in the Boy Scouts of America?" Mones asked.

"Um, I'm not sure it has ever been a problem. It is a situation that we wish would not happen," Marshall replied.

Mones took another run at it: "To the best of your knowledge… when was the problem of the sexual abuse of Scouts by Scoutmasters first recognized by the BSA?"

"Define 'problem,'" Marshall replied.

"Well, what do you think I mean by the word 'problem'?"

"I don't know. That's why I'm asking you."

"So when I say…'sexual abuse by Scoutmasters is a problem,' you want to know what the word 'problem' means?"

"Uh-huh."

Lewis's lawyers had played a clip of the exchange during their opening statement to jurors, hoping they'd interpret Marshall's verbal tap dancing as evasive, or worse.[23]

Mones used Marshall's two days on the stand to elicit a range of testimony, including that the Boy Scouts had not placed Dykes into the Ineligible Volunteer files until an inexplicable four years after his initial conviction, and it had done so then only because a civil lawsuit had been filed. Marshall also testified that the BSA had never disclosed the existence of the perversion files to parents and local Scouts officials and had never mined them for information that might help the organization do a better job of protecting kids.

That's not to say that the youth group was oblivious to the dangers that lurked in Scouting. The official *Boy Scout Handbook* covered all kinds of potential perils, Mones pointed out, including the mishandling of perishable food on campouts and the errant lopping off of youthful digits with axes. He highlighted a section of the handbook that described the close relationship between a boy and his scoutmaster, depicting the adult as "a wise friend to whom the Boy Scout can turn for guidance on all kinds of problems and issues, including sex," and another passage noting that "a far greater degree of intimacy" is built into overnight outings and camping trips than formal meetings in church basements. But when Mones asked if the handbook contained any explicit warnings about the potential for sexual abuse of Scouts by their leaders, Marshall said it did not: "None that I can see."[24]

Mones also quizzed Marshall about the BSA's former policy of putting some suspected abusers on probation in lieu of the blacklist. He trotted out several glaringly questionable examples approved by Paul Ernst, who had been in charge of the perversion files from 1971 to 1993, a period that overlapped Dykes's abuse of Lewis. The files from that period are loaded with correspondence between Ernst, a former accountant with no expertise or education in child sexual abuse, and similarly untrained local Scouts officials who found themselves dealing with accused molesters in their troops. In many of the letters, Ernst asked for newspaper clippings, police records, or other corroborating evidence to justify excluding the alleged abusers. Sometimes, even in the face of strong evidence of abuse, he allowed them to continue to work with boys, often at local officials' urging.

Michael Nonclerg was a Pennsylvania scoutmaster placed in the files in 1972 after he had admitted to "acts of perversion" with several troop members. After he had agreed to seek professional treatment, the local Scouts official had suggested Ernst drop the matter, telling him, "If it don't stink, don't stir it." Nonclerg had resigned, but Ernst had allowed him back into Scouting four years later to lead a different troop, putting him on two years' probation.[25] Ernst had later extended the probation by two years after the scoutmaster was accused of punching a boy in his troop.

Mones also recounted Ernst's handling of the case of an Alaska Scout leader, air force sergeant Kenneth A. Burns, Jr., who was accused in June 1981 of sleeping nude with Cub Scouts and showing them pornography. The local leader kicked Burns out of the pack, but Ernst overruled his request to boot him from Scouting altogether. "I will agree that sleeping nude and showing the boys pornographic books indicated very poor judgment when dealing with Cub Scouts," he wrote. "I do not know, however, that this is a serious enough offense to refuse registration anywhere he might try to register unless there are more instances."[26] Burns was ultimately accused of molesting up to a hundred boys before being convicted of a sex crime in Utah in 2007.[27]

Wrapping up his examination of Marshall, Mones circled back to the Scout official's earlier reluctance to call sexual abuse in Scouting a "problem," ostensibly because he believed that the BSA was one of the safest youth organizations in the country.

Was it a safe organization for the former Scout who testified last week that Dykes had abused him? Mones asked.

"No, for that particular instance, no," Marshall said.

Was it safe for the seventeen Scouts Dykes had admitted molesting? Mones asked.

"For that situation, no," Marshall replied.

"And it was not one of America's safest organizations for Kerry Lewis, correct?"

"That would be correct."

"And, finally, sir," Mones said, "isn't it still the position of the Boy Scouts of America today that it was one of the safest organizations in America for the thousands of boys whose stories are sitting in those file boxes there, boys who were abused by Scoutmasters and adult volunteers?"

Smith, the Boy Scouts' attorney, objected, and Judge Wittmayer instructed jurors to disregard the question. But Mones had made his point.[28]

*   *   *

I⟶ᴛ ᴡᴀs ᴊᴜsᴛ ᴏᴠᴇʀ a week into the trial when Kerry Lewis took the stand on March 23. His mother, Helen, had just finished telling the jury about how Timur Dykes had cultivated a positive relationship with her family and was everything a scoutmaster should be. Or so she'd thought until he had been arrested in Tillamook. Kerry's father, Jimmy, would testify that until the arrest, he, too, had considered Dykes a trusted family friend.

Kerry himself had nothing but fond memories of his early time with Dykes. He wasn't alone. All of the boys in Troop 719 had looked up to the rugged young man who was roundly regarded as "cool," a father figure to some, a sort of Pied Piper of the outdoors to others. "He's larger than life, a survivalist," Kerry said. "You just wanted to soak knowledge up from him. Kind. Nice. He always went out of his way for everybody." Dykes's reputation as a mountain climber took on near-mythic proportions among the Scouts in his troop, Lewis said. "That was huge. I mean, nobody does that. That's, that's death-defying."[29]

Lewis recalled having been "starstruck" by Dykes as a young boy. He had been more than a little flattered when the Scout leader had complimented his agility in climbing the ropes on a wooden rig he'd set up at the church before one of the weekly meetings. One of the smaller boys in the troop, Kerry had gone up against a bigger kid and clearly outperformed him. "Timur started praising me, telling me that—not me, but all of the other boys—that's how you do it, that's how you are supposed to win the game," he said. "I was on Cloud Nine. It was pretty cool. I knew I had him hooked....I wanted to get his attention from mountain climbing. And I showed him that I could do it, and he saw it, and he made a big deal about it." From then on, he said, Dykes had included him in everything.

"Did you believe that Dykes cared for you?" his lawyer asked.

"Oh, yes," Kerry said.

"Why?"

"He told me he did."[30]

Dykes frequently pumped up the boy's confidence, convincing him he could succeed at anything he tried, including becoming a fighter pilot: "He basically always told me I was going to be fine; that he didn't have to worry about me. I was one of the few kids he didn't have to worry about. That said it all to me. That I was going to be great."

At the beginning of the trial, Lewis's attorneys had shown jurors photos of the boy and Dykes. Some had been taken by Kerry's family, including a picture from Christmas 1983 of him and Dykes playing an electronic football game. Others were photos of Kerry shot by Dykes on rock-climbing trips. Jurors also viewed a clip from a videotaped deposition of Dykes taken just three weeks before the trial. In it, he admitted to having molested Kerry once, fondling the boy's genitals while he slept, but only for "a couple of minutes at best."

Lewis did not remember that particular incident, he said, but there were five others that he did recall. Four had occurred in Dykes's apartment, where he had spent fifteen or twenty nights, always sleeping in Dykes's bed. It was his spot, and his alone among the other Scouts. The first time Lewis recalled being abused, he had awakened suddenly to find himself "laying on top of Timur," something that had not happened before. He could feel Dykes's erect penis pressing against his midsection, Lewis said. He was eleven years old and didn't know what to make of it, other than that he knew something was not right: "The only memory, in my head, was I was screaming 'wrong, wrong, wrong.'"[31] He said he had pretended to be asleep and, after a while, rolled off of Dykes. He and Dykes hadn't discussed the incident afterward. Once he'd gotten out of the bedroom, he'd tried to forget about it. "I put it out of my head, out of my mind," he said. "I wanted to go camping."

Like many children who are molested by adults, Kerry did not tell anyone about it right away. He testified that, as a child, he had been warned about men who were sexually attracted to boys. But it was always in the context of "stranger danger," he said, some creep in a van trying to lure kids with candy or a ruse about a pet dog. No one had ever warned him that someone like Dykes, a trusted adult—a *scoutmaster*—could be a predator.

Dykes's abuse continued over the next year, with three similar incidents occurring at the apartment. A fourth took place at the Lewis home, the weekend Dykes babysat Kerry and his siblings while their parents were in Klamath Falls on the job search. His brothers and sister were in bed, and he and Dykes were sitting on the couch, he testified, when the Scout leader reached over, took the boy's hand, and slid it up his leg, inside his shorts, touching his penis with it.

A week later, Dykes was arrested in Tillamook while on the camping trip with Kerry and the other boys. Kerry never saw him or spoke to him again.

Now, testifying more than twenty years later, he tried to assess the toll Dykes's abuse had taken on his life. As a twelve-year-old he'd been filled with self-confidence. He wasn't a big kid, but he was quick and fearless, a self-styled daredevil. Whether it was jumping off the roof of the house, tying knots in Scouting, playing baseball, or doing stunts on BMX bikes with his pals, Kerry had fancied himself "best in the West" at everything. "I was something special," he said. "I was number one. I was the best." In grade school, he got A's and B's. By the time he was in high school, his marks were slipping and his self-confidence had evaporated: "It very quickly disappeared. I don't remember having any, actually. It was gone."[32] Dykes's abuse had stolen it from him.

Lewis had made no secret of his alcohol and drug abuse, which continued to be a struggle. He said he wouldn't try to blame Dykes and the Boy Scouts for all of his troubles but that he'd learned through counseling that he suffered from anxiety and depression, so severe at times that he "won't even reach over and grab the remote to change the channel," much less get out of bed, for days on end. Now, at thirty-seven, it had all left him feeling "faulty" and empty. Hollow.

"I feel like the whole world got an instruction manual to life and I didn't," he told the jury. "I always miss things. I misunderstand things. And it seems common knowledge to the rest of the world."

Gary Schoener was among a parade of dueling expert witnesses. The Minnesota psychologist had built his practice on evaluating sex offenders, assisting their victims, and advising religious groups and other organizations on how to deal with abuse. His previous clients had included the BSA. Lewis's legal team had hired him to analyze the perversion files the Boy Scouts had turned over. Until then, Schoener had had no idea they existed. The Boy Scouts had never mentioned the files to him, much less shared their contents, even though he had testified as an expert witness for the BSA in a sexual abuse lawsuit in the 1990s and consulted with individual troops and local Scout executives on other occasions.

At the Lewis trial, Schoener said he had been "impressed and flabbergasted" by what he had read. Despite his decades in the field, he'd never seen anything on a par with the wealth of information the Boy Scouts had collected on child sexual abuse, information that would have been invaluable to others studying the problem. "The Boy Scouts possessed a greater knowledge of the incidence and prevalence of sexual abuse of boys by people in leadership positions than, to my knowledge, existed anywhere," he testified. "They had a great deal of detail from these files about the ways in which it occurs, who does it, how it is done, and such things as the tendency of people to try to get back in, even after they were prosecuted, to try to gain access to kids. So, my main opinion is it is an extraordinary body of information."[33]

Unlike Marshall, the BSA official who had repeatedly balked at using the word *problem* to describe sexual abuse in Scouting when he had testified, Schoener said the existence of the perversion files clearly demonstrated it: "You don't need a system if you don't have a problem." By not analyzing their own files or sharing their data with others who could use it to help curb child sexual abuse, the Boy Scouts had squandered a rare and valuable opportunity, he said. "They had enough knowledge and information to intervene in a much more forceful and effective way. And by not doing so, they guaranteed that there were going to be a number of people involved in their programs that were going to pay a price."

Kerry Lewis was one of them, he said.

The BSA presented its own expert assessment of the files by Janet Warren, a professor of psychiatry in neurobehavioral sciences at the University of Virginia. Warren was the university's liaison to the FBI's behavioral sciences unit. She trained others how to conduct forensic evaluations and had researched violent crime and sexual victimization. She, too, had been asked to review the files and tasked seven of her best graduate students to code them and help build a database of the information and determine how it might be put to good use.

Warren had come away with a decidedly different take than Schoener's. She had concluded that "there's nothing in these files that we could analyze that would further the research field." In her view, the perversion files demonstrated the Boy Scouts' diligent pursuit of wrongdoers, "a very sustained effort by the local Council[s] to actually investigate these offenders" and run them off "if there were <u>even</u> a whisper or suspicion." Contrary to Lewis's lawyers' contention that the Boy Scouts had routinely kept parents in the dark, Warren said she had seen cases in which they not only were informed of the allegations but participated in meetings with local officials about how to handle them. Sometimes, she said, it had been the parents who had put a halt to abusers' formal expulsion, deciding, "We're satisfied that this guy is out of our life, and we don't want to proceed."[34]

In sharp contrast to Schoener's contention that the Boy Scouts had fumbled a great opportunity to protect children, Warren said that the youth group had met or exceeded the standard of care at the time for informing others about sexual abuse. She also disputed the notion, pushed by the plaintiff's attorneys, that the Scouts had dodged that responsibility by issuing public service ads that spoke to the general dangers of child sexual abuse but did not mention that Scout leaders might also be perpetrators. The number of sexually abusive scoutmasters was actually quite small, she said, and specifically naming them as potential abusers would have only frightened parents. She also said it wouldn't have been right to single them out without mentioning all of the other groups of potential molesters, including schoolteachers and Little League coaches. "To create a hysterical fear that every Boy Scout leader was going to sexually abuse your child without contextualizing it…would have been an improper presentation of information that was very relevant and close to everyone's hearts," she said.

Not surprisingly, other expert witnesses called by both sides also disagreed on the extent of damage Lewis had suffered as a result of Dykes's abuse. Jon R. Conte, a University of Washington professor with a PhD in social welfare, examined Lewis twice at the request of his attorneys. He concluded, among other things, that Dykes had been "the significant non-parent relationship of his life" and was helping him move from childhood to adolescence when he sexually abused him. "I think the betrayal, being hurt by somebody who you admired and looked up to and was this important person who was teaching you the Scout way and the Mormon way of values, I think the betrayal and the loss…in that relationship is more significant than the actual sexual behavior."[35]

The sexual abuse had diminished Lewis's "internal ability to manage life," contributing to his tendency to self-medicate with drugs and alcohol, Conte said. Lewis had also suffered from anxiety and depression, he said, but those weren't the most serious effects. As often happens in these situations, he said, the traumatic experience had stunted the boy's emotional development. "My experience with Mr. Lewis is that if you shut your eyes and don't know that he is a father and the other things that he does as an adult, he sounds to me emotionally and feels to me emotionally like in some ways an adolescent."

Lorah Sebastian, a Portland psychologist, evaluated Lewis for the BSA. She seemed to downplay Dykes's abuse of Lewis by describing the incidents as "sexual encounters"—between an eleven-year-old boy and a man in his midtwenties—and said they had not had a significant negative impact on him. She found no evidence of post-traumatic stress disorder and said that his substance abuse problems did not stem from Dykes's abuse. Instead, she cited an inherited tendency to use drugs in Lewis's family history and said that his difficulty sleeping, depression, and irritability likely had more to do with that than with sexual abuse. "Methamphetamine abuse can lead to all of the symptoms that he's having currently," she said. "And the return to normalcy after use of methamphetamine can be quite slow."[36]

Eugene Grant, the volunteer president of the Cascade Pacific Council, was called as a defense witness and introduced a new villain in the Dykes saga: the parents of Kerry Lewis and the other abused boys.

Grant, a Portland real estate and land use lawyer who had been a Boy Scout and later served as a scoutmaster and in various other leadership roles, said he'd never seen nor heard of anything like Dykes's involvement with Lewis and the others. Yes, the Boy

Scouts encouraged close, trusting relationships between boys and their adult scoutmasters, he said, but this was "a complete aberration." He laid the blame at the feet of moms and dads who should have known better than to let their kids spend nights at Dykes's apartment, no matter that the Boy Scouts at the time had no rules against sleepovers.

"I mean, any parent that does that ought to be sent to jail," he said. "That is just wrong, and it should have never happened."[37] It was nothing short of criminal, he said, and he reiterated his contention that the Cascade Pacific Council bore no responsibility for what had happened to Kerry Lewis.

Lewis's mother, Helen, was floored. "It was like a slap in the face," she said. "Believe me, don't think I didn't slap myself, for why didn't I see this earlier, why didn't I know? But for him to sit there and make me feel like I should be in jail was just shocking."[38]

THREE WEEKS AFTER OPENING statements and the testimony of some thirty witnesses, closing arguments began on April 8, with Lewis's attorney Kelly Clark hammering on the themes of his case in chief: The BSA had kept files for decades on thousands of sexual abusers but refused to acknowledge that it had a problem. It had fought to keep the files secret in an effort to protect its public image, and it had willfully ignored information that could have helped protect kids. In eighty-five years, Clark said, the Boy Scouts had never analyzed the perversion files, insisting that it couldn't be done, even though a retired LAPD detective working for Lewis's legal team had done it in just three weeks. He also mocked a defense contention that in the early 1980s sexual abuse had been less prevalent in Scouting than in society at large, dismissing that as cold comfort to the parents of the boys who'd been molested by Timur Dykes. He argued that the evidence warranted a $4 million judgment for Lewis's pain and suffering, and he urged the jurors to take it a step further by hitting the Boy Scouts with punitive damages for concealing the dangers to children. "They had the information," he said. "They kept the secrets."[39]

In his closing argument, BSA lawyer Chuck Smith said that the jury should blame no one but Timur Dykes for what had happened to Kerry Lewis. He called Dykes "the consummate con man" who had fooled everyone—the church, the Lewis family, the Boy Scouts, the police. Nothing in all of that justified punitive damages, he told the jurors.[40]

Smith's closing was followed by that of Paul Xochihua, the Cascade Pacific Council's attorney, who took a far sharper approach. He questioned the motives and attacked the credibility of Kerry Lewis, his family, and other plaintiff's witnesses, including the abused former Scouts who had testified. Lewis had seemed to be doing just fine, Xochihua said, before his mother had called him in 2007 to discuss the lawsuit against the Boy Scouts she'd heard about on TV. Judge Wittmayer had forbidden the attorneys to mention at trial that Lewis had already received a settlement from the LDS Church, but that didn't stop Xochihua from hinting at it.

Sure, he told the jury, Lewis might have had some earlier financial issues, but once "he left his wife and daughter in New York to come here to be involved in this lawsuit," things seemed to have turned around: He now had a house in Klamath Falls, a pickup truck, and a couple of all-terrain vehicles he frolicked around in on the sand dunes on weekends.[41] The defense attorney also pointed out what he called discrepancies in Lewis's testimony, including whether Dykes had actually placed the boy's hand on his penis while sitting next to him on the couch or had merely moved it under his shorts and up his leg in that direction.

Clark got the last word, and he used his rebuttal to blast the defense for having one attorney, Smith, say it did not blame the victim while the other, Xochihua, attacked him "seven ways from

Sunday" and all but called Lewis a liar. Clark defended his client as "an honest guy" who sometimes struggled to put concepts and feelings into words. The Boy Scouts, on the other hand, had chosen "membership, money and manpower over the safety of children."

Closing arguments wrapped up at 4:30 p.m. that day. Wittmayer told the jurors it had been a long day already, so he sent them home with the usual admonishment not to discuss the case with anyone and a reminder that they would need at least nine of twelve votes for a verdict.

Deliberations began at 9:00 a.m. the next day, a Friday, but that day came and went without a verdict, as did the following Monday. Just before 10:30 a.m. on Tuesday, Wittmayer called the lawyers to his courtroom and then summoned the jury. "Has the jury reached a verdict?" he asked.

"We have," foreman Roger Fisher said, and handed the signed verdict form to the clerk, who gave it to the judge.

Both organizations had been negligent, the jurors found, and they had damaged Kerry Lewis to the tune of $1.4 million. The jury apportioned the negligence at 60 percent to the Boy Scouts of America, 15 percent to Cascade Pacific Council, and 25 percent to the LDS Church, which would not have to pay its share because it had already settled. That left Lewis with a net award of $1.05 million.

But that was not the end of it. Question number seven was the one that would rock America's largest youth organization: "Is the Plaintiff entitled to punitive damages against the Defendant Boy Scouts of America?" Answer: Yes. The jury let the Cascade Pacific Council off the hook for punitive damages, which are intended to punish and deter bad behavior. The jurors were instructed to come back in a week for a second phase of the trial to determine the extent of the BSA's "reprehensibility" in failing to protect Lewis and how much it would have to pay.

Twenty-seven years after he was abused by his scoutmaster,

Kerry Lewis had won his case. It had begun as a "Jack Doe" proceeding to protect his privacy but ended with Lewis permitting his name and likeness to be published. After the verdict was read, he sighed and hugged his mother. The lawyers for the Boy Scouts left the courthouse without commenting.

Instead of apologizing and promising to do better or simply offering something diplomatic about respecting the jury but being disappointed in the verdict, the BSA promptly released a statement denouncing the panel's decision, right after it was read. As with most significant BSA statements over the years, it was issued by a spokesman, not by the chief Scout executive, in this case Robert Mazzuca. But it is hard to imagine that it was not approved at the highest levels. For an organization that prided itself on its public relations acumen, blasting the very jury that was about to decide how hard to hammer it with punitive damages was a woefully ill-timed move. Smith, the Boy Scouts' trial attorney, had learned of the statement before it was issued and tried to quash it but had been overruled by BSA officials. "I couldn't shut it down," he recalled. "It spit right in the face of the jury."[42]

BY THE TIME COURT reconvened for the punitive phase on Tuesday, April 20, the Boy Scouts of America had deleted the statement from its website. But Clark wasted no time seizing on it in his opening remarks, to underscore his contention that BSA officials were still in denial. "They have not accepted responsibility for what they allowed to happen to Kerry Lewis and others like him," he said. "In fact, I'd like to show you a piece of evidence that will prove just the opposite. Ladies and gentlemen, last week within about an hour of your verdict coming in, the BSA posted on its national website—"[43]

That was as far as he got before Smith objected. Wittmayer sent the jury out of the courtroom, and Smith asked him to bar the statement from being read into the record. "Its only purpose really is to introduce evidence that's going to inflame this jury," Smith told the judge, who was having none of it.

"That's what the Boy Scouts of America invited when they posted this on their website—commenting on the evidence presented at trial that the jury obviously accepted," Wittmayer said. "Incredible that they did that." The judge overruled the objection and Clark picked up where he'd left off, projecting the statement on a screen. For good measure, he asked the audiovisuals guy to "blow it up a little" to make sure jurors could see it clearly.

"We are gravely disappointed with the verdict," Clark said, reading from the Boy Scouts' statement.

We believe that the allegations made against our youth protection efforts are not valid. We intend to appeal. We are saddened by what happened to the plaintiff. The actions of the man who committed these crimes do not represent the values and ideals of the Boy Scouts of America. The safety of the young people currently in the Scouting program has never been in question during these legal proceedings.

The case focused on a discussion about what society and the BSA knew about child abuse approximately three decades ago. This is a longstanding societal issue that every youth-serving organization must address. Based on the standard of care at that time the BSA believes it acted responsibly, and that the evidence presented during the trial does not justify the verdict.

Clark gave jurors a moment to digest the statement. "This is the most telling and most recent evidence about whether the Boy Scouts of America accept responsibility for what happened to Kerry Lewis in light of what happened to others like him," he said.

Smith tried to mitigate the damage with a series of witnesses detailing the strides that Scouting had made in protecting children since Dykes had abused Lewis. They discussed the mandatory background checks instituted in 2003 for all new volunteers and paid staffers. They talked about the Scouts' "two-deep" rule, preventing any adult from being alone with a Scout.

Assistant Chief Scout Executive James J. Terry, Jr., a top national official, touted the creation in 1988 of an expert advisory panel of psychologists, psychiatrists, and researchers to help the Boy Scouts develop a new Youth Protection Training Program. In an apparent attempt to blunt criticism that the Boy Scouts had never analyzed its own data, Terry said that one of the experts, Dr. David Finkelhor, had sent a couple of researchers to study the files but they had yielded no useful information.

"There was nothing in those files that really could be of assistance to him in the kind of analysis he wanted to do, correct?" Lewis's attorney Mones asked.

"That is correct," Terry said.[44]

Finkelhor later disputed that assertion.[45] But all the jurors heard was that the blue-ribbon panel had worked hard to make Scouting safer. The same jurors who a week earlier had decided by a 9–3 vote that the defendants were liable for $1.4 million in compensatory damages retired to deliberate for a second time, weighing a demand for $25 million in punitive compensation.

Margaret Malarkey was in her midtwenties when she was seated as a juror. She had a bachelor of arts degree in cultural anthropology from the University of Oregon and worked for a Portland nonprofit that served immigrants and refugees. Her dad was an Eagle Scout, and she had kept his merit badges and other Scouting mementos as cherished keepsakes. She believed in the intrinsic value of Scouting and still does, but her faith in the BSA was put to the test during the trial with each new piece of damning evidence and testimony, none more powerful than the Ineligible Volunteer files.

"We were the first 'civilians' to see the P files, the perversion files. I remember when they brought them in, literally in big boxes on a dolly, dolly after dolly. We spent about a full day silently going through the files and sharing them with each other. It was like, 'Oh, my God, look at this: here's a scoutmaster who was caught molesting boys and then he's let go from that troop and six months later he pops up in the next county!' Or another guy who's caught in '57. And in '63. And in '68. And then again in '72."[46]

As they worked through the files, Malarkey and her fellow jurors saw the same patterns emerge: "Scout leaders accused of sexual assault and molestation and trauma to little boys, year after year, decade after decade, with all of the information funneled back to the national headquarters," she said. As the jurors deliberated, one refused to consider that the Boy Scouts were at fault, Malarkey said, and kept talking about how Lewis would use the money from a damages award for drugs and partying. But most of the others quickly reached the same, infuriating conclusion about the Boy Scouts of America. "They knew. They totally fucking knew," she said. "And they didn't do anything....They covered it up out of a sense of self-preservation."[47]

Malarkey said she wanted to hit the Scouts with the entire $25 million in punitive damages. Instead, the jury deducted the 25 percent of liability that had been apportioned to the Mormon Church and issued a verdict for $18.5 million in punitive damages—the largest judgment in the youth group's hundred-year history.

"We sent a message to the Boy Scouts, but it was also a message to any other organization that might put self-preservation and PR and image above holding predators accountable," she said. The trial, and what she'd read in the confidential files, had left her shocked and saddened. "How many of those boys could have been saved from that abuse and trauma and the lifelong burden of the aftermath of that?"[48]

Kerry Lewis was happy it was all over, joking at a postverdict press conference that he looked forward to going home and mowing his lawn. A reporter asked if he had any advice for victims who had yet to come forward. "It's very scary, but take that first step and reach out," replied Lewis. "Ask for help. Regardless whether it's a lawyer, a counselor, a therapist, anybody, just ask for help, and you'll get it. Don't be scared even though it is scary. You can do it. I did it."[49]

CHAPTER 9

THE LID COMES OFF

No court shall be secret, but justice shall
be administered, openly and without
purchase, completely and without delay.

—*Oregon Constitution, Article 1, Section 10,*
the "open courts" clause

Straying from its long-standing strategy of quietly settling sexual abuse lawsuits would prove costly for the Boy Scouts of America in the Kerry Lewis case in 2010 and for years to come. But the most damaging fallout was yet to come, with the publication of the closely guarded perversion files and the long-buried secrets they held.

Judge John Wittmayer had ordered the Boy Scouts to turn over 1,247 of the files to Lewis's lawyers, who introduced them as evidence at trial in Portland. Wittmayer also placed the files under a protective order, which barred their public release during the court proceedings and required them to be returned to the Boy Scouts right afterward. It took almost no time for reporters covering the trial to recognize the files' newsworthiness and try to pry them loose. On the second day, William McCall of the Associated Press dropped by to see Wittmayer and took the first stab at it.

"What he said was his editors in New York are asking whether at the conclusion of the trial they would have access to the I.V. Files," Wittmayer later told attorneys for both sides. "And I said, 'Well, generally things that happen in court are public, but if there was a request, I would certainly give all of the litigants an opportunity to weigh in on that issue.'"[1]

After the trial, Wittmayer extended his earlier restrictions on the files. By then, the AP had allied with other news outlets, including the *Oregonian*, the *New York Times*, Oregon Public Broadcasting, Courthouse News, and Portland TV station KGW, to petition the court to open the records. Wittmayer granted the media's request, on the condition that the names of victims and others who had reported sexual abuse be redacted. But he stayed his decision and ordered the files to remain sealed pending an anticipated legal challenge by the BSA, a contentious process that would stretch out for the next two years.

While that legal tug-of-war was working its way through the Oregon courts, the *Los Angeles Times* launched its own examination of the perversion files, collaborating with the Canadian Broadcasting Corporation's newsmagazine, *The Fifth Estate*, on an investigation of Rick Turley, a Canadian Scout leader who had abused boys in southern California and British Columbia in the 1970s.[2]

Turley's file, from September 1979, was nine pages long and included the basics: He was a Canadian Air Force reservist living in Victoria, single, twenty-six years old, six feet two and 195 pounds with red hair. The file also contained letters between Boy Scouts officials in California and at the national office, detailing allegations that Turley had molested three boys at Lost Valley Scout

Reservation in San Diego County.[3] When confronted with the accusations, Turley, the camp's program director, confessed to the abuse, "expressed concern" for what he'd done, and immediately packed up and headed home to Canada.

The boys' parents agreed not to press charges if Turley left town, so no one called the police. Boy Scouts officials at the camp falsely attributed his abrupt departure to "family problems," an explanation that A. Buford Hill, Jr., a retired Orange County Scout executive, defended in 2011. "We were following exactly the national recommendations of the Boy Scouts of America and its board who set up the rules," he said. "You do not want to broadcast to the entire population that these things happen. You take care of it quietly and make sure it never happens again."[4]

But it did happen again with Turley, just as it had with so many other sex offenders who had slipped back into Scouting after being blacklisted.

When he returned to British Columbia, Turley again became active in Scouts Canada, which is akin to but separate from its US counterpart. The joint *Los Angeles Times*–CBC investigation revealed that he had molested Canadian Cub Scouts as early as 1971, eight years before the BSA had placed him in its confidential files. His modus operandi was to turn up at their homes in uniform with a sash full of merit badges and a spiel about being a prominent scoutmaster. He would charm parents and offer to take their boys out for a swim or a drive, then ply some with alcohol before molesting them.

In early 1975, Turley showed up at the La Puente, California, home of Eddy Iris, whom he'd met at a local Scout meeting. Friendly, engaging, and right on cue, Turley told the boy's mother he was "one of Canada's top Scout leaders" and asked her if the eleven-year-old Eddy could show him around town. Off they went to play miniature golf, take a demo flight in a small plane at Fallbrook Airport, and spend the night together in a sleeping bag in the mountains. "He was knowledgeable about things that I liked," Iris, then forty-seven, told the *Times* in 2011. "He was extremely friendly. He paid attention to you."[5]

If something bad happened in the mountains that night, Iris said, he didn't remember it. The next day, he and Turley returned to the airport, where the Scout leader stole a Cessna 172, a single-engine plane. Once aloft, he turned to Eddy and said, "You do realize you've been kidnapped, don't you?" The terrified boy feared that Turley would open the door and push him out,[6] but the kidnapping was foiled when the plane ran out of gas and had to make an emergency landing on a Mojave Desert airstrip.

Turley was arrested and later pleaded guilty to felony child stealing. He was committed to a state hospital in San Bernardino County as a mentally disordered sex offender. He was released after eighteen months and less than a year later was working at a Boy Scouts camp not far from the hospital. He would spend the next three summers among southern California Scouts before being expelled from Lost Valley.[7]

Turley's ultimate undoing came nearly twenty years later, in 1995, when his girlfriend told police he'd confided in her his sexual attraction to children. He was convicted of five counts of sexually abusing Canadian Scouts and spent five years in prison. Over two decades, authorities said, he had molested at least fifteen boys on both sides of the border. When *Los Angeles Times* reporter Jason Felch and a CBC team with a camera crew surprised him one night in 2011 at the Alberta truck stop motel where he was working, Turley stood outside the office in the glow of a neon OPEN sign, acknowledged his criminal history, and conceded that he'd been "a monster" earlier in life. He said he'd tamed his sexual impulses and "had no plans on ever offending again." Looking back, even he was surprised at how often he'd gotten away with abusing Scouts. "It was easy," he said. "Kids were easily accessible."[8]

*   *   *

TURLEY'S STORY PIQUED THE *Los Angeles Times'* interest in what else might be in the perversion files, which had largely existed in obscurity before the Portland trial. Some had been submitted as evidence in lawsuits two decades earlier and had been the subject of Patrick Boyle's nonfiction 1990s book *Scout's Honor*. But that had been before most people had even heard of the internet and long before scandals in the US Catholic Church, at Penn State University, and in USA Gymnastics helped propel the issue of child sexual abuse to new levels of public awareness in the new millennium.

In 1988, lawyers for a Virginia boy who'd been molested by Scoutmaster Carlton Bittenbender had forced the Boy Scouts to hand over 231 perversion files spanning the years 1975 to 1984 as evidence of the BSA's knowledge of sexual abuse in its ranks. The trial had attracted national media attention, which had fizzled out after the BSA had prevailed in the case, convincing a jury that it had not been responsible for the actions of a rogue scoutmaster.[9] The wider BSA sexual abuse story had also fallen off the public's radar and likely would have stayed there if not for Boyle, a *Washington Times* reporter whose reporting on the 231 files resulted in a multipart series for the newspaper in 1991.[10]

A year later, armed with Boyle's stories and records he'd collected from other lawsuits, Sacramento attorney Michael Rothschild persuaded a California judge to order the BSA to hand over a larger group of nearly 1,900 files covering 1970 to 1991 for his lawsuit involving Scoutmaster Allen Lee Trueman, who by then had been convicted of molesting eight boys.[11]

Rothschild is one of only a few people outside the top echelon of Scouting who have seen the physical files, not just copies of them. After deposing Paul Ernst, the Scouts official who had overseen the confidential records, Rothschild asked to have a look at them. Ernst obliged, took him to a nearby room, and opened some of the metal filing cabinets stuffed with manila folders on abusive scoutmasters. "I kept a straight face, but I said to myself, 'This is gold,'" Rothschild said.[12]

The Trueman lawsuit was settled, but the judge did not order those files sealed, so Rothschild shared them with Boyle and with other lawyers. Boyle used them to publish his book, which profiled some of the most egregious cases and offenders. It wasn't a runaway bestseller, but it had legs, serving for years as a reference guide for other journalists and for plaintiffs' attorneys suing the BSA. He eventually put the records into storage, where they sat until a Seattle lawyer, Tim Kosnoff, asked to copy them. Years later, in 2011, Kosnoff shared them with the *Los Angeles Times*.

The newspaper sought to do what the BSA had never done: analyze the files to identify trends and patterns of behavior by abusive leaders and volunteers. Scouts officials had long insisted, in sworn testimony in court and in depositions for lawsuits, that studying the records would not yield information that could bolster their efforts to protect boys, even though some of their own expert advisers disagreed.

Over the next year, *Times* reporters read thousands of pages of perversion files, an eye-popping, stomach-turning collection of unspeakable acts against children committed by adult Scout leaders and volunteers across the country. The files covered the biggest cities to the smallest burgs, ranging in size from a cover sheet with a couple of pages to enough paperwork to fill a three-ring binder. Some described the abuse in graphic detail. Others only hinted at it with vague euphemisms such as "improper relationship" and "corrupting the morals of a minor." Many contained newspaper clippings on criminal proceedings against the abusers, and some included angry and anguished letters from parents alerting Scout leaders to the predators in their sons' troops.

The *Times* documented patterns of grooming behavior by abusive Scout leaders who had often enticed their youthful victims with pornography and alcohol, bought them gifts, lavished them with one-on-one attention, and seemingly taken a keen interest in the things they enjoyed: TV, board games, swimming, hiking, and, of course, camping and other Scouting activities. The patterns were so distinct and so common that it sometimes seemed that the abusers had all worked from the same script.[13]

The files also documented what Scout leaders and the organization had or hadn't done in response to abuse allegations. The numbers told a troubling story of neglect and cover-up as local Scouts officials failed to report hundreds of suspected child molesters to police and often hid abuse allegations from parents and law enforcement. Scouts officials routinely urged abusive leaders to quietly resign and disappear and then, as in the case of Rick Turley at Lost Valley, helped them cover their tracks with bogus explanations ranging from the mundane ("business demands") to the ridiculous ("chronic brain dysfunction" and "duties at a Shakespeare festival").[14]

In most of the cases reviewed, the Boy Scouts learned about alleged abuse from local police or other authorities already investigating it. But in more than five hundred instances, Scout leaders heard about it from boys, parents, staff members, or anonymous tips. In about four hundred of those incidents—or 80 percent—the *Times* found nothing in the files to indicate that the Scouts had reported their suspicions to authorities. And in more than a hundred of those cases, Scouts officials had actively sought to conceal the abuse or enabled the accused molesters to hide it, at times justifying their actions by claiming they were trying to spare young victims from embarrassment.[15] Local police and news outlets sometimes played along with the ruse, ostensibly to protect the boys but at least as if not more often to shield the organization from bad publicity.

Over the two decades covered by the files, at least 125 men continued to molest Boy Scouts after the first allegations against them surfaced.[16] They would sneak back into the program by falsifying personal information—sometimes simply by changing a first name or middle initial—or find other ways to skirt the registration process so they wouldn't be checked against the blacklist.

Some abusers went to great lengths to conceal their crimes, but ingenious trickery wasn't always necessary. Some of the most egregious predators were hiding in plain sight as prominent members of their communities: doctors, lawyers, politicians and police officers, schoolteachers, men with families and sterling reputations and years of faithful service to Scouting. In some cases, it seemed, Scouting rewarded them by looking the other way when they were caught molesting boys.

ARTHUR W. HUMPHRIES OF Chesapeake, Virginia, had been active in Scouting for more than fifty years and was by all accounts the model leader. He'd served the Boy Scouts in a variety of capacities since the 1930s and had won presidential citations for outstanding leadership from Gerald Ford and Ronald Reagan. He had earned the Scouts' top award for distinguished service, the Silver Beaver, and was active in his local Methodist church and Sunday school. In 1972, the retired electronics technician and father of three adult sons helped organize a troop at a local rehabilitation center for disabled boys and stayed on as their scoutmaster.[17] In 1978, he received the Chesapeake mayor's Outstanding Service Award for his work with disabled boys.[18]

Six years later, in May 1984, Humphries was arrested and charged with molesting boys, including severely disabled members of Troop 472, the unit he had founded and led. He pleaded guilty that September to thirty-one felony counts involving twenty boys, some of whom he had photographed in the nude. At the time, the Scouts' executive director of Tidewater Council, John B. Terwilliger, told a newspaper reporter that he was as surprised as could be: no one in the council had had any indication of Humphries's behavior until he had been arrested and charged.[19]

But that was not true, and Terwilliger must have known it.

In May 1978, one of the boys in Humphries's troop accused him of assaulting him on a camping trip. In an interview that Terwilliger himself ordered, the boy told a district executive for the Scouts that Humphries had followed him into a bathroom and performed oral sex on him. "He then told me to do the same and I did," the Scout said. "Mr. Humphries told me not to tell anyone about this."[20]

The boy said that Humphries had abused him twice more, once during that camping trip and again the following September, when he had gone to the Scout leader's home to work on a merit badge for citizenship. According to Humphries's confidential file, a Chesapeake police detective had sat in on the interview and signed his name as a witness to the handwritten transcript, which also contained this notation by the Scout executive who had conducted it: "This statement will not be used in a court room or as an official complaint to the police."

The Scouts dropped the matter after the boy, in a second interview conducted by the director of the rehabilitation center that sponsored the troop, said he had not been sexually abused by any of his Scout leaders. Humphries was apparently never questioned about the boy's allegations, and three years later, when he applied for a post at a national Scouting event, Terwilliger wrote a letter endorsing him for it. "I believe the attached letters of recommendation and the newspaper write-up will give you a well-rounded picture of Art," he wrote. "If selected, I am sure that he would add much to the handicapped awareness trail at the 1981 Jamboree."[21]

Humphries worked with Scouts until he was arrested again in 1984. He was convicted of abusing twenty of them, some as young as eight, and was sentenced to 151 years in prison. One boy Humphries had molested a decade earlier as an eleven-year-old Scout

grew up to be an abuser himself.[22] Keith M. Gardner, who was convicted as Humphries's accomplice and sentenced to sixteen years
in prison, testified that the Scout leader had blackmailed him by
threatening to publish snapshots of him as a child having sex with
other boys. "He said the photos would go in the newspaper," Gardner said. "I hated myself."[23]

In June 2012, more than two years after the verdict in the Kerry
Lewis case, the Oregon Supreme Court rebuffed the Boy Scouts'
efforts to quash Judge John Wittmayer's order. It unsealed the
1,247 files admitted as trial exhibits, accepting the petitioners'
argument that "lifting the veil of secrecy on child sexual abuse" is
the best way to combat it. The court ordered the files released after
the redaction of names of victims and others who had reported
abuse, to protect them from embarrassment and retaliation. The
Boy Scouts responded with a video statement by Chief Scout Executive Mazzuca, who doubled down on the BSA's long-standing
assertion that the records should remain sealed.[24] "We've kept
these files confidential because we believe that victims deserve
protection and that confidentiality encourages prompt reporting of
questionable behavior," he said. "It removes the fear of retribution
and assures the victims and their families that they receive the privacy that they deserve."

Beginning on August 4, 2012, two months before the release
of the Oregon records, the *Los Angeles Times* published a series of
investigative stories based on its review of the files, along with
fresh reporting from interviews, court documents, and other public records. The paper also published a database of the files, as well
as some 3,200 less detailed case summaries, at long last opening
the records to public scrutiny.

"The BSA had this vast knowledge base of sexual abuse that
they sat on and did not educate the Scouts or their parents about,

and kept it from the public," said Paul Mones, one of Lewis's attorneys. "The importance of the *Times'* release of those files was that people then had the ability to do a search online."[25]

For the first time, men who had been molested as Boy Scouts could punch in the names of their abusers, their troop numbers, or their hometowns and validate their experiences and perhaps come to grips with them. Labeled "Inside the Perversion Files,"[26] the database immediately drew former Scouts searching for information about their abusive scoutmasters or for clues to why they had been singled out for abuse. Like their perpetrators, the survivors were from all backgrounds and all geographic regions. Some were well into their seventies and eighties by then. Many had pushed the details of their abuse deep into the recesses of their memories and found that as painful as the accounts were to read, it helped them grapple with questions about their own masculinity and sexuality.

Non-Scouts who scoured the database included lawyers looking to bolster their clients' claims, as well as people who suspected that their acquaintances or relatives might be among the alleged abusers. Some were surprised and deeply disappointed by what they found; others were disturbed that their long-standing suspicions were finally confirmed, including one man who discovered that his grandfather was on the blacklist.

The *Oregonian* and some law firms subsequently posted their own searchable databases of the files from the Lewis trial. News outlets around the country plumbed the records to localize the sex abuse scandal by naming and reporting on perpetrators in their own communities. Men who believed they'd gotten away with molesting Boy Scouts decades earlier suddenly found themselves on the wrong end of reporters' phone calls or, even worse, on the front pages of their local papers.

CHAPTER 10

A FINE LITTLE TOWN

R odger L. Beatty must have thought he was in the clear. After all, it had been thirty-six years.

On July 1, 1976, the same day that five Boy Scouts in Newport, Pennsylvania, accused him of sexually abusing them, Beatty resigned as scoutmaster of Troop 222, citing new and pressing demands of his job as a county drug and alcohol counselor.[1] Soon after, he slipped out of town, unencumbered by criminal charges and, thanks to Boy Scout officials' help in concealing his actions, trailing not so much as a whiff of wrongdoing.

Beatty, then twenty-nine with a bachelor's degree in social work, went on to enjoy great success in his academic and professional lives. He earned a master's degree in psychological science from Penn State University and a doctorate from the University of Pittsburgh's School of Social Work. He spent most of his career in AIDS-related public health and education programs geared largely to the LGBTQ community. He held several posts with the Pennsylvania Department of Health, enjoying a reputation as a tireless advocate for people on the margins of society. He was an assistant professor in the University of Pittsburgh School of Public Health's department of infectious diseases and microbiology, and his research focused on HIV prevention and its relationship to substance abuse and sexual minorities.[2] In 1981, the National Jaycees honored him as "Outstanding Young Man of the Year."[3]

For three and a half decades, Beatty's sexual abuse of Boy Scouts had been his secret. The accusations against him lay buried in the Ineligible Volunteer files; his stood out for several reasons, and not just the egregiousness of the abuse his young accusers had described in graphic handwritten statements. It also echoed patterns found in perversion files spanning decades, including the BSA's practice of allowing predatory leaders to resign under false pretenses and evade criminal consequences.

In many of the most serious scenarios, the abusers had been caught and prosecuted or had resurfaced in other troops and reoffended. But in Beatty's case, there was no indication that he was ever held to account for what happened in Newport in 1976. Unlike most of the BSA's confidential files, Beatty's included some of his victims' names, making it possible to track and compare how his life, and the lives of his young accusers, had played out over the previous three and a half decades.

In late summer 2012, a *Los Angeles Times* reporter reached out to Beatty by phone at his home and at his University of Pittsburgh office, leaving messages with just enough detail to get his attention: "I'd like to speak with you about your time as scoutmaster of Troop 222 and your reasons for leaving so abruptly."[4] All went unanswered, as did emails sent to his Pitt account. At the reporter's request, someone in his office finally checked with Beatty, who confirmed that he'd received the messages and said he would respond. He never did, so the reporter went to see him.

Beatty lived in a nice two-story brick Colonial built in the 1920s, fifteen steps up from the sidewalk in a well-kept neighborhood in northeast Pittsburgh. Parked facing the house a short distance away, the reporter waited and watched for signs of life for a half hour and then climbed the cement steps and knocked on the door. No answer. Back to the car to wait some more, hoping the neighbors wouldn't take him for a burglar casing their homes. Maybe Beatty wasn't home. Maybe he didn't live there anymore. Maybe this was all a waste of the reporter's time and his newspaper's limited travel budget.

Finally, at about 8:00 p.m., there was a little flurry of activity as three or four people went up the steps and into the house. The reporter waited a few minutes to let them settle in and then knocked on the door again. This time it was answered by a man who was much too young to be Beatty, then in his midsixties.

"Hi, I'm hoping to speak with Rodger Beatty," the reporter said, in as casual a tone as he could muster. "Is he home?"

"You're here to see *Rodger*?" the man asked, obviously taken aback. "Rodger isn't here....He's in the hospital. He had a stroke and isn't able to talk to you or anyone else."

It was the reporter's turn to be taken aback. "I'm really sorry to hear that," he said. "Is he going to be okay?"

"We don't know yet," the man said and then cut the conversation short, agreeing to pass along a business card to Beatty when he was feeling better.[5]

The next morning, cruising along the Pennsylvania Turnpike toward Newport two hundred miles to the east, the reporter couldn't shake the uneasy thought of Beatty's falling ill shortly after he'd started leaving him messages a couple of weeks earlier. It must have been quite a jolt to get a call like that out of the blue, decades and a sterling career after the abuse allegations had surfaced and seemingly been put to rest.[6]

THE PUBLIC LIBRARY ON North Fourth Street housed a collection of Newport High School yearbooks, including the 1981 edition of the

Blunita with Carl Maxwell, Jr.'s, smiling senior picture and description below it: "short 'n' sweet...gymnast...artistic...Ambition: to be a famous interior designer in New York City." About a mile away, on South Fifth Street, stood the tidy frame duplex where Carl had grown up, several blocks uphill from the river, with a front porch looking out in the other direction, at the woods across the street. His widowed seventy-five-year-old mother still lived there and was napping in a comfortable chair in the living room when Carl came to the door in jeans, a sweatshirt, and a baseball cap, a grown-up and somewhat wearier version of the kid in the yearbook photo. A former bartender forced into early retirement by pulmonary hypertension, he spent much of each year in the resort town of Rehoboth Beach, Delaware, and just happened to be in Newport for a couple of days to visit his mom and their ailing cat, Jasper.[7]

Though he would eventually find himself out of step with the majority of residents in the ultraconservative county that has voted Republican in every presidential election since 1964, Carl remembered Newport as a fine little town, a great place to be a kid in the 1970s.

Like other Boy Scouts, he and his pals were taught to respect their scoutmaster, a personage cast in successive editions of the BSA handbook as not just an authority figure but also a trusted friend, adviser, and mentor. At first, the members of Troop 222 happily accepted Beatty's invitations to his home to work on their merit badges or sleep over on the nights before camping trips or special Scouting events.

Beatty lived alone in a little house, really not much more than a rustic cabin, on the edge of a golf course owned by the Newport American Legion post. It was old, with creaky floors and sparse furnishings, and it was in the middle of nowhere. You had to walk or drive across the golf course to get to it, and if you wandered too far from it in the wrong direction in the dark, you'd step off a cliff and plunge into a rock quarry. The way Carl remembers it, the place was straight out of a horror movie. It was so far removed from any other houses that even if you screamed into the night, no one would hear you. "It looked like the kind of place where bad stuff would happen," he said, "and it did."[8]

Carl's recall of events and details was uncanny, virtually identical to what was in Beatty's perversion file and nearly verbatim to the written statement he'd given to Scouts officials thirty-six years earlier and hadn't reviewed since. He recalled the mattresses that Beatty had spread out on the living room floor for the Scouts to sleep on after he retired to his room—only to creep back out a short while later to attack them one by one. "I remember the first time for me," Carl said. "The lights were turned off and the moon was out, and I could see it shining through a crack in the blinds. Then all of a sudden it got dark and then it got light again, and you could tell someone passed through the light."[9]

He knew it was Beatty.

"He started at one end of the room and worked his way right down," he said. Beatty never uttered a word during the assaults, after which he would "just go back to his bed and snooze, sweet dreams." Beatty never spoke of the abuse the next morning, either: no sheepishness, no remorse, no nothing. Instead, he'd make nice by taking the boys to get milkshakes or letting them motor around the golf course in his Chevy Vega. It was all so confusing to the thirteen- and fourteen-year-old Scouts who had looked up to him as their leader.

The assaults went on for several months in the spring and early summer of 1976, until Carl and his best friend, Scott, decided they could take no more of it. "I knew on every single level of my being that it was so wrong, so, *so* wrong," Carl said. He and Scott talked it over with the other three Scouts in their little clique and then told their parents. By then Carl's family had noticed changes in his personality and behavior: he was more withdrawn, his schoolwork was suffering, and he was starting to shut down emotionally.

The good news was that his parents believed him immediately, in sharp contrast to the experience of one of his friends, whose mom and dad refused to accept that their son had been molested.

Carl said his dad "wanted to kill Rodger," and he remembers him coming out of the house with pistol in hand. Alas, the elder Maxwell did not gun down Beatty, but Carl thinks he and a friend paid him a punishing visit. "I think they had a couple of beers, and I think they beat the hell out of him," he said. "That would be my guess if I knew my dad and his buddy....I'm sure they beat the hell out of him."

Days after they came forward with their allegations, Carl and the other boys were summoned to meet that July 1 with Scouts officials from the troop and higher up the organization's chain of command. One at a time, they met in the basement of Incarnation United Church of Christ, in rooms the congregation used for hoagie sales and other fundraisers and special events. For the better part of a day, the officials asked questions and the boys answered them and then scratched out their statements.

"All I heard was belts unbuckling and snaps opening and zippers coming down," one Scout wrote, describing the first of many alleged attacks at Beatty's house. One such assault had occurred the night before a ten-mile hike.[10] "He asked some scouts to stay over at his house and we said yes," one of the boys wrote. "I knew what was going to happen but somehow I fell asleep. I woke up and he had my pants down and then he rolled me over on my stomach and pinned me down and had sexual intercourse with me. But I was too scared to say anything and too scared to tell anybody." The same Scout also accused Beatty of raping him at the Spring Camporee after he awoke to find the Scout leader inside his tent.

One of the other boys wrote that he had joined the troop because Beatty had helped his dad with a drinking problem and his mom thought that Scouting would be good for him. Twice while sleeping over at Beatty's place, he had awakened in the morning with his pants pulled down. Once he woke up to find Beatty performing oral sex on him. "It went on for about an hour and then he said thank you when he was done," the Scout wrote.

Another said he'd been warned about Beatty's behavior but didn't believe it because "he did a lot of nice things for our family," so he had agreed to sleep over. "That night he seduced me," he wrote. Yet another Scout described his experience: after looking at travel photos Beatty had shot while serving in the army in Europe, he and the boys had watched a movie. After they had fallen asleep, Beatty had assaulted them.

Carl remembers going to that meeting at the church without his parents, because he "wanted to be a big boy" and he didn't want to pain them with the details of what had happened to him. Afterward, he fully expected Beatty to be taken away in handcuffs. "We and our families were told, or at least my family was told, that it would be taken care of, that the authorities would be notified and Rodger Beatty would be taken care of," he recalled. "And that was pretty much the end of it."[11]

Carl never saw Beatty again. Up until the day in 2012 when the *Los Angeles Times* reporter dropped in on him, he did not know what became of the scoutmaster after he had left Newport. When he learned that Beatty had been allowed to resign and avoid any legal consequences, he was incensed. "All of us boys—two of them's dead now—but all of us were scarred, and scarred for life by that," he said. "I'm sorry, but that's not something a thirteen-year-old boy puts out of his mind. And he got away with that."

Carl's childhood best friend, Scott, joined the air force after high school, and died in a car wreck on the Autobahn while serving in Germany. Their pal J. P. Culhane was also killed in a traffic accident, but his stepbrother, Mike Kunkel, still lived in Newport in 2012, married to his hometown sweetheart, Shawn, with two teenage daughters and a job as a produce merchandiser for an independent grocer. Like so many other survivors of childhood sexual abuse, he had never told his wife about what had happened to him, until the night he sat for an interview at a table in his backyard.[12]

"It was a big bomb to drop on her," said the fifty-year-old Kunkel. He spent eight years in the marines after high school and another nineteen in the Army National Guard, including a tour in Iraq. He recalled that his parents had been having problems and met Beatty while seeking counseling through the county. He and J.P. could have benefited from some more structure in their lives, he said, so they joined Scouting at Beatty's urging. Kunkel was at something of a loss to explain why Beatty's abuse had gone on as long as it did. The boys' naivete probably had a lot to do with it, he said, and so did Beatty's position as their leader.

"I look back at it and say, 'You're a victim,' but back then it was like, hey, he was my scoutmaster," he said. "...I wasn't proud of it. In fact, I was embarrassed about it. It was something that happened. It was vile, it was foul, but it was something you don't talk about. You move on."

Kunkel said he had not suffered "debilitating effects" from Beatty's abuse, but always kept in mind that "people like that are out there." He recalled the time a few years earlier when a man had kept riding past the family's house on a bicycle to "eyeball" his daughters playing outside. He'd told the guy if he stopped in front of his house one more time, it would be the last thing he ever did. He was just as blunt in his reaction to the news that Beatty had suffered a massive stroke, his response unmasking the anger he'd quietly carried for years. "My first thought is...I hope he dies and rots in hell," Kunkel said.

On the same date the five Scouts wrote out their statements accusing Beatty of sexual abuse, Beatty submitted his resignation letter to Arthur Lesh, the institutional representative for the church that sponsored Troop 222. His letter made no mention of the allegations. "For some time, the demands of my job have been increasing and it now appears shifting again with more travel, etc.," he wrote. "I fully realize this is very sudden and not at a very opportune time, but I have been left with very little choice in the situation. I am sure that you will be capable of securing a sound individual to continue great Scouting experiences in the Newport area. I have certainly appreciated the fine cooperation and consideration from all involved these past very quick three years."[13]

Lesh responded to Beatty with a letter that also omitted any reference to the abuse allegations. And then, even knowing the real reasons for the resignation, he went a step further. "I might add that it is with extreme regret that I accept your resignation on behalf of the Troop committee," he wrote. "We appreciate the services you have rendered as Scoutmaster of Troop 222, Newport, Pennsylvania, for the past three years."[14]

In 2012, when he was in his seventies, Lesh said in an hourlong interview in his Newport living room that he did not recall much about what had happened more than three decades earlier. But he did remember Beatty and the allegations against him, and he said he had believed the boys who had made them, in part because "there were so many of them." When asked why he would have written such a conciliatory letter to a man accused of molesting Boy Scouts—and why no one had called the police—Lesh said he and other adults involved with the troop were too shocked and embarrassed to do so. "Nobody wanted to discuss it publicly," said Lesh, who as a boy had been one of the original members of Troop 222. "Nobody was too proud that it even happened or was allowed to happen."[15]

RODGER BEATTY NEVER RECOVERED from his stroke. He never regained consciousness before dying just weeks later in November 2012.[16] His death prompted an outpouring of sympathy on Facebook from his friends and professional colleagues, some of whom told the *Times* they simply could not reconcile the abuse allegations with the Rodger Beatty they had known.

"Rest in Peace dear Rodger," one wrote.

"To all who hold Rodger near to their hearts, may you find comfort and peace in the many beautiful memories that you have had with this gentle man," wrote another.

The University of Pittsburgh published its own obituary, recounting Beatty's numerous accomplishments and quoting some of his colleagues, including Anthony J. Silvestre, who had headed the search committee that had hired him. "For 30 years, his research and policy development helped state and federal agencies improve drug and alcohol as well as infectious disease services for many populations...he spent countless hours in the field as a volunteer in dozens of governmental, professional and community organizations, working directly to improve services and to reach people too often marginalized and forgotten." The only reference to his time in Newport was near the end of the obit: "Shortly before Beatty fell ill this year, the Boy Scouts of America's ineligible volunteer file was revealed, listing Beatty among those accused of, but never charged with, abusing scouts in past decades."[17]

Carl Maxwell regrets not getting a chance to confront Beatty about what he'd done to him as a boy. In 2012, when he learned that Beatty was comatose in a Pittsburgh hospital, he toyed with the idea of driving there and trying to get in to see him, but his mother talked him out of it. Although Maxwell considers himself "a God-fearing Christian" who would not revel in another's misfortune, he admits to hoping that Beatty knew that his "dirty little secret" was finally out in the open before he died.

"I would like to think that his brain fried," he says. "That's evil to say, but what he did was evil. He was an evil person....A lot of people don't get to see karma work, but I believe that I had a firsthand experience of karma. I've got to continue to believe that because that's the only thing I'm ever going to get, that's the only kind of closure I will ever have from him."[18]

Carl is nothing if not resilient and not nearly as bitter as he has the right to be. His bad memories of boyhood do not cast long shadows over the good ones. The "dinner whistle" still sounds each day at noon in Newport, and it takes him back to his frolics in the woods with three sets of cousins, bellying up to a real soda fountain downtown, running up the steps and swinging open the door to the garment factory where his mom worked, and seeing "all them women, all them sewing machines, and all the noise they made, the women who set zippers, the pressers, the people who did the buttons."

Those are the images he prefers to remember. "Newport was the perfect place for a young boy to grow up," he says. "I have the best memories, the memories of all the good times. You can't ever take away the good feelings of growing up in a small town like that."

CHAPTER 11

THE FLOODGATES OPEN

The verdict in the Kerry Lewis trial not only sent shock waves through the highest echelons of the Boy Scouts of America but also prompted a search for a national director of its Youth Protection program. The BSA offered the job to Michael Johnson, a Plano, Texas, police detective. He had worked narcotics, street patrol, and SWAT but had spent most of his twenty-eight-year career with the suburban Dallas department investigating child sexual abuse and exploitation cases.[1]

Johnson was born and raised in San Antonio, where his mother, a nurse, was a descendant of one of the region's first Black landowners. His father was in the air force, so the family moved around a lot, to Virginia and Hawaii and then back to the Lone Star State. Michael landed a scholarship to play football at Southwest Texas State University, now Texas State, where he studied criminal justice. Along the way, he learned how to get along with all kinds of people, "the rednecks, the cowboys, the Hispanics, the rich white kids." He counted all of them among his friends.[2]

"And I always had this thing—I didn't like bullies," he said.

"And there were some guys that were bullying the mentally chal-
lenged kids, and I would end up taking up for them and getting
in some fights....I don't like people who pick on people who are
vulnerable. So for me, law enforcement was a real logical choice."[3]

Johnson, who gained a national reputation as an expert in child
abuse investigation and prevention and took on the public persona
of "Detective Mike," investigated hundreds of cases, although none
involved the Boy Scouts. He was also the founder of the Children's
Advocacy Center of Collin County and its multidisciplinary team
and trained investigators, prosecutors, social workers, and others
how to investigate all manner of crimes against children. By 2010,
he was feeling the effects of a rewarding but high-burnout job, so
he welcomed the opportunity when the Boy Scouts recruited him
as its first full-time Youth Protection director that July.

"To be able to basically double my salary and work Monday
through Friday, eight to five, and be a normal person? To me,
that was a great deal. And I really believed it when they sold me
on the idea that they really wanted to make some major changes
and show they were committed to keeping kids safe, you know,
post–Portland, Oregon, and 'ground zero.'"

It didn't take long for Johnson to feel like an outsider in the
insular organization. He and others have described it as "cultish,"
where many in leadership had grown up in Scouting and spent
their entire working lives there. He found many of those at national
headquarters to be "truly nice people," while some seemed naive
about issues such as child sexual abuse, some of them willingly
so. Having come from the similarly insular background of law
enforcement, he wasn't entirely surprised, and for the first couple
of years he sought to navigate his new world in ways that would
ensure that his BSA superiors would respect and listen to him. "I
kind of knew there are going to be some challenges," he said. "I just
thought I was going in to help better educate these ignorant people
who still think the earth is flat."[4]

Johnson had been in his new job for about two years when a large group of the BSA's Ineligible Volunteer files hit the internet in 2012. The searchable databases posted by the *Los Angeles Times* and later by other media outlets and law firms[5] led to the phone lines at BSA's local councils across the country and at the national offices where Johnson worked buzzing with calls from sexual abuse survivors, men who'd read the redacted files and recognized themselves or their abusers; men who'd managed to tamp down the pain of their boyhood experiences for years and were now retraumatized and needed to talk with someone about it. Many of their calls were funneled to Johnson,[6] inundating him and others on the national staff.

"I'm talking hundreds of calls, and some of them are just incredible," he said. "We were taking calls up till midnight, working weekends....We had men talking about committing suicide—literally. We had men calling and talking about how terrible their life has been. Some of them were so bad, so crisislike, that we had to connect them immediately with resources....But many times, we were having to do some crisis intervention right there."[7]

Johnson referred those who needed professional help to support systems he'd come to know and trust over his career—mainly child sexual abuse hotlines and children's advocacy centers. That put his approach at odds with BSA's standard practice of urging abuse victims to rely on the organizations that sponsored their troops, including Catholic and Mormon congregations, for help and counseling. The BSA's preferred response was not in the best interest of abuse survivors and their families, Johnson said, but it *definitely* benefited the churches and other chartering groups that faced possible criminal or civil liability themselves. His reaction to that practice was "not no, but hell no!" he said, and his vocal resistance to it contributed to long-running friction with his BSA superiors.[8]

Some of the survivors' phone calls were fielded by BSA lawyers, who had a different agenda than Johnson. They tended to view the callers less as abuse victims and more as potential litigants who could damage the Boy Scouts' brand and reach into the deep pockets of the BSA, with its $1.2 billion in assets, and they were right: the public release of the perversion files would unleash a wave of new, potentially costly lawsuits.

Tim Kosnoff, a veteran Seattle sex abuse attorney, had a long track record of successfully suing the Boy Scouts of America. Fresh out of law school in 1980, he wanted to be a criminal defense attorney and landed a job in the Law Office of the Cook County Public Defender in Chicago. Looking for a change of scenery six years later, he found it in Washington State's San Juan County, a remote, sparsely populated cluster of islands in the Salish Sea north of Puget Sound. After working there for two years as a deputy county prosecutor, he pulled up stakes again and headed seventy-five miles south to Seattle, where he switched to criminal defense, representing drunk drivers, drug offenders, and the occasional murderer.[9]

Kosnoff's career track changed dramatically in 1995, when seventeen-year-old Jeremiah Scott picked his name out of the Yellow Pages, walked into his office, and told him of having been repeatedly sexually assaulted years earlier by a Mormon Sunday school teacher named Brother Frank Curtis. Kosnoff had never worked on the civil side of the justice system but was intrigued by the teenager's story, finding it hard to believe that the Church of Jesus Christ of Latter-day Saints would knowingly harbor a violent child rapist. He took on Scott's case and sued the Mormon Church, which led him to a half-dozen states and a trail of Curtis's victims—and the discovery that the church had helped shield the serial molester. In September 2001, Kosnoff settled Scott's lawsuit for $3 million, then one of the largest sexual abuse payouts on record.[10] The resulting publicity brought more of Curtis's victims out of the shadows and more sex abuse lawsuits by Kosnoff against the Mormon Church, followed by a slew of litigation naming the BSA.

Kosnoff said the BSA had made "a colossal mistake" in taking the Lewis case to trial, departing from its time-tested strategy of quietly settling such claims with confidential agreements. "Once they did that and then the rest of the perversion files got out into the public, they opened up the floodgates," he said. "That was a pivotal moment in the story of the Boy Scouts of America and their legal woes."[11]

THE LEGION OF ABUSE survivors combing the database included former Scouts from suburban Chicago, who searched the files for information on their abusive leader, Thomas E. Hacker, the Boy Scouts' most prolific known abuser. Although Hacker was already serving a one-hundred-year prison term for molesting more than a hundred boys from 1961 to the late 1980s,[12] his file would yield previously undisclosed details of his abuse and provide grounds for new lawsuits by more than a dozen Illinois men who accused the BSA of negligence and fraudulently concealing what it had known about Hacker's history.[13] The case also opened a window on the twisted psyche of one of America's most dangerous pedophiles when Hacker freely shared his thoughts and motivations in a pretrial deposition.

One of the plaintiffs had been ten in 1983 when Hacker had begun assaulting him; the attacks had continued for three years. He was now about forty but had kept his molestation a secret, a common defense mechanism among survivors of child sexual abuse, many of whom never share their experiences with anyone. "I did not tell my parents, family, spouse or friends, initially because I thought I would get in trouble," he said. "I did not want those people close to me to think any differently of me or know what was happening. Once the abuse ended, I did everything in my power to move on from the abuse."[14]

But he was unable to do that, even though he had achieved considerable success by earning a master's degree and embarking on a career, according to a child sexual abuse expert who examined him. Jon R. Conte, a University of Washington professor of social work retained as an expert witness for the plaintiff, said the former Scout's life had been profoundly changed by reading Hacker's perversion file. Until then, Conte said, the man had not realized that the BSA and its Chicago Area Council had known that Hacker was a pedophile years before he was abused. "He was consumed with anger over the fact that he had been hurt...and [the Boy Scouts] knew it, yet they did nothing over the years to approach him or help him," Conte said.[15] The former Scout had long suppressed his psychological injuries, Conte said, including anxiety, rage, self-blame, shame, difficulty concentrating, mistrust of others, intimacy problems, sexual concerns, helplessness, and hopelessness. Rather than linking those ill effects to his boyhood abuse, the former Scout had gone through life thinking that it was just the "way he was," Conte said. "...The quality of his life has been significantly made more negative by the abuse and the years that he did not understand the impact that the abuse had on his life."[16]

The Boy Scouts sought to dismiss the lawsuit, claiming that it was time-barred under Illinois's two-year statute of limitations for personal injury claims. But a state appeals court rejected that argument in 2016, finding that the former Scout had "had no reason to know or suspect any wrongdoing on the part of the Boy Scout defendants" until he read Hacker's file.[17]

The thirty-five-page document lays out three decades of abuse by a self-acknowledged master manipulator who was five feet seven, weighed 160 pounds, and preyed upon young boys in Catholic Church activities, park programs and Scouting.[18] Hacker, a genial, mild-mannered elementary school teacher and later a park district director, first came to the Boy Scouts' attention in 1961, when three Indiana boys accused him of sneaking into their tent at night and molesting them on a camping trip. He was suspended as scoutmaster but was reinstated when criminal charges were dismissed for lack of evidence. Nine years later, he landed in the perversion files when he was convicted of "assault and battery with intent to gratify sexual desires" involving multiple Scouts at the school where he taught. A judge suspended his one-to-five-year sentence and put him on probation.

"This man should not be allowed to register in the Boy Scouts of America at any time or any place," an Indiana Scouts official wrote to the national headquarters at the time, conceding that he and others had dropped the ball in 1961 when they had failed to muster enough evidence to prosecute Hacker. He also recalled being pressured by a local Scouts official to go easy on Hacker. "At the time, a prominent member of my board called me to say that he knew the family, that Tom was a fine young man, and asked that he not be placed on our 'red flag' list," he wrote. "Because of no concrete evidence, at the time, we did not do this, for which I have had many hours of regret."[19]

That should have been the end of Thomas Hacker's time in Scouting. But despite his 1970 conviction in Indiana, another one the following year in Illinois for "taking indecent liberties with a child," and a 1976 arrest for grabbing a boy, throwing him to the floor, and pulling down his pants, he continued to find his way back into the program, sometimes by simply changing his middle initial or using an alias, Thomas Edward, to avoid being matched against the blacklist.

By 1983, Hacker was a volunteer merit badge counselor and committee chairman with Troop 1600, sponsored by a Catholic church in suburban Chicago, where he served as de facto scoutmaster and met the ten-year-old boy who would sue the BSA thirty years later. The youngster had joined Troop 1600 because many of his friends were in Scouting and his parents believed it would instill in him the positive values embedded in the Scout Oath and the Scout Law. "Both I and my parents trusted Mr. Hacker because he was an acting Scoutmaster and an important leader in the troop," he said. "I did not believe that Mr. Hacker was an individual that would harm me, given his role in Scouting."[20]

He could not have been more wrong about that. It is "undisputed" that Hacker molested the boy for three years, according to the Illinois appellate court decision that allowed the lawsuit to move forward. Hacker's repertoire of abuse of boys included fondling, mutual masturbation, oral sex, and anal rape, the court said. "Plaintiff estimated that Hacker abused him on 100 occasions.... Some of Hacker's sexual abuse of plaintiff occurred in a group setting, with other Boy Scouts present. During the period of Hacker's abuse, plaintiff experienced extreme emotional distress and physical pain."[21]

Hacker's abuse of the Scout, which included a threat to kill his parents, ended in 1986, probably when he aged out of the predatory leader's target demographic, prepubescent boys. Hacker would lose interest in them as sexual objects after about age thirteen but remained close enough with the older Scouts to use them to help him recruit and groom younger ones. When Hacker was arrested on new allegations in 1988, Boy Scouts officials alternately denied that he was in the confidential files and refused to confirm it. "Obviously, he's not on that system. It would have come up," Kenneth Walters, a top official with the Chicago Area Council, erroneously told the *Chicago Tribune*. Barclay Bollas, a national Scouts spokesman, would say only that "we consider that list confidential."[22] It was so confidential, Walters would later testify, that even he had been stonewalled when he had contacted the national headquarters to find out if Hacker was in the files.

Twenty-eight years after he had first been accused of molesting Boy Scouts, Hacker was convicted in 1989 of five counts of aggravated criminal sexual assault against three Scouts. That April, the Illinois Department of Children & Family Services informed the Boy Scouts of America that Hacker had molested at least thirty-four boys, but the BSA made little or no effort to identify and locate his victims. At the time, the Boy Scout he'd brutalized for three years told police and investigators from the state agency that Hacker had molested other boys but not him.[23] It was a lie born of shame and embarrassment that he would live with for the next twenty-five years, until joining the other former Scouts in suing the BSA in 2013.

DURING THE DISCOVERY PHASE of those lawsuits, the men's Chicago attorney, Christopher Hurley, drove five hours downstate to Big Muddy River Correctional Center to take Hacker's deposition. At seventy-six, he had served about a quarter of his hundred-year sentence and was housed in the state prison's "C" wing, where all of the inmates were sex offenders. "I go in there and they bring in this meek little guy who couldn't be more friendly," Hurley said, describing Hacker as "a professional con man" trying to downplay his crimes. "A big part of what he was trying to spin was that he just got a little out of hand and never meant to hurt anybody, which was just total bullshit."[24]

Over the next few hours, the talkative Hacker told Hurley that his father had been an alcoholic who had beat his mother and that his grandmother had sexually abused him until he was about thirteen—not that he was making any excuses for his own behavior, mind you. "Let's just say I had a very troubled childhood, that I turned outside the family for care and love and, obviously, didn't do a very good job of that," Hacker said.[25]

He traced the roots of his own abusive behavior to his youth, when he had discovered that he "enjoyed seeing the nakedness" of children he babysat. That had led to "enjoying the hugs and affection" of boys when he was in high school and to his becoming an adult volunteer in Scouting. There he had found easy pickings among the boys, whose trust he had gained by pumping up their self-confidence and indulging their interests. His master's degree in psychology had come in handy in manipulating them, he said. "Well, basically, all boys that age like adventure, outdoor activities, people that will pay them attention, people that will spend time with them and be patient and show them skills that they don't have and they want to have," he said. "Unfortunately for the children involved....I had a lot of background education that was used in inappropriate manners."[26]

Hacker denied having committed any rapes, but he freely admitted to having performed oral sex on boys and getting them out of their clothes by talking them into skinny-dipping or telling them it was unhealthy to sleep in their underwear. He might have been inured to the harm he had caused, but he was not oblivious to it, recalling one boy who'd been so mortified after being made to strip that he had gone into his tent and wouldn't come out until the campout ended. "He wouldn't take part in any activities, he wouldn't go to eat, he wouldn't go swimming, he wouldn't do anything," Hacker said. "I saw him many times after that and when his parents were with him, he would speak to me. When [they weren't with him], he would look away. And then I knew that I had damaged that child."[27]

When Hurley asked him how many boys he'd hurt in that way, Hacker said he couldn't even hazard a guess, much less remember all of their names. "There are just so many," he said. "I mean, it's horrible to say, but there's so many out there that I made sure that I saw them naked. I mean, we're talking lots and lots and lots of kids." More than a hundred? Hurley asked. "Well, in Scouting alone there were more than a hundred," he said. "Gosh, there were probably a hundred in three or four years."[28]

In contrast to his fuzzy memory about who and how many he

had molested, Hacker had a remarkably clear-eyed and articulate assessment of the damage caused by child sexual abuse. When reading his deposition transcript, it is hard to tell if he is speaking from his experience as an adult perpetrator, a childhood victim himself, or both.

"There's slews of things that it can do," he said. "Number one, with a child ready to reach puberty there is then the lifelong fear that they could be homosexual....There's the shame that they feel....There's the embarrassment of having maybe somebody discover it and then talk to them about it or, in other words, they build up secrets and inside these secrets they become isolated from other people....They're hurt and they don't have anybody to talk to about it. The shame is too heavy for them. The guilt is too heavy, like it's their fault instead of the perpetrator's." They also might grow up thinking that "sex is dirty."

What about trust issues? Hurley asked.

"Oh, yes, I forgot that," Hacker said. "That's probably the biggest. You can't trust authority figures. I mean, here's a school teacher, here's a Scout leader, here's a person that's in charge of a park district I trust—the parents trust, they trust, and then, all of a sudden, the trust is broken. They may never trust another authority figure for the rest of their lives."[29]

Early on, the BSA lawyers were adamantly opposed to settling those lawsuits, according to Hurley and Paul Mones,[30] who worked with him on the Illinois cases. But with a potentially devastating witness such as Hacker waiting in the wings, the Scouts' attorneys apparently came to realize that they were playing a losing hand as the cases moved toward trial[31]—sixteen separate trials, actually, scheduled for one a month over a year and a half. On the eve of each trial, the BSA capitulated and offered a settlement, Hurley said, with the largest coming in at more than $9 million. By the time all of the agreements were signed in 2018, the Boy Scouts had paid a huge price for the abuse perpetrated by one man, Thomas Hacker, and the BSA's failed response to it—a total of $89 million.

"He was just a monster," Hurley said. "The amount of harm he did is so huge, so tremendous. He had unfettered access to these kids—and nobody was looking out for them."[32]

Thomas Hacker died in prison in June 2018. He was eighty-one.

PART III

—

THE FALL

CHAPTER 12

THE LONG SLIDE

The $89 million in Hacker lawsuit settlements helped grease the skids for the 110-year-old organization's slide into bankruptcy. But it was hardly the sole impetus for that drastic move, which was long in the making. The BSA had been pummeled for years by declining membership, spending that had exceeded revenue, the ongoing sexual abuse scandal, and other factors, including a long-standing and controversial membership policy banning openly gay boys as members and gay adults as leaders.

In 2012, the BSA doubled down on its no-gays rule, which the US Supreme Court had upheld in 2000 in *Boy Scouts of America v. James Dale*[1] and which many supporters perceived to be embedded in the Boy Scout Oath, in the part that reads "to keep myself physically strong, mentally awake, and *morally straight*" (italics added).

"Scouting believes that same-sex attraction should be introduced and discussed outside of its program with parents, caregivers, or spiritual advisers, at the appropriate time and in the right setting," the BSA said in announcing its extension of the ban after a confidential two-year review. "...The BSA is a voluntary, private organization that sets policies that are best for the organization. The BSA welcomes all who share its beliefs but does not criticize or condemn those who wish to follow a different path."[2]

The decision drew widespread criticism as discriminatory and out of step with much of the country, which was steadily moving toward accepting, if not fully embracing, homosexuality and gay rights. Same-sex marriage had been legal in some states since 2004, beginning with Massachusetts. By 2009, polls by the Pew Research Center and ABC News/*Washington Post* had shown that a majority of Americans supported such unions. Still, the BSA dug in. Contrary to media reports, it said, it had "no plans" to change its membership policy.[3] But less than a year later, it did just that.[4]

Under pressure from LGBTQ rights groups and others, and after conducting what it called "the most comprehensive listening exercise in its history"[5] by holding more than 250 town hall meetings across the country and polling more than 1 million of its members, the BSA's 1,400-person National Council voted in May 2013 to rescind the ban on gay boys but left in place the prohibition of gay adults.

The move was hailed as a good first step by those who opposed the gay ban, including corporate sponsors Intel Corporation and UPS, which had pulled their financial support; many former Eagle Scouts; and elected leaders, including President Barack Obama. Proponents of the ban, including the Catholic Church, the Church of Jesus Christ of Latter-day Saints, the Southern Baptist Convention, and the Family Research Council, a right-wing, evangelical Christian advocacy group, condemned the policy shift as "the beginning of the end" of the Boy Scouts.

In fact, neither side was happy with the split-the-baby compromise, which seemed to defy logic by allowing gay boys into Scouting, only to deem them ineligible again once they became gay adults.[6]

Meanwhile, the Boy Scouts' shrinking youth membership was

down to 2.6 million by 2013, about half what it had been at its zenith in the early 1970s. Under pressure to repair its reputation and resuscitate its numbers, the BSA's executive board elected a new member, Robert Gates, the widely respected former CIA director for President George H. W. Bush and secretary of defense for presidents George W. Bush and Barack Obama.[7] Gates, plainspoken and pragmatic, had orchestrated the Obama administration's repeal of the US military's discriminatory "Don't ask, don't tell" policy, which allowed gays and lesbians to serve, but only if they didn't make their sexual orientation public.

Gates supported a similar lifting of the BSA's ban on gay adults, but he took a deliberate approach to it. At the Boy Scouts' national annual business meeting in May 2015, Gates, by then elevated to national president, told the leadership that local councils in New York and Denver were already defying the policy and others were likely to follow suit. More legal challenges were all but certain in the near future, and the odds were good that Scouting would lose in court this time around. "I must speak as plainly and bluntly to you as I spoke to presidents when I was director of CIA and secretary of defense," he told the BSA crowd. "We must deal with the world as it is, not as we might wish it to be. The status quo in our movement's membership standards cannot be sustained."[8]

Gates's push to open the ranks to gay leaders was not universally accepted by BSA officials in Irving, to put it mildly. Michael Johnson, the BSA's director of youth protection, had supported lifting the ban and welcomed Gates's advocacy of doing it. Johnson, who had been in that job since 2010, said it had been a constant battle trying to convince BSA officials that homosexuality did not translate to pedophilia and child sexual abuse. He was more concerned about "overly zealous religious white males" than he was about allowing gay people into Scouting, and he had "the experience and the research" to support that view—a view to which some others in the top tier of BSA leadership were openly hostile.

"They referred to him as, and you can quote me, 'Bob Gates and his merry band of faggots' coming into the national office to tell them what to do and how to run the organization."[9]

In the end Gates would prevail. Two months after he addressed BSA leaders at the annual business meeting, the organization's national executive board voted to lift the ban on openly gay and bisexual adult leaders and employees, effective immediately.[10] Among those who welcomed the change were Eagle Scout Zach Wahls, the son of a married lesbian couple from Iowa and the executive director of the advocacy group Scouts for Equality. He declared that the Boy Scouts of America was now "an organization that is looking forward, not back."[11] But not everyone was celebrating.

Catholic leaders "went nuts," Johnson said. The move did not sit well with the Mormons, either. The churches' disenchantment threatened to be costly for the BSA, accustomed as it was to "kissing the ring" of both powerful religious institutions. "At the end of the day, the bottom line for the Boy Scouts is money," Johnson said. "It's registration. It's boys. And who brings them in? It's not the Boy Scouts of America. It's the churches."[12]

The LDS Church was the Boys Scouts' oldest and largest sponsor, whose youth members for generations had filled about 20 percent of the rolls. LDS leaders expressed concerns about lifting the ban but agreed to remain aligned with Scouting after receiving assurances that the church could appoint troop leaders who adhered to its religious and moral beliefs,[13] which included that gay men could hold leadership roles—as long as they did not act on their homosexuality. In January 2017, a year and a half after opening its membership to gay adult leaders, the BSA announced that it would accept transgender boys.

Over the next few months, it also became known that the Boy Scouts of America was seriously considering welcoming girls into its ranks, a move that the Girl Scouts viewed as a blatant attempt to bolster the BSA's flagging membership at their expense. At one point, representatives of a high-powered strategic communications firm hired by the Girl Scouts of the USA reached out to reporters with offers to enlighten them on how "the Boy Scouts are in financial peril and looking to girls to solve their problems."[14]

In August 2017, the national president of the Girl Scouts, Kathy Hopinkah Hannan, sent a blistering letter to BSA's national leaders, accusing them of "surreptitiously testing the appeal of a girls' offering to millennial parents" and of being "inherently dishonest" about their intentions.[15] "I am also deeply concerned about reports of aggressive posturing by Boy Scout leaders towards Girl Scout leaders at recent 'family meetings' outlining the proposed girls program," she wrote in her three-page letter. "This includes everything from disparaging and untrue remarks about Girl Scout programming, to subtle implications about the weakness of Girl Scouts' long term market strength." In closing, she said, the BSA would do better to go after the 90 percent of American boys who were not already in Scouting. She suggested that the BSA start by concentrating on the African American and Latino boys it had "historically underserved and underrepresented" and leave the girls to the Girl Scouts.

Two months later, in October 2017, the BSA said it would accept girls.[16] The following spring, it announced that it would change the name of its program for older youth members from Boy Scouts to Scouts BSA and said girls could begin signing up in February 2019. That was the last straw for the Mormons.

In May 2018, the LDS Church said it would sever its 105-year ties with the Boy Scouts of America at the end of 2019 and launch its own youth program. The BSA's changes were simply too much to brook, one key Mormon leader said at the time. "The reality there is we didn't really leave them; they kind of left us," said M. Russell Ballard, acting president of the Quorum of the Twelve Apostles. "The direction they were going was not consistent to what we feel our youth need to have...to survive in the world that lies ahead for them."[17]

The Mormon exodus meant that the BSA would enter 2020 with some 425,000 fewer dues-paying members than it had had the year before. It was a huge hit to its programming and prestige, not to mention its coffers. With every departing Mormon Scout went registration fees, some $14 million when calculated at the regular annual rate of $33 per youth member. The actual revenue loss is unknown but probably smaller, however, because Scouts in LDS-sponsored troops paid a discounted registration fee negotiated confidentially by the church and the BSA. What is clear is that the loss of LDS-sponsored troops pushed the BSA's membership down to about 1.7 million, marking the first time since World War II that it had dipped below 2 million.[18]

Even more trouble loomed for the Boy Scouts. Legislators in several states, including New York, New Jersey, California, Arizona, and North Carolina, passed or were considering laws that would ease the statutes of limitation on sexual abuse lawsuits. The legislation varied but generally opened temporary "look-back windows," clearing the way for victims of past sexual abuse, even that occurring decades earlier, to sue for damages in cases that otherwise would have been time barred. New Jersey's law, for example, allowed those who had been molested as children to sue until age fifty-five or within seven years of discovering that the abuse had harmed them, while California's Child Victims Act raised the maximum age to sue from twenty-six to forty or within five years of recognizing harm. The first of the look-back laws took effect in 2019, with others coming online the next year.[19] By then, conditions were ripe for a tsunami of costly new litigation against the Boy Scouts.

Paul Mones, the plaintiffs' attorney who had won the $19.9 million jury award in the landmark Kerry Lewis trial in Portland in 2010, said that the Boy Scouts' timing could not have been much worse. The organization now found itself in a "steel-encased tidal wave" of public support for victims, as attitudes about child sexual abuse had shifted dramatically in the two decades since the *Boston Globe*'s reporting had pushed the Catholic Church's sexual abuse scandal into public view. Back then, the acts of pedophile priests had often been seen as "idiosyncratic," the work of a few bad apples, he said.

Fast-forward to 2019, after what he called a "never-ending staccato" of high-profile scandals engulfing other large organizations—private schools, Penn State University, US Olympic swimming and gymnastics teams among them—and sexual abuse in the Boy Scouts was now seen as an "institutional" problem. And the institution was about to pay dearly for it.

"People all over the country started saying, 'Wait a second, what about justice for these people?'" Mones said of BSA sexual abuse victims. "And the thing that brought the Boy Scouts down, honestly, was not the [previous] lawsuits but the change in the law. They could not withstand the thousands of cases" that were coming. "That's when the Boy Scouts of America really got behind the eight ball."[20]

RUMORS OF A BSA bankruptcy had swirled for months, but the first solid indication came in December 2018. Quoting unnamed sources, the *Wall Street Journal* reported that the BSA had hired the top-tier law firm Sidley Austin to explore a Chapter 11 filing.[21] The Boy Scouts did not dispute the report and responded to it by releasing a letter to its employees that said it was considering all options to ensure that its local and national programming would continue uninterrupted. *Journal* readers' reaction to the story ran the gamut from blaming the Boy Scouts for ignoring or mishandling sexual abuse allegation, to blasting the organization for all but destroying American manhood itself. "They betrayed the time-tested values

of Christian masculinity upon which the organization was built,"
one wrote. "By embracing LGBT issues and feminism, the group
lost its identity and its core supporters: duty-driven conservative
Christian men and their sons."

Bankruptcy as an option for the Boy Scouts was not a new idea:
dozens of Roman Catholic dioceses, religious orders, and USA
Gymnastics had sought similar protections from abuse survivors
who had sued them. Lawyers and other advocates for survivors said
that the bankruptcy process often shortchanged them, denying
traumatized people their day in court and treating them as unsecured creditors in a cold-blooded financial proceeding. Whether it
involves religious groups or Scouting, the bankruptcy system as a
venue for child sex abuse claims inherently favors the institutions,
according to Marci Hamilton, a University of Pennsylvania political science professor and the founder and CEO of CHILD USA, a
nonpartisan think tank that advocates for victims of child abuse
and neglect. Bankruptcy courts are "geared to make the institutions whole and make it possible for them to go forward," she said,
while treating victims as bystanders.[22]

Over the next few months, Boy Scouts officials remained
tight-lipped about their bankruptcy plans and their mounting
legal woes. Repeatedly prodded by reporters, they would not say
how many sexual abuse lawsuits had been filed over the years or
how much the BSA had paid out in settlements and judgments. (At
that point, the gargantuan Hacker settlements had not been disclosed.) Plaintiffs' attorneys at the time estimated the number of
pending lawsuits to be in the hundreds, but no one except the Boy
Scouts of America, its legal counsel, and its insurers had a firm grip
on the actual count.

By then, the BSA and its lawyers were also tangling with some
of their insurers, which refused to cover claims and settlements,
contending that Scouting could have done more to prevent the
abuse. The dispute wound up in court, where the Hartford Accident

and Indemnity Company and First State Insurance Company, among other insurers, argued that the very existence of the perversion files demonstrated that the Boy Scouts had failed to adequately protect children against sexual abuse or warn their parents of the risks.[23] The fallout foreshadowed an even larger legal battle to come between the BSA and some of the nation's biggest insurance companies in bankruptcy court.

The BSA had long insisted that it had kept no running count of abusive Scout leaders and their victims. That changed in May 2019, when Jeff Anderson, a veteran sex abuse attorney, called a news conference in New York to announce a startling revelation: a researcher hired by the BSA to study a more complete set of its confidential records, covering the years 1944 to 2016, had identified 7,819 suspected abusers and 12,254 victims. News outlets across the country trumpeted the story, under headlines that echoed one in the Los Angeles Times: "Boy Scout Sex Abuse Scandal's Stunning Toll: Over 12,200 Reported Victims."[24]

Janet Warren, the University of Virginia professor of psychiatry and neurobehavioral sciences who had been an expert witness for the BSA at the Kerry Lewis trial, had disclosed those numbers a few months earlier while testifying in an unrelated lawsuit Anderson was litigating in Minnesota. Warren had testified that she and a team of computer coders contracted by the Boy Scouts had come up with those totals after spending five years analyzing the perversion files. It marked the first time that the Boy Scouts had acknowledged tallying the predators and their prey; until then, a procession of BSA officials and expert witnesses had testified under oath in lawsuits that the organization had never counted the perversion files or analyzed their contents, contending that there was little value in doing so.

Anderson, Mones, and other plaintiffs' lawyers insisted at the time that Warren's figures, while the most definitive to date, still vastly understated the true extent of sexual abuse in Scouting, largely because so many molesters were known to have had multiple victims and so many of the victims were reluctant to come forward. Thomas Hacker alone admitted to having more than a hundred victims, many of whom had never reported the incidents to authorities or even discussed it with their families. CHILD USA, citing US Department of Justice data and more than a dozen other studies, found that 86 percent of child sexual abuse goes unreported altogether and that victims who do disclose it often wait well into adulthood; the average age of disclosure is fifty-two.[25]

By the summer of 2019, sexual abuse and personal injury attorneys were busily lining up clients to sue the Boy Scouts under the newly relaxed statutes of limitations, with an eye toward a potential bankruptcy that would put an automatic stay on lawsuits already filed in state and federal courts.

Tim Kosnoff, the Seattle lawyer who had sued the Boy Scouts on behalf of hundreds of abuse survivors over the years—and who had provided the *Los Angeles Times* with the perversion files for its searchable database—teamed with two law firms to launch a national marketing campaign dubbed Abused in Scouting. In short order, their newly formed coalition signed 350 clients ranging in age from fourteen to ninety-seven, with claims spanning decades and forty-eight states. Most of the 234 alleged abusers they identified were men who were not named in the perversion files, which they said was evidence of a bigger universe of predatory Scout leaders than previously known. "Consequently, the number of children who have been abused in Scouting is much larger than the BSA has ever disclosed," Kosnoff said. "It is time the BSA is held to account fully for this atrocity."[26]

In a Hail Mary effort to stave off bankruptcy, the Boy Scouts' lawyers met with Kosnoff, Mones, and other key plaintiffs' attorneys in the late summer and early fall of 2019 in Los Angeles and New

York. Nothing came of the first meeting, at Sidley Austin's Century City offices, so a second session was scheduled a couple of months later in New York, with representatives of some of the Scouts' major insurers participating, as well as attorney Paul Finn, who served as a mediator.

"So the November meeting, it was just a lot of sitting around, you know, jaw, jaw, jaw," Kosnoff said, describing lengthy presentations on the Scouts' complicated web of insurance coverage. "At one point, Finn says, 'Well, come on, come on, just give me a number, any number.'...So I think I threw out, 'Okay, $500 million,' and somebody took that back to the Boy Scouts, and they guffawed and said, 'You're crazy.'...So that went nowhere."

But it could have, Kosnoff said in late 2022, when the Boy Scouts' legal fees and other bankruptcy expenses were north of $200 million and mounting. "It is a sweet irony that they probably could have gotten this case resolved at that meeting in November, without bankruptcy, for an amount that was probably about where they are now just in administrative expenses in the bankruptcy," he said. "The reality of it is that they could have basically bought us for a song."[27]

The Boy Scouts' lawyers outlined their version of the negotiations in a bankruptcy filing. They said it had become apparent to them that the plaintiffs' attorneys believed that the BSA's local councils had significant assets that should be added to the national organization's holdings in bankruptcy—a nonstarter for the Boy Scouts. The Scouts' attorneys also noted that the other side seemed unwilling to take the BSA's word for the "nature and extent" of the organization's available assets. "Accordingly, the BSA recognized in late 2019 that there were no meaningful prospects for a pre-arranged global resolution," they wrote.[28]

As 2019 gave way to 2020, the BSA's rumored bankruptcy filing became a foregone conclusion; it was no longer a question of *if* the BSA would seek to reorganize under Chapter 11 but *when*. The answer came shortly after midnight on February 18, 2020, when the Boy Scouts of America filed its voluntary petition in US Bankruptcy Court in Delaware.[29]

A COMMON MISCONCEPTION ABOUT bankruptcy protection is that the companies or organizations that file are broke. Some are, but the BSA was not—far from it. At the end of 2019, it still had more than $1 billion in assets, consisting largely of cash, stocks and bonds, real estate, and an art collection built around Norman Rockwell paintings. It also had 261 local councils with their own valuable holdings,[30] some 2.1 million dues-paying youth members, a legion of adult volunteers, and every intention of continuing to operate as it had for the last 110 years.

But it also had big problems, some of them buried in the details of the nonprofit's annual federal tax returns known as Form 990s, and in BSA's treasurers' reports and notes attached to annual reports. Among other things, the documents revealed that youth membership had declined by nearly 30 percent since 2009, the year before the landmark Kerry Lewis verdict, when BSA had had 2.9 million registered youth members. The ranks of adult volunteers had also thinned significantly, down to 770,000 from multiyear highs of more than 1 million earlier in the decade.

The BSA's total assets still amounted to $1.2 billion, roughly the same as over the last decade. But its net assets, the value calculated by subtracting the organization's liabilities—including legal settlements and insurance costs—were dwindling. From a peak value of $702 million in 2014, net assets had fallen to $408 million in 2019 and were on their way down to $254 million two years after that.

The records showed that the BSA also consistently spent more than it took in from a variety of revenue sources, including membership dues, contributions, investment income, and funds generated by four High Adventure bases. Sales of Scouting merchandise routinely grossed more than $100 million a year for everything from uniforms to camping equipment to an 8½-inch-tall, silver-plated rendition of the Boy Scout statue that stands outside national headquarters in Texas and retails for $229.99.[31]

In only one year in the previous decade had the BSA not been in the red when its expenses were subtracted from its revenue: in 2014, it had been about $9 million in the black, but every other year it had finished in the hole, with a string of spending deficits ranging from $18 million to $58 million, with even worse to come in 2021, when it hit negative $95 million. Meanwhile, at various times in the preceding decade, Chief Scout Executives Robert Mazzuca, Wayne Brock, and Michael Surbaugh had hauled in compensation packages worth more than $1 million a year each.

Even as the BSA steadfastly refused to publicly disclose how many times it had been sued and how much it had paid out in settlements and judgments, its risk managers closely tracked that information in an electronic system called Riskonnect, which included historical and current data on claims, claimants, dates of abuse, settlement amounts, and defense expenses.[32] The Boy Scouts' lawyers who had access to that information did not sugarcoat the financial picture, laying out the organization's deepening troubles in a lengthy debtor's brief filed with the bankruptcy petition.

"As widely reported, the BSA is currently a defendant in numerous lawsuits related to historical acts of sexual abuse in its programs," it noted, offering its first-ever public breakdown of litigation: 275 cases pending in state and federal courts across the country and about 1,400 additional claims not yet filed as lawsuits. In just two years, from 2017 to 2019, the Scouts had shelled out $150 million in settlements,[33] including the $89 million paid to the plaintiffs in the sixteen lawsuits involving Thomas Hacker. The BSA was bleeding money at an unsustainable rate.

"The BSA cannot continue to litigate abuse claims in the civil tort system, especially in light of the recent changes in state statutes of limitations and corresponding increase in the number of pending claims," its lawyers said in justifying the bankruptcy. "...In addition to depleting its assets, continued case-by-case litigation or individual settlements with abuse victims would do little to dispel the cloud of uncertainty that lingers over the BSA's organization."[34]

The bankruptcy put a freeze on all of the pending lawsuits and required that new ones be handled as claims in that venue instead of in state or federal court. The idea was to compile all of the claims by a "bar date" to be set by the court, then settle them all at once with payments from a pool of money contributed by the Boy Scouts of America, its insurers, and some chartering organizations. Scouting's local councils, which held billions of dollars' worth of real estate and other assets, were not part of the initial bankruptcy action but would later agree to contribute to the victims' compensation fund.

Some former Scouts who had lawsuits pending at the time denounced the bankruptcy. Eager for their days in court, they suddenly found themselves in legal limbo, stuck in a long line with all of the other unsecured creditors. The resolution of their cases was certain to be delayed—perhaps by years.

For the Boy Scouts, the reorganization would be a make-or-break proposition, its lawyers argued; it was the only way that Scouting could equitably compensate those who had been abused and still be able to carry out its mission to serve America's youth and their families.

It was the only way Scouting could survive.

CHAPTER 13

THE NEW MESOTHELIOMA

The tone of the infomercial was at once reassuring and urgent: If you are among countless innocent children sexually molested by Boy Scout leaders, it's not too late to seek compensation. But the clock is ticking. *Now is the time to act!* "You are not alone," the disembodied narrator says. "Come forward and get the help and healing you deserve. Protect tomorrow's children—identify your abuser and help put a stop to the cover-up....Call Abused in Scouting for a free confidential consultation. We have skilled and compassionate people standing by to take your calls."[1]

That ad and countless others produced for mass tort law firms by "client acquisition" marketers flooded TV and radio airwaves, cable channels, and the internet for most of 2020—right up until November 16, the filing deadline set by a bankruptcy judge for claims in the BSA's Chapter 11 reorganization. Because individual lawsuits against the BSA were put on hold by the bankruptcy, sexual abuse survivors who wanted to pursue litigation were left with no option but to file a claim. The come-ons were so ubiquitous that the Boy Scouts' lawyers noted in court papers, dyspeptically, that they had aired thousands of times in recent months and were popping up everywhere, "during episodes of *Law & Order*, during movies on the Sundance TV channel, during *The Three Stooges* on AMC, and during an NBA game on NBA TV, among other programs and channels."[2]

By the fall of 2020, sexual abuse in the Boy Scouts had become the "new mesothelioma." The outreach to BSA abuse survivors mirrored previous high-profile mass tort lawsuit efforts such as asbestos exposure, weed killers, prescription drugs, talcum powder, and hernia mesh implants. They all contributed to advertising buys that routinely totaled more than $100 million a year.

The beating hearts of the various marketing campaigns were the call centers that fielded inquiries from potential clients and hooked them up with lawyers who would represent them on contingency, for up to a 40 percent slice of any eventual settlement. One of the most successful of the operations was run by Andrew Van Arsdale, a fortyish attorney with a bachelor's degree in sociology from Montana State University and a juris doctor from the University of San Diego Law School, class of 2018.[3] He formed the AVA Law Group, which was branded with his initials and was small enough to share a 1,900-square-foot San Diego storefront office space with six other law firms.[4] Van Arsdale might have been a newly minted member of the bar, but according to his online biography, the Boy Scouts campaign was hardly his first mass tort rodeo: "Andrew has worked directly with over one hundred and fifty plaintiff law firms that handle mass tort cases in the assistance of their marketing and screening criteria since 2008."[5]

That was the year that he and a partner founded Reciprocity Industries LLC, a small software development and pay-per-click marketing company in downtown Billings, Montana. The company's call center, on the top floor of a three-story office building, served as the marketing and client recruitment arm of Abused in Scouting, a coalition of lawyers comprised of Van Arsdale and two seasoned plaintiff's attorneys, sole practitioner Tim Kosnoff from Seattle and Stewart Eisenberg of the Philadelphia personal injury firm of Eisenberg, Rothweiler, Winkler, Eisenberg & Jeck.[6]

Kosnoff, who had sued the Boy Scouts multiple times over the previous two decades, had reached out to Eisenberg and Van Arsdale after the *Wall Street Journal* had reported in late 2018 that the youth organization was considering bankruptcy. Kosnoff was new to the world of mass tort litigation, which allows multiple plaintiffs with similar injuries to collectively sue the same defendant while preserving their individual damages claims. Eisenberg's firm had mass tort experience and a history with Van Arsdale, who brought not only his marketing expertise but also connections to satellite carriers and cable networks and access to affordable remnant ad buys. The three attorneys agreed that Kosnoff and Eisenberg would finance the operation and Van Arsdale would staff it. "I think I put up $100,000 and Eisenberg, Rothweiler put up $100,000 and we cobbled together our first thirty-second television ad and it ran...at the end of February and beginning of March 2019," Kosnoff said. "I had no idea whether, or how many, people would respond to that. The first month we maybe had thirty clients who came forward."[7]

That pace would quicken dramatically over the coming weeks. Abused in Scouting lawyers soon had 500 clients and then 1,200—and the numbers only multiplied after the Boy Scouts filed for bankruptcy protection in February 2020. Judge Laurie Selber Silverstein's claims-filing deadline of November 16 loomed as the finish line for mass tort law firms racing to sign up as many clients as possible.

VERONICA STENULSON GREW UP in Billings and was nineteen in the summer of 2020 when she went to work for Reciprocity Industries, a job she'd learned about from former middle and high school classmates who were employed there.[8] She spent her first two weeks training on "the legal stuff" and other aspects of handling sensitive calls from men of all ages, from every background, and from all parts of the country, men who had been abused as Boy Scouts. "We also learned, like, how to have a heart when it comes to these guys and how to talk to them about it," she said. "A lot of times it was their first time ever talking about what had happened to them.... So we had to be very, very charismatic and nice to them."[9]

Stenulson, the youngest "intake professional" in the thirty-person call center, worked five days a week, from 1:00 to 10:00 p.m. She earned about $12 an hour in base pay, with a weekly bonus of $200 if she hit her goal of signing up twenty claimants and an extra $100 for every ten sign-ups on top of those, incentives that Van Arsdale said are common practice in the call center business. She fielded about seventy-five calls a day, asking each potential client the same qualifying questions: When and where were you abused? What was your troop number? What was your abuser's name? What did he do to you? How often did he do it?

It was awkward sometimes, but Stenulson said she had quickly gotten the hang of it, and rejected fewer than a dozen of the six thousand prospective claimants she figures she spoke with during four months on the job.[10] Most of her "turn-aways" were prank calls, especially early on, or "ones where there was abuse, but it wasn't the exact type of abuse the law firms were looking for," she said. "So yeah, we tried to do pretty good on rejecting because if there was something there, we tried to get it right. Everyone deserves some sort of reimbursement for what happened to them."[11]

Callers who asked how much they stood to collect were given necessarily vague answers. A compensation fund for victims had yet to be established, and it was anyone's guess how many former Boy Scouts would be able to claim a share of it. Stenulson said she had been instructed to tell prospective clients that their lawyers would shoot for no less than $100,000 per claim and would keep

40 percent of any award as their contingency fee.[12] Clients who wound up getting nothing would owe their lawyers nothing.

Those who met the filing criteria were handed off to Reciprocity case managers to complete proof-of-claim forms with a checklist of alleged abuse ranging from "touching outside of my clothing" to "the penetration of some part of my body." The twelve-page forms were signed under penalty of perjury by the abuse survivors or their lawyers or legal guardians and then submitted to the bankruptcy court online or by mail.

The call center's employees worked in cubicles, wore telephone headsets, and were divided into four competing teams, each with a leader, an intake worker, a cyberspecialist, and two case managers. Stenulson's group was nicknamed "The Cool Ones" and was a top producer.[13] Reminiscent of Alec Baldwin's "Always be closing" spiel in the 1992 movie *Glengarry Glen Ross*, whiteboards placed around the office kept a running tally of sign-ups, so the intake workers always knew how their teams stacked up. Unlike the beaten-down real estate salesmen in the movie, Stenulson said she was never unduly pressured to hit her goals, although managers sometimes urged staffers to change claimants' details to make them "more viable," something she said she had refused to do and Van Arsdale denies ever happened. But everyone was aware of the deadline, and the energy level in the call center amped up as the November bar date approached.

Stenulson and her coworkers were competing not just with each other but also with law firms and marketers around the country with similar phone banks and ad campaigns. Some of the marketers worked as aggregators, paid by the number of leads they generated or retention agreements they got signed. Some campaigns were backed by hedge funds that financed their operations in exchange for a piece of the future proceeds, essentially placing bets on how successful the mass tort lawyers would be. One BSA analysis showed that in just three months leading up to the bar date, ads and informercials aired more than eleven thousand times across ninety-one media markets, focusing heavily on major population centers including New York, Los Angeles, and Houston.[14] All followed more or less the same script: *Time is running out. Act now. Call this number.* Sign-up volume was the name of the game.

Mass tort campaigns featured such familiar faces as Dr. Wendy Walsh, a popular TV psychologist, self-help guru, and former Fox News contributor who has also fronted infomercials for litigation involving everything from baby powder to covid 19–related nursing home deaths. Walsh's own sexual harassment allegations against Fox's star bloviator, Bill O'Reilly, helped crush his career during the #MeToo movement.[15] In Boy Scouts infomercials, Walsh served alternately as interviewer and interviewee. In one she serves up questions to plaintiffs' attorney Jeff Herman, quizzing him in his role as a sexual abuse expert. In another, she is the guest expert herself, offering her thoughts not just on past abuse in Scouting but on the warning signs today's parents should be on the lookout for.

"You know, I hate to say it," she begins. "There are lots of great men out there, many of them good fathers. But you've got to question a man who would want to spend his free time on the weekend with children instead of adults, right? So if he's inviting kids for overnight trips and sleepovers, if he's contacting single mothers because many of these predators know that single mothers need the childcare, so they often will date women who are single mothers so that they can have access to the kid. If they're just spending too much time with a child, and having too much interest in your child, find out if they're following your child on social media. Find out if they're texting them privately."[16]

Walsh is a headliner in the talent pool at Consumer Attorney Marketing Group (CAMG), a Los Angeles firm that offers one-stop shopping for law firms craving a slice of the mass tort pie. CAMG's website touts its track record of "institutional sex abuse campaigns" across the country, of both the Scouting and clergy varieties, and it offers a choice of advertising options—off the rack or tailor made: "CAMG has a library of available shorter form commercials and our exclusive sex abuse infomercial that can be branded for your firm. Our in-house production team can also film spots featuring lawyers from your firms in our state-of-the-art production studios....Our exclusive sex abuse infomercial provides nearly 30 minutes to engage and inform the audience, as well as build trust so they feel comfortable calling." Those who phone in, according to the company, will find intake staffers who are well trained, available to answer questions, and happy to help with the all-important next step of "converting a caller into a client."[17]

Always be closing.

In September 2020, the Boy Scouts of America was preparing to launch its own $6.8 million advertising campaign, to urge sexual abuse survivors to file claims in the bankruptcy.[18] The ad blitz would feature print, television, radio, and online spots in English and Spanish that the Scouts billed as "clear, accurate, impartial, informative, and sensitive to survivors"—all of the things, the BSA contended, that the messaging being pushed by the mass tort law firms was not.

Lawyers for the Scouts asked bankruptcy judge Laurie Selber Silverstein to restrict the opposing law firms' advertising, claiming it was rife with "false, misleading and one-sided statements" that could damage the reputation, brand, and goodwill of the BSA. Among other things, the Scouts' lawyers alleged that the plaintiffs' attorneys' ads falsely promised anonymity to prospective claimants and told them that compensation was "ensured." They also accused the lawyers and marketers of using BSA's logo and trademarks without permission and of ignoring "the robust, expert-informed youth protection program the BSA has put in place" to make it one of the world's safest youth organizations.[19]

"Failure to curb the ongoing advertising campaigns described above could have disastrous consequences for these chapter 11 proceedings," the Scouts' lawyers warned. For good measure, their motion included a copy of a letter that Jessica C. K. Boelter, a partner at the law firm Sidley Austin, the Scouts' bankruptcy counsel, sent to the official Tort Claimants' Committee—a panel of nine abuse survivors appointed by the US Trustee to represent the interests of all who filed claims—asking it to be distributed to law firms in the case and demanding that they "immediately and permanently cease and desist from publishing these misleading and damaging advertisements."[20]

Not surprisingly, the plaintiffs' firms pushed back. They decried the Scouts' motion to scuttle their advertising as "a thinly veiled attempt to minimize participation" and diminish the leverage of the claimants in an effort to limit the BSA's liability. They also contended that the Boy Scouts' lawyers had shown no evidence that the mass tort solicitations were false or misleading.

Silverstein heard arguments on the BSA's motion but did not grant it, saying it was too broad and raised First Amendment issues. A week later, however, she ordered that law firms no longer promise anonymity to prospective clients or predict the size of the potential compensation trust fund or the individual payouts they might receive.[21] With those restrictions in place, the ads and infomercials were allowed to continue.

By all accounts, however, the solicitation of Boy Scout claims had been brisk at Reciprocity Industries in Billings and at call centers elsewhere. Van Arsdale and his fellow Abused in Scouting attorneys, Kosnoff and Eisenberg, signed up some seventeen thousand claimants by the court's bar date. That was several thousand more than the entire universe of victims identified the previous year by the Boy Scouts' expert, Janet Warren. "We knew that the number of boys that were abused in the Boy Scouts was of epidemic-type proportions, I mean, just huge numbers," Van

Arsdale said. "But we didn't think that they'd come forward like they did. That surprised us."[22]

Van Arsdale was not the only one taken aback. Hours before the close of business on the last day to file a claim, the BSA acknowledged a "gut-wrenching" response by sexual abuse survivors. Pre-bankruptcy estimates of the number of potential claims had varied widely, from several thousand to some multiple of that, maybe even as high as the 12,254 victims counted by Warren, the BSA researcher, in her study of perversion files spanning 1944 to 2016.[23] But no one, including the BSA, had expected anything close to the final tally of 92,700 claims. Even after weeding out 10,500 duplicates, the remaining 82,209 claims dwarfed the number of victims in the Catholic Church's sex abuse scandal two decades earlier, when John Jay College of Criminal Justice researchers had found that 10,667 individuals had made allegations of sexual abuse against priests from 1950 to 2002.[24] The bulk of the BSA claims were from the years 1960 to 1990, with annual tallies ranging from 1,085 to 2,839.[25]

"We are devastated by the number of lives impacted by past abuse in Scouting and moved by the bravery of those who have come forward," the organization said. "We are heartbroken that we cannot undo their pain."[26]

The organization said it was "deeply sorry" and promised to work as expeditiously as possible to compensate survivors fairly and continue with its mission of helping boys become men and teaching them patriotism, courage, self-reliance, and kindred virtues. To make those payments, it would set up a Victims Compensation Trust, overseen by an independent trustee who would divvy up the money and distribute it to claimants. The BSA and its insurers would fund the trust, but how much each would contribute was subject to negotiation. The local councils, which chartered the community groups and churches that sponsored troops, faced pressure to contribute but were not debtors in the bankruptcy.

How much the individual claimants would receive would depend on the eventual size of the trust fund, how many survivors were vying for shares of it, and the severity of the abuse they had suffered. It was generally accepted that the more serious the abuse, the greater would be the compensation, but at that early stage the parameters had not been set. Nor had a process been established for vetting the claims.

All of that and more would be spelled out in the Boy Scouts' reorganization plan, which would have to be approved by an "overwhelming" majority vote of the claimants and ultimately confirmed by Judge Silverstein. But first would come a steady torrent of nearly ten thousand motions, objections, declarations, orders, and other pleadings,[27] along with months of head-knocking negotiations and jockeying for position by lawyers representing the disparate interests in the case. No one expected a quick and easy resolution. Sexual abuse survivors hoping for a quick payout on their claims were sure to be disappointed, and those whose pending lawsuits had been stayed by the bankruptcy were frustrated to boot.

In the meantime, the bankruptcy filing would continue to take its toll on the finances of the Boy Scouts of America—and the emotional health of abuse survivors stuck in legal limbo.

CHAPTER 14

LETTERS FROM HELL

I never realized how much damage I endured
until trying to compose a letter. I have avoided
mentioning it, much less discussing it my entire
life. I am humiliated to have a story like this....To
put it in writing, black and white, is tormenting.

—*A Boy Scouts sexual abuse survivor*[1]

Attorneys for some of the 82,209 claimants in the Boy Scouts' bankruptcy urged them to write to Judge Laurie Selber Silverstein, detailing their sexual abuse and describing its impact on their lives. More than a thousand did, beginning in May 2021, weighing in from across the country and from all rungs of the socioeconomic ladder. Their abuse ran the gamut from a single instance of fondling to multiple rapes spanning several years. Their letters were a compilation of heartbreak and human wreckage strewn across generations and all fifty states.

As young as six or seven when they had been molested, some of the boys are now in their eighties and nineties. Many had silently shouldered the weight of their abuse since it had occurred, unable or unwilling to share their experiences or seek the help they needed. Others had come forward immediately, only to be accused by their parents of lying or told to keep quiet and never again speak of what had happened to them: One recounted being raped six times *after* his mom and dad had refused to believe that his troop leader had sexually assaulted him on a camping trip.[2]

Their accounts are penned in block letters, written out longhand, typed on computers, or pecked out on old typewriters with misaligned characters. Some are shaky, barely legible chicken-scratching, and some are florid, nearly perfect cursive. They are as short as a paragraph, as long as a master's thesis. One former Scout tapped out his letter on a smartphone, all fifteen pages of it, single-spaced. Dozens were sent from prisons. All are part of a bankruptcy claims process in which a court-approved settlement trustee will put a dollar amount on their suffering.

Over the last fifty years or so, the awareness and understanding of child sexual abuse in the United States have evolved and grown, with researchers generally agreeing that it can seriously affect the physical and mental health of victims well beyond childhood and often for the rest of their lives. Not everyone experiences it in the same way or suffers the same symptoms, which can include nightmares, sleep and eating disorders, post-traumatic stress, self-harm, inappropriate sexual behavior, and a laundry list of other ill effects.

In missives ranging from unintelligible to eloquent, the abuse survivors vent their anger, pain, humiliation, disappointment, regret, despair, shame, and guilt, all while ripping the scabs off their struggles with trust issues, panic attacks, alcohol and drug abuse, suicide attempts, sexual dysfunction, failed relationships, divorce, broken families, lost careers. They wonder if their abuse led to their being gay or to their homophobia or both, or if it is what caused them to become child molesters themselves. They fear for their own children's well-being. They attach boyhood photos of themselves in their Scout uniforms with their merit badge sashes as painful illustrations of innocence stolen and longing for what might have been. They lament life as it is.

"I will go to my grave without ever being loved or hugged," one says.

"I am a devastated human being," says another.

BEFORE POSTING THEIR LETTERS to the online docket, the bankruptcy court redacted survivors' names and other identifying information, along with most graphic descriptions of abuse, while leaving intact their deeply personal accounts of lives forever changed.

They include old men who hope for nothing more than to live long enough to see the Boy Scouts of America held to account for what happened to them decades ago. "I am 85 years old and do not have much time," a rape survivor wrote. "I would like to see justice done before I pass on." A ninety-two-year-old man from the coal country of southern Utah said his family had already been ravaged by the Great Depression when his abusive Scout leader had made his life much worse by stealing his "teen age years, high school prom's etc school day's and basketball, boxing team and dating the girls you sorta had a crush on."[3] One aging survivor had kept his ordeal to himself since he was thirteen but had finally shared it with a loved one: "I am 87 years old and have had to conceal this abuse secret for 74 years, not ever revealing this atrocity to my wife, who is no longer with us, my parents nor anyone else. Recently I told my daughter and I cant describe the feeling of relief."[4]

While some say that no amount of money will ever make things right—"A billion dollars cannot give me back what was taken from me"—many implore Silverstein to punish the BSA with big payouts to survivors—big enough, they hope, to put the

113-year-old organization out of business. One man who wrote
that he had been repeatedly raped by a Scout leader in the 1960s
said he will not accept any of the "blood money" from the bankruptcy, pledging instead to give his share to the children's camp
where he volunteers.[5]

Among the more common threads are survivors' vivid recollections of their abusers' menacing promises. "He threatened that if I
told anyone ever that he would kill me and my mom," one wrote.
"...I was a little boy. I didn't want my mom to be hurt or mur-
dered."[6] So he kept quiet. Indeed, the threats and the physical and
psychological power differential behind them—men in positions
of authority holding sway over young boys—all but guaranteed
victims' silence. So did the fear instilled by many predators that no
one would believe them, anyway: *I'm a grown man, you're just a kid.
It's your word against mine.*

In Johnson City, Tennessee, one survivor followed his older
brother into Scouting, only to be molested by a troop leader at
a state park. "[On] our way back to our camp site he told me if I
told anyone he would kill my brother and parents," he says. "He
told me I better not quit coming to Boy Scouts because my parents would ask questions." The abuse continued for three years,
extending to one of his friends. "We never told anyone about what
he did to us," the former Scout wrote, blaming it for a lifetime
of substance abuse and emotional problems. "...Both my parents have passed away and I never told them why I was the way
I was....I am 56 yrs old now and have spent my whole life by my
self."[7] His friend died of brain cancer a few years ago and took
their secret to his grave.

Wrenching letters describe parents who sided with abusive
Scout leaders, accused their sons of fabricating allegations, or punished them for the aberrant behavior the abuse likely triggered. A
fifty-two-year-old former Scout recalled that when he was twelve,
a southern California troop leader had sexually assaulted him and

"beat the crap" out of him. "He punched my face so hard that he broke my nose & I loss vision in my left eye. My ribs were bruised & he told my mom that all this were done by older boy scouts," he wrote. "...She believed him so I never talked about anything to anyone ever. I took 40 years to be able to say that I was raped by a Boy Scout leader."[8]

It was no secret in the small town where one boy grew up that his family couldn't afford to buy him a Scout uniform. His troop leader knew it, too, and offered to help. Alone with the boy, he told him to take off his shirt so he could measure him for one. Then he molested him, the first time of many. The Scout, who until then had sung in his school choir, played drums in the band, wrestled, and run track, suddenly dropped out of everything. "My relationship with my Mom and my brother would never be the same again," he wrote. "I could still see the love in her smile and in her eyes but as she would walk away I would catch glimpses of the shame she felt....My brother, almost immediately started distancing himself from me....We haven't spoken in decades....I just wasn't the same boy anymore."[9]

Another former Scout recalled having the time of his life as a squad leader in a troop in the 1970s—until his scoutmaster began abusing him. When he acted out, he wrote, his stepfather, unaware of what was driving his misbehavior, decided that he needed "a 'good 'ol fashioned' ass beating" to fix it. "I guess it must have flipped a switch because once he started, it <u>never</u> ended, he used a belt, switch, elec. cords and once a 2×4 stud basicly anything he could lay his hands on." With nowhere to turn, the boy climbed to the roof of his school's auditorium and jumped off, slamming onto the pavement three stories below. "There I was a 13 yr. old trying to end my life. When I arrived at the hospital the priest from my church gave me my 'last rights' then I died," he says. "The Drs. brought me back twice, that day. I had survived 28 broken bones—I lost 1/2 of my shredded left lung. I was in a halo for 8 mo.'s and a cervical collar for a year and all that time I was still being abused by my trusted scout leader."[10]

While others also attempted suicide, or at least contemplated it, some thought about killing their abusers instead. One recalled getting a gun and plotting to shoot the Scout leader who was molesting him but ultimately couldn't pull the trigger. Another fantasized about slaying the man who had abused him in 1968, shortly after he had finished third grade and joined the Scouts. His two most enduring childhood memories are of (a) hawking glazed doughnuts for a dollar a dozen, and earning a dime on each sale, and (b) being groped in his underwear by his scoutmaster. More than fifty years later, his long-festering anger emanated from a particularly disturbing letter to the judge in which he wished his abuser a "long and miserable life." "If I ever was to cross paths with him, I would have no problem pulling my pocket knife out and stab him in the head. While I'm cutting his throat, I would be reminding him who I was and why I'm killing him," he wrote. "Your Honor I would have no problem cut his head off and put it on the hood of my car with a sign saying this man ruined my trust, ruined my life."[11]

JUST AS THEIR CHILDHOODS were twisted and warped by their sexual abuse, some survivors say it also affected how they raised their own sons and daughters. Now in his early seventies, one recounted his abuse by a Scout leader in Palmdale, California, beginning when he was eight and continuing through his teens. His first marriage fell apart because he couldn't communicate his feelings, and he was unable to hold good jobs because he couldn't see his own worth. One of the worst things was realizing, as an adult, that his children were collateral damage. "I will never forget the pain in my heart the day one of my grown sons came to me and asked me why I didn't love him enough to have shown him affection, tell him I love him and spend time with him as a child," he says. "He didn't know I didn't let him sit on my lap, or give him a bath or play with him much because I was afraid that somehow, sometime, if I let this innocent activity happen, I might be triggered to recreate the abuse I had experienced."[12]

Some letters came not from former Scouts but from their parents or wives. One writer recalled that when her husband was a boy his father had committed suicide at Christmas, so his mother had signed him up for Scouting to fill the void. "Instead of goodness, fun and friendships, it was a molestation nightmare!" she wrote. "My husband has been scarred for life....He's almost 57 years old and he shakes, stutters and cries like a tiny boy when he speaks to me about how he was violated," she says. "He has gone through hell, the shame he feels, no matter how many times he's told by a therapist, or by all of us who love him, that it was not his fault." The perpetrator is in prison, but her husband is, too, in a way, and so is his family: "This heinous crime...continues to violate his life, my life, his mother's life, his daughter's, the entire family's lives, and will do so until we die! [He] has a life sentence to cope with this, and so do we."[13]

Several of those abused became abusers themselves, including one who wrote that he has "hurt 3 young boys" and believes that "if this didn't happen to me, I would not have done that."[14] Another said his scoutmaster had molested him after grooming him with pornographic magazines and movies. By his mid-teens, he was doing the same thing to other boys, including his nephews. He's now serving a life sentence in a California prison for molesting his eleven- and thirteen-year-old stepdaughters.[15]

Though the vast majority of sexual abuse in Scouting is committed by men, the letters reveal isolated incidents of boys being molested by women, as in the case of a sixty-one-year-old former Cub Scout whose den mother had abused him every Friday while "inspecting" him before the weekly meeting. He said that the experience had been "uncomfortable, humiliating, demoralizing, and scared me to this day."[16]

Not all the victims were boys. A ninety-one-year-old woman recalled being sexually assaulted by a Scout leader in Indiana in the early 1940s. She was twelve or thirteen and volunteering with a local Cub Scout pack when he followed her home from a meeting and raped her. "It's been very hard on me because I have kept this a secret, not even telling my 96-year-old husband that passed away this year. We were married 70 years," she wrote. "...Last night I didn't go to sleep until 3AM because I kept reliving what happened to me as a young girl."[17]

One letter is from a woman who was raped as a teenager by a university music instructor, the leader of her Explorers post. He was always nice to her, gave her rides to meetings and special events, and befriended her mother after learning that the family was struggling. "He seemed to really care about those problems and about me," she wrote, then described the time he drove her to a hotel and sexually assaulted her on the way home from an event. "He made me feel like I owed it to him because he cared about me. I guess he knew he didn't need to threaten me not to tell because I was afraid of my parents who were sometimes violent."[18] She said the abuse had been "a huge factor" in the failure of her first marriage.

Her story is echoed by a woman who was in Explorers in West Virginia. "I was just turning 17 years old. I was active in sports, had good grades, and had a boyfriend. I had what I thought was the beginning of a bright future," she wrote. Her adult mentor raped her in the back seat of his car as she "kicked and screamed trying desperately to get away from him." Afterward, when she told him she was a virgin, "He just threw his head back and laughed and laughed like he had just gained a prize." It would be the first of at least six such attacks that she told no one about for years. Even now, only a few people know. "Life for me has been a series of horrible choices," she wrote. "Alcohol, drugs, and very poor choices of men. For a very long time I would not even speak to a man for fear he would hurt me. All of this because of what I went through with the Boy Scouts of America."[19]

AT LEAST ONE LETTER shed new light on a sexual abuse case whose full scope had not been previously disclosed, publicly or in the perversion files, even though it had played out in criminal courts and in the news media. Maryland Scout leader David MacDonald Rankin[20] was convicted in 1988 of eleven counts of child abuse and sentenced to fifteen years in prison for molesting nine boys in a bizarre scenario in which he "initiated" them into a clique of Troop 740 he called "the Rowdies" by making them have sex with him—and each other. Rankin, a gun store manager in his late twenties who was an Eagle Scout and a US marine, expressed remorse at his sentencing, telling a judge that he had never intended to harm the Scouts. "They were like sons and little brothers to me," he said. "If I could turn back the hands of time, I would."[21]

So would the boys he molested, including a now-middle-aged man who wrote a seventeen-page letter to the bankruptcy judge, asking her not to redact the excruciating details of the abuse Rankin had inflicted on him and others. It included rape, penetration with a broomstick, mutual masturbation, forced oral copulation, psychological battery, and death threats. "The true extent of the abuse has never come to light," he wrote. "More boys were involved, and more incidents of sexual abuse occurred. It wasn't a handful of times. It was a repeated pattern over a couple of years with eight to 10 different Scouts, likely more....If I personally suffered 50 to 70 incidents over a nine-month period, based on what I heard from other boys...it's possible to estimate the incidents of sexual abuse numbered between 300 and 500 times, maybe more."[22]

He said that Rankin, who had died in 2014,[23] "operated with the mentality of a teenage bully wrongly empowered by an organization that saw him as a model leader" and noted that he now feels "immense shame" over his own inability to stop him. He has PTSD and flashbacks. He has trouble sleeping and difficulty making friends with men and maintaining relationships with women. His first marriage ended in divorce.

"After it happened, I wanted nothing more than to forget and deny—it's likely part of the mind's way of coping and healing," he wrote. "Now that I've reached middle age, I realize I've dealt with the demons for 35 years and they are not going away. I've tried to forget through sports, writing, medicine, therapy, spirituality, religion, work, travel, relationships, self-help, etc., but scars from the sexual abuse are open wounds that are part of me." Every retelling of his experience "triggers similar feelings of anger and helplessness, of being ruined and beyond help, hopeless, dead inside, misconfigured into someone I didn't want to be against my volition, lost in a thousand-mile stare like a shell-shocked soldier." Still, he hopes that his story will serve as a cautionary tale for others.

"I had a suburban upbringing and attended Catholic schools. I excelled at sports, had many friends, and earned good grades. My parents were involved in my life. We went to church every Sunday," he said. "It's wrong to think that only females or outcast males, children of divorce, suffer from sexual abuse. I'm proof it may affect anyone."

CHAPTER 15

A MELTING ICE CUBE

At a bankruptcy hearing in February 2022, an attorney for the BSA's outside counsel, White & Case, likened his client's financial condition to "a melting ice cube," warning against unnecessary delays. The longer this drags out, Glenn Kurtz told the court, the greater the costs to Scouting's shrinking fortunes. "At some point, it's just money that's coming out of the estate, as it tries to continue to operate long enough to emerge and continue its mission," he said, "so we really have a very critical situation for the debtors."[1]

If anyone should have known about the mounting costs of the Boy Scouts' bankruptcy, it was Kurtz. As the head of his global firm's commercial litigation practice, he billed his services to the BSA at $1,900 an hour, racking up an average of fifty hours a week en route to a whopping $1.15 million tab just for February, March, and April 2022. But Kurtz was far from alone among amply compensated White & Case attorneys working on the bankruptcy: court records show that twenty of his colleagues clocked in at between $1,060 and $1,470 an hour, while associates just a year out of law school charged $770 per hour.[2] All told, during that three-month period, White & Case charged the Boy Scouts $14.7 million, not including expenses, and netted $11.7 million after a 20 percent "holdback" of fees eligible to be paid later. By the end of 2022, the BSA had paid White & Case more than $52 million since retaining it in September 2020.[3] By July 2023, the firm's BSA fees topped $70 million, plus $2.7 million in expenses.[4]

White & Case's big guns weren't the only ones cashing big checks from the Boy Scouts of America. As the bankruptcy debtor, the BSA was obligated to pay not just its own financial advisers, consultants, and attorneys but also those of committees representing the abuse survivors, unsecured creditors, and future claimants, those who might come forward later.

For those keeping score in dollars, three and a half years into the BSA's bankruptcy, it was White & Case, $73 million; Pachulski Stang Ziehl & Jones, $40 million; and Sidley Austin, $11 million; sexual abuse survivors, $0.

While those firms were among the top billers as the bankruptcy dragged on through its fourth year, together they accounted for *less than half* of the fees and expenses the Boy Scouts had shelled out to lawyers, accountants, financial experts, property appraisers, and other professionals since filing for Chapter 11 bankruptcy on February 18, 2020. By midsummer 2023, the swarm of attorneys had rung up a collective tab of nearly $300 million.[5] By then, some lawyers were charging upward of $2,000 an hour, with individual billings topping $5 million. Even the fee examiner the BSA hired to watchdog all those billings cashed in, banking more than $1.1 million for his efforts.[6]

The huge bites taken out of the Boy Scouts' funds did not escape the attention of Judge Laurie Selber Silverstein, who sounded the alarm after billings hit the $100 million mark barely a year into the case. "I think that is a staggering number," she said during a hearing in March 2021, urging the parties to get into gear, "and progress needs to be made. Victims need to be compensated appropriately. and the Boy Scouts' mission needs to continue.... Every dollar going to professional fees is a dollar that comes out of some creditor's pocket"[7]—i.e., the pockets of former Scouts who'd been molested as boys. Thousands of them would end up with less from the bankruptcy than some of the BSA's lawyers made before taking their first bathroom break on any given day.[8]

BANKRUPTCY COURTS HAVE THE power to control fees, but they have been corrupted by the competition to attract lucrative cases to their venues, said Lynn LoPucki, a University of Florida law professor and bankruptcy expert. Simply put, the courts don't want to lose business by alienating the attorneys who are driving it, so their fees are rarely questioned or constrained. Delaware, where the BSA's case was lodged, became a major competitor in the 1990s, when it landed thirteen of the fifteen largest bankruptcies, an 87 percent share of a lucrative market, LoPucki said. "It's a valuable industry for this tiny state. Most years it's probably more than a billion-dollar industry, and when bankruptcy booms, it can be billions for the state of Delaware."[9]

That helps explain the big fees but doesn't address another key question: How did the Boy Scouts' bankruptcy wind up in Silverstein's court in the first place, considering that the BSA is headquartered in Texas and had no business presence in Delaware, a venue with a reputation for being friendly to corporate debtors? That required a little creative lawyering by the Boy Scouts' attorneys.

From the outset, the BSA has insisted that its 250-plus local councils, which held billions in assets including investments, campgrounds, and other valuable real estate, operate independently of the national organization and thus should not be debtors in the bankruptcy. To shield the councils and their extensive holdings from creditors, the BSA's strategy was to grant them what are known as nondebtor or third-party releases from liability in any global settlement, in exchange for their contributions to the compensation fund. The hitch in that plan, which would also release from liability insurance companies, as well as churches and other chartering organizations that agreed to contribute to the victims' fund, was that bankruptcy courts in some jurisdictions, including the one encompassing the BSA's home state of Texas, were averse to such "nonconsensual" releases and likely would not approve them in this case.

Ah, but Delaware was different.

Nicknamed "The First State," it is home to about one million people—and roughly the same number of businesses. Delaware followed the lead of another small state, South Dakota, which revived its dying economy in 1980 when it attracted the behemoth Citibank by freeing it from caps on the interest it charged its credit card holders.[10] Delaware in turn enacted usury laws that allowed banks to set their own lending rates, so financial institutions and other businesses flocked there—at least on paper—to take advantage of its corporate-friendly regulations and tax laws. Delaware has become an "onshore haven," according to LoPucki and other critics who have dubbed it the Cayman Islands of the Eastern Seaboard.

"They have a huge incorporation industry there," LoPucki said. "Fifty-five percent of all large public companies are incorporated in Delaware, and that's because Delaware will let management do whatever the hell it wants." And, he contends, so will Delaware bankruptcy judges. "Bankruptcy is just an add-on. It's another thing that Delaware can do for Delaware corporations."[11]

The hurdle for the BSA was that it was not a Delaware corporation. It was incorporated in 1910 in Washington, DC, initially set up shop in New York City, and eventually moved its corporate headquarters to Irving, Texas, in 1979. Bankruptcy laws allow companies to file where they are incorporated, where their principal place of business or assets are located, or where one of their affiliates has filed for bankruptcy. Since the BSA had no affiliates in Delaware, that would seem to limit its filing options to DC or Texas, but it didn't. No Delaware affiliate? No problem. In July 2019, the Boy Scouts solved its dilemma by simply creating one, Delaware BSA, LLC, just in time to meet a requirement for companies to be "domiciled" in the state for 180 days before filing a Chapter 11 petition the following February.

Delaware BSA, LLC consists of little more than its digital record on the state's Division of Corporations website.[12] When it filed for bankruptcy, it listed assets of $0 to $50,000. Three years into the case, its monthly operating statement filed with the court showed that it still had zero employees and total assets of $10 in cash.[13] With no income, no one on the payroll, and no apparent business function, it looks to have been nothing more than a corporate shell on which the national organization could piggyback its own Delaware bankruptcy—which was exactly what the BSA did, immediately after its new "affiliate" filed its Chapter 11 petition on February 18, 2020.

Georgetown University law professor Adam Levitin, who, like LoPucki, has written extensively about the flaws and excesses of the US bankruptcy system, has called Delaware BSA, LLC an illusion, "a Potemkin Village of an affiliate." He has cited it as a prime example of gaming the system through "forum shopping," in which debtors such as the Boy Scouts choose venues they think will treat them most favorably, in this case by approving third-party releases.[14] "I am hard pressed to think of a case where an affiliate was so blatantly created solely as to create venue," he wrote. "Other cases have relied on affiliates that have at least engaged in some modest business....BSA's behavior here is really outrageous to anyone who isn't inured to it by virtue of having lived as a professional inside the bankruptcy system for too long, and it's even more outrageous that its creditors should have to foot the bill to correct its forum shopping."

Notwithstanding Levitin's protestations, the Boy Scouts' forum shopping was not seriously contested in court, and its bankruptcy proceeded apace. LoPucki's take on it calls to mind the famously hopeless line from the 1974 movie starring Jack Nicholson as the jaded private eye Jake Gittes: "Forget it, Jake. It's Chinatown." As LoPucki put it, "Well, you go to your lawyer, and you explain your problem. And the lawyer tells you 'I got a solution for this.' And you hear the solution. And it seems really sleazy to you, but the lawyer says that's the way this is done. In Mexico, you give fifty dollars to the cop that pulls you over....In Delaware, you just go to bankruptcy court."[15]

Bipartisan bankruptcy reform legislation in Congress, including most recently a Senate bill cosponsored by Massachusetts Democrat Elizabeth Warren and Texas Republican John Cornyn, has gone nowhere.[16] Their Bankruptcy Venue Reform Act of 2021, which would have required businesses to file where their headquarters or principal assets are located, while cracking down on the blatant creation of affiliates such as Delaware BSA, LLC to establish venue, had the backing of forty-three attorneys general from red and blue states across the country.

Warren and Cornyn's Senate bill stalled out, as had a similar previous House effort. LoPucki places much of the blame for that on former senator and current president Joe Biden, he of the great state of Delaware. "I think they have the votes, but they can't get it to come up for a vote. The leadership won't let it happen, because they are embarrassed by it, or they fear Biden would veto it," he said. "It's astonishing. You don't think of the United States as a corrupt country generally. But this is just flourishing corruption. I don't think there's any other word for it. And nobody can fix it."[17]

WITHIN A COUPLE OF weeks of Silverstein's admonition to hold down costs and keep the case moving, the Boy Scouts of America filed a 379-page placeholder reorganization plan on March 1, 2021. Even as the work in progress that the BSA acknowledged it to be, the plan was short on specifics and, in the eyes of the claimants and the attorneys who represented them, shorter still on the cash and assets it offered to contribute to the settlement trust.

The BSA said its local councils had agreed to chip in at least $300 million, a fraction of the real estate and other assets held by the 261 entities that chartered the churches and other organizations that sponsored troops.[18] In California alone, Boy Scout councils owned more than $250 million in real estate, according to an analysis by Seattle attorney Michael Pfau, whose firm represented more than a thousand claimants. "It appears very clear the Boy Scouts are trying to conceal the fact that these councils are not paying a fair amount, and worse, they are trying to force abuse survivors to give up their claims for close to nothing," he said.[19]

For its part, the BSA would contribute the yet-to-be-determined proceeds from its insurance policies and the sale of some of its assets, including gas and oil wells, a couple of buildings, and a collection of art, including more than fifty oil-on-canvas paintings and other works by Norman Rockwell. An artist and illustrator known for patriotic themes and all things Americana, Rockwell was hired as a teenager to do pen-and-ink drawings for *The Boy Scout Hike Book* and was soon named art director of *Boys' Life*, the BSA's monthly magazine, which used dozens of his paintings to adorn its covers beginning in 1913.[20] Art critics have said that much of what he did for the Scouts over the span of sixty years was not his best work, largely because the BSA often dictated the content of the pieces it commissioned. His illustrations for the *Saturday Evening Post* would prove to be more valuable, with one, *Saying Grace*, bringing more than $46 million at auction in 2013[21] and others fetching as much as $22.5 million each.

The Boy Scouts initially assigned no values to its Rockwells. In subsequent bankruptcy filings, however, it listed appraisals of

$1 million to $3 million each for at least twenty of the paintings, including *The Scoutmaster* ($2 million), *On My Honor* ($2 million), and *High Adventure at Philmont* ($3 million). Pending their sale, the Rockwells and the rest of the Boy Scouts' art collection, which also includes works by other painters and illustrators such as Walt Disney, Carl Clemens Moritz Rungius, Howard Chandler Christy, and Joseph Christian Leyendecker, were to remain on exhibit at the Medici Museum of Art in Warren, Ohio.[22] The collection, valued at some $59 million, was still there in April 2024.

The BSA's initial reorganization plan lacked proposed contributions by its many insurers, with which it continued to negotiate. In its filing, the BSA promised to "work with all parties" and said it would provide more details in the coming months but insisted that the plan "demonstrates considerable progress" in the bankruptcy. That was a view clearly not shared by many plaintiff attorneys and members of the Tort Claimants' Committee representing survivors.[23]

"The plan violates every word and the spirit of the Boy Scout Oath that each of us took as kids," said John Humphrey, an abuse survivor himself and chairman of that panel, which estimated that the Scouts' proposal, without insurers' contributions, would pay an average of $6,100 per claimant. That compares to the approximately $1.3 million per survivor that the Archdiocese of Los Angeles agreed to pay in a $660 million settlement of sexual abuse claims in 2007 and is a fraction of what survivors in other institutional sexual abuse settlements have received.[24] "The BSA and its local councils are not making the effort necessary to provide a modicum of compensation to men and women whose lives were changed forever by BSA's and the local councils' failure to protect them as children," Humphrey added.

His comments were mild compared to some others.

"It's really disgraceful," said attorney Paul Mones, who had won the nearly $20 million judgment against the Boy Scouts in the

Kerry Lewis trial in Portland in 2010 and represented other clients in the bankruptcy. "Considering the enormity of the problem, are they taking care of survivors as they should? I don't think so."

Tim Kosnoff, a member of the Abused in Scouting coalition representing some 17,000 of the 82,000 claimants, dismissed the reorganization plan as "dead on arrival" in the upcoming balloting by survivors and called instead for the nuclear option, the Boy Scouts' liquidation. "This plan is pouring salt in the wound, and it is an insult," he said.

It didn't help that at the top of the list of unsecured creditors, the vast majority of them abuse survivors, sat three former BSA chief Scout executives—Wayne Brock, Robert Mazzuca, and Roy Williams—with claims ranging from $1.1 million to $2.3 million each for future pension payments.

CHAPTER 16

LET'S MAKE A DEAL

In 2002, a few months after Tim Kosnoff won a hefty settlement in the Jeremiah Scott case, the *Boston Globe* rolled out its exposé of sexual abuse in the US Catholic Church. The newspaper's Pulitzer Prize–winning reporting focused public attention not just on the predatory clergymen it unmasked but also on the big-picture issue of child sexual abuse in America. Powerful institutions that had dismissed it as the isolated acts of individuals were now being held to account for their negligent responses to it.

While studying up on the BSA and reviewing prior litigation involving it, Kosnoff happened upon Patrick Boyle's book *Scout's Honor: Sexual Abuse in America's Most Trusted Institution*, which he considered a remarkable chronicle of Scouting's efforts to quietly remove sexually abusive leaders over a twenty-year period beginning in the 1970s.[1] Boyle, a former *Washington Times* reporter, had kept copies of the perversion files he'd obtained from lawsuits in Virginia and California, and he agreed to share them with Kosnoff, as he had with other attorneys who had asked for them.[2]

Kosnoff had the documents scanned and gave Boyle a digitized copy. Then he read and analyzed the dossiers and used them to allege a pattern of negligence by the Boy Scouts and secure a settlement in a lawsuit brought by brothers Tom and Matt Stewart, who had been abused as boys by their suburban Seattle scoutmaster, Bruce Phelps.[3] Through discovery in the Stewart case, Kosnoff and Mark Honeywell, an attorney he worked with on it, obtained an additional 3,200 perversion files dating to 1947.[4] In all, the two lawyers had some 5,100 complete files and less detailed summaries. They hired someone to create a database of information that could be searched and sorted to produce a variety of useful facts: abusers by year and date; the numbers of unmarried abusers and those with children in Scouting; abusers by geographic location or affiliation with the Catholic or LDS churches; convicted sex offenders; repeat perpetrators; and on and on. Honeywell figured that such detailed information could be useful in proving at trial that the BSA had been well aware of its long-standing sexual abuse problem and had neglected to address it.

When the lawsuit settled, Honeywell thought it would be a shame to waste such a valuable resource and sent analyses of the two sets of files to the Boy Scouts' lawyers on a compact disc, free of charge, no strings attached. "We provide it with a genuine desire and expectation that BSA will make productive use of these two studies in terms of their educational efforts, perhaps alerting local councils of the various 'red flags' to consider when accepting applications for volunteers in various scouting positions, how to better guard against the re-entry of 'booted' volunteers, and to generally obtain some statistical benefit from this exhaustive collection of information in BSA's possession," he wrote to the Scouts' lawyers. "Our true hope is that some good will come of this exchange."[5]

Honeywell never heard back from the BSA or its lawyers.[6]

By 2012, Kosnoff had sued the BSA on behalf of hundreds of former Scouts, earning a reputation as a hard-nosed, media-savvy advocate for abuse survivors—and one who made a handsome living at it. By 2014, he had turned sixty, his marriage had been dissolved, and he was winding down his law practice with an eye toward retirement. He had a fifty-five-foot sailing yacht built and shoved off from the East Coast for Puerto Rico, where he lived aboard it. He stopped taking on new clients, whittled away at his pending caseload by phone and computer, and relied on a Texas forwarding service for his mail.[7]

Then, in late 2018, Kosnoff read a *Wall Street Journal* story about Boy Scouts officials mulling over bankruptcy amid mounting sexual abuse lawsuits and decided to "unretire," believing that thousands of abuse survivors were about to lose their shot at holding the youth organization accountable. "I thought about it, I paced, I considered what it would mean to jump back in, and made the decision that I wanted to, and if I could find lawyers that would do it with me, that I would do it," he said.[8] And do it in a big and potentially lucrative way.

That was the genesis of his association with Stewart Eisenberg and Andrew Van Arsdale and the collaboration that became known as Abused in Scouting. The lawyers' mass tort marketing campaign took off in early 2019, a year before the bankruptcy was filed. They signed up dozens of clients and then hundreds and then thousands,[9] positioning Kosnoff and Abused in Scouting as major players in the bankruptcy when proceedings formally commenced in 2020.

Or so he thought.

Long on candor and short on diplomacy, Kosnoff can be aggressive, blunt, and abrasive—and those are the *nicer* things that people say about him. His detractors sketch him as a kind of mad-bomber barrister, intent on blowing up the bankruptcy and maybe himself along with it. The "largest pedophile ring on earth" is how he has often described the Boy Scouts of America, calling for its demise: "Let 'em fail—burn it to the ground."[10]

As the bankruptcy played out, it was inevitable that Kosnoff would get sideways with the opposing lawyers. And with his allies. And with the judge presiding over the case. Much of the friction grew out of his contention that the Boy Scouts' 250-plus local councils—with their wealth of assets—should be debtors in the bankruptcy right alongside the BSA, which sought to shield them from creditors by insisting that they were legally separate and financially independent of the national organization.[11]

By June 2020, four months into the proceedings, Kosnoff had grown "extremely frustrated" with James Stang, the bankruptcy counsel to the nine-member Tort Claimants' Committee appointed by the US Trustee to represent the fiduciary interests of all the abuse survivors. Kosnoff pushed the TCC, unsuccessfully, to bring in a top litigator to file a lawsuit within the bankruptcy to force the consolidation of the local councils' assets with the BSA's, a move that would sweeten the settlement pot and, by extension, fatten the plaintiffs' lawyers' contingency fees.[12]

By then, Kosnoff also was unhappy that Abused in Scouting represented thousands of claimants but had only one of nine members on the TCC, and he contended that his group's "voice and bedrock principles" were being ignored. He fired off an email intended to elicit other plaintiffs' lawyers' support for his position, explaining that it was time for Abused in Scouting (AIS) to flex its collective muscle in the case. "Here is the message," he wrote. "We control 80% of the claims, i.e., our coalition controls the case. We are not going to do anything to help grease the gears for Stang and the dimwits, including speeding up the insurance analysis....Nothing happens until AIS says so."[13]

Unfortunately for Kosnoff, he had hit "reply all" to a previous email and misfired his "Stang and the dimwits" message to many more people than he had intended, including Stang, who did not take kindly to it. Months later, Stang and the committee cited the email in opposing a request to participate in mediation sessions by the newly formed Coalition of Abused Scouts for Justice, of which

Kosnoff and his Abused in Scouting cohorts were members. The TCC accused Kosnoff and AIS of "scheming to exert their control over the entire process, including over the mediators, BSA, Local Councils and the Tort Claimants Committee" and said they were attempting to manipulate the process to unduly benefit their clients.[14]

Kosnoff defended the email as merely advancing his clients' best interests, and he disputed the committee's contentions. But by then a deep rift had opened between Abused in Scouting and the TCC. Kosnoff cut his ties to the committee and, having also grown disenchanted with the Coalition of Abused Scouts for Justice, withdrew from that group in September 2020, as did Andrew Van Arsdale's AVA Law firm. When the third member of Abused in Scouting, the Eisenberg, Rothweiler firm, refused to leave the Coalition of Abused Scouts for Justice that November, Kosnoff stopped communicating with it directly.[15] All of that created an awkward situation in which the three Abused in Scouting firms were estranged and giving divergent legal advice to the seventeen thousand clients they shared, while still legally bound to cooperate with one another in the bankruptcy.

As 2020 gave way to 2021, mediation continued among the Boy Scouts, its insurers, the TCC, and the Coalition of Abused Scouts for Justice, which had been let into the settlement talks after Kosnoff was shut out. The goal, as it had always been, was to come up with a reorganization plan that could be approved by "an overwhelming majority" of the 82,200 claimants and sent to Judge Laurie Selber Silverstein for confirmation. In the meantime, Kosnoff took to Twitter to roast his adversaries.

At various times throughout the bankruptcy, he labeled other plaintiff lawyers "mass tort mobsters," "cowards and capitulators," and "shysterettes." He blasted the attorney for one insurer as "all hat and no cattle" and "a total windbag," calling him a poseur and likening him to "the big shot who sits down at the $25,000 poker table with 50 bucks in his pocket pretending he's a 'player.'" He scorched the Coalition of Abused Scouts for Justice as "nothing but a bunch of fast-buck-sell-out-the-victims-mass-tort-lawyers who don't give a spit about the survivors" and said he was ashamed that he had once been allied with them.

Some of his harshest tweets targeted Judge Silverstein, whom he referred to as "Her Royal Highness" or simply LSS. "Silverstein is so deep in the BSA's old kit bag, I'm amazed she can even breathe," he wrote in one tweet, while calling for her job in another: "She should resign now....She is a shill for the Boy Scouts of America. She's draped in a black robe under the authority of the U.S. Constitution. Impeach."

NEGOTIATIONS CONTINUED BEHIND THE scenes for most of 2021 but jumped into the headlines that fall, when Rothweiler, a cofounder of the Coalition of Abused Scouts for Justice and Kosnoff's estranged Abused in Scouting colleague, trumpeted a tentative settlement of nearly $1.9 billion.[16] Rothweiler's group, which billed itself as a coalition of twenty-six law firms representing some sixty thousand claimants, endorsed a plan that included contributions of $250 million from the BSA, $600 million from its local councils, $787 million from insurer Hartford Financial Services Group, and $250 million from the Church of Jesus Christ of Latter-day Saints. A committee representing Catholic Church interests did not immediately pony up settlement money but dropped its opposition to the plan and agreed to support Scouting through at least 2036, giving a vital boost to the BSA's flagging membership. "The $1.887 billion is just the start," Rothweiler said at the time. "Current negotiations with insurers and chartered organizations are ongoing, and if appropriate settlements can be reached, they will add significant funds to compensate survivors."[17]

Even at $1.9 billion, the compensation fund would yield only a fraction of the eighty-two thousand claims' true value, according to its opponents, who contended that the plan let the Boy Scouts and other responsible parties off the hook for billions more in damages from decades of abuse. "We can't tell you how to vote, but we can frankly tell you this plan sucks," Doug Kennedy, a cochair of the TCC, which had estimated total damages from the abuse at more than $100 billion, said at a virtual town hall meeting for survivors that October 7. "That's not the legal term. That's the survivor term—it sucks."[18]

Rothweiler pushed back, urging the 82,200 claimants to approve the plan when voting opened later that month. "Voting yes will promptly deliver a degree of justice and closure to survivors, and accountability for the Boy Scouts organization," he said, blasting the TCC as "the Party of No: no settlements, no reorganization plan, no guaranteed payment for survivors whose cases are beyond the statute of limitations, and no end in sight to the litigation."[19]

Kosnoff was livid, calling the $1.9 billion proposal "chump change," and "an utter fucking betrayal" of BSA abuse survivors.[20] With voting set to begin, he banged out a five-page "Dear Clients" letter slamming Rothweiler and urging them to vote no, reiterating his reasoning: the settlement amount was insufficient; the local councils weren't paying their fair share; the Hartford had agreed to contribute only a fraction of the amount its Boy Scouts coverage required; Rothweiler and his coalition were more interested in a quick payday than the equitable treatment of survivors; and other, nonsettling insurers were certain to appeal, potentially delaying resolution of the bankruptcy for years.[21]

"The BSA Plan is a disaster for all survivors," he wrote. "We can only go up from here. But first survivors have to send a resounding message to all of the players that the BSA Plan is a big fat **NO!**"

At that point in October 2021, Kosnoff and the Tort Claimants' Committee were on the same side in opposing the plan. Because he lacked the email capability to send out his letter to thousands of Abused in Scouting clients on short notice, Kosnoff asked John Lucas, a Pachulski Stang attorney working for the committee, to distribute it for him. Lucas edited it and had an assistant loop out the letter, which was intended only for AIS clients. But it also inadvertently landed in the inboxes of seven thousand claimants represented by other lawyers. Once again, a misfired Kosnoff communiqué would roil the BSA bankruptcy, as it had with his "dimwits" email. It was a major screwup, and it created bafflement and hard feelings—and so much heat that Stang, who apparently had not read the letter before it had gone out, was compelled to distance his law firm and the Tort Claimants' Committee from it in a full-throated retraction. "My firm and the TCC sincerely apologize for any confusion caused by our distribution of Mr. Kosnoff's email and letter," he wrote. "We acknowledge that the email and letter contain inflammatory language directed against another lawyer and his law firm. The TCC does not agree with, and affirmatively rejects, all statements made by Mr. Kosnoff in his email and letter about the Eisenberg firm and Mr. Rothweiler."[22]

The errant letter was more than embarrassing; it wound up as the subject of a hearing in Silverstein's court, and it cost Stang's law firm $2 million to quell concerns that it could taint the voting process. To resolve the matter and quiet the uproar, Pachulski Stang pledged to contribute $1.25 million to the reorganized Boy Scouts of America's Youth Protection program and to forgo $750,000 of its legal fees.[23]

In December 2021, with balloting coming to a close, the $1.9 billion settlement offer was increased to about $2.7 billion, with an additional $800 million contributed by another major Boy Scouts insurer, Chubb Ltd.'s Century Indemnity Company. The TCC now estimated that the settlement would work out to an average of

$28,000 per claim, although some plaintiffs would receive more and others less, depending on several factors including the severity of the abuse and where and when it had occurred. Stang's partner Richard Pachulski, another of the TCC attorneys, contrasted it to a recent settlement with USA Gymnastics and the US Olympic & Paralympic Committee, which had agreed to pay some five hundred sexual abuse survivors about $800,000 each. "In a case involving horrific abuse of children, average payments of approximately $28,000 do not begin to justly compensate survivors," he said.[24]

After two contentious months of voting, the offer failed to garner "overwhelming support"—defined as 75 percent—from the nearly fifty-four thousand abuse survivors who cast ballots. A preliminary tally released in early January 2022 showed that the reorganization plan had been approved by 73 percent, just shy of what was needed for Silverstein to confirm it.[25] With a confirmation hearing already scheduled, the prospects for her approval looked bleak. But just a month after the failed vote was announced, negotiators for the BSA and lawyers for thousands of sexual abuse survivors struck a deal that allowed the reorganization plan to move forward.

The Tort Claimants' Committee, which had adamantly opposed the plan just a few months earlier, now supported it. Among other things, the revised plan called for the BSA to hire a "youth protection executive" to oversee policy and training, filling a vacancy created by the recent departure of Youth Protection director Michael Johnson, who would go on to blast the BSA's continuing "high risk of child sexual abuse" and accuse it of resisting meaningful reform. The new plan also called for updating existing criminal background checks, enhancing sexual abuse incident reporting, and "exploring opportunities" to make public the Volunteer Screening Database, formerly known as the perversion files, and share it with other youth-serving organizations. The "exploring opportunities" language was guaranteed to spark skepticism among those who had watched the BSA refuse to share its blacklist and fight for decades to shield it from the public. Still, the modifications sufficed to win the support of the Tort Claimants' Committee. "With these accomplishments in hand, the TCC recommends that all survivors vote to accept the new and improved plan," cochair Humphrey said.[26]

The Coalition of Abused Scouts for Justice had already supported the initial offer and hailed the enhanced one as "a positive outcome" of intense negotiations, for which Rothwell claimed credit. It also teased the prospect of more money for survivors. "The $2.7-billion compensation fund built through the Coalition's efforts during 2021 isn't the end," it said. "We are committed to working together with our plan partners to further grow the fund, ensure key protections for current and future Scouts and make certain that survivors receive the best and fastest avenue to closure, as well as fair, just and equitable compensation."[27]

The Boy Scouts of America also supported the plan, while remaining "steadfast in our commitment to equitably compensate survivors and preserve the mission of Scouting."

Staunch opponents continued to say that the proposal had shortchanged the 82,200 claimants and was unconstitutional because it had provided nondebtor releases to chartering organizations and other potentially liable parties. The US Trustee, the bankruptcy system's government watchdog, also objected on the grounds that the plan violated the due process cause of the Fifth Amendment and that its third-party releases were not authorized by the bankruptcy code. Although in a distinct minority, Kosnoff and some other plaintiffs' attorneys stood fast against the plan.

"The new agreement does not change the fundamentally illegal nature of the third-party releases contemplated under this plan," said Gilion Dumas, a Portland, Oregon, attorney with sixty-seven clients with claims. Lawyers for more than seventy former Scouts from Guam also objected, their claims mostly stemming from abuse by the late Reverend Louis Brouillard, a scoutmaster and Catholic priest. He "was one of the most prolific child sexual abusers in scouting history," according to the Guam claimants' attorneys, who opposed releasing the Archdiocese of Agana from liability.[28]

In the end, the reorganization plan's backers prevailed when enough "no" voters changed their ballots to "yes." On March 11, 2022, just days before Silverstein would convene a confirmation hearing, the Boy Scouts announced that 85 percent of the votes were now in the affirmative column, enough to constitute the "overwhelming" majority needed to move forward. "We are enormously grateful to the survivor community whose bravery, patience, and support has been instrumental in the formation of this plan," BSA National Chair Dan Ownby said. "Our hope is that the confirmation of the BSA's Plan will bring this financial restructuring process to an end, providing survivors with equitable compensation, and the closure they deserve while preserving the mission of Scouting for young people for years to come."[29]

But as Ownby and the 82,209 claimants would soon discover, the longed-for happy ending would not come anytime soon. The plan still had to be confirmed by Silverstein and subsequently blessed by a federal judge. Then it would likely face legal challenges and appeals. The gulf separating sexual abuse survivors from the compensation they sought remained wide and deep.

CHAPTER 17

INTO THE MATRIX

This is a case about trust—or more accurately—lack
of trust. Boys and their families put their faith
in a lionized institution, which failed many
of them. These boys—now men—seek and
deserve compensation for the sexual abuse
they suffered years ago. Abuse which has had
a profound effect on their lives and for which
no compensation will ever be enough.

—US Bankruptcy Court Judge Laurie Selber Silverstein[1]

On March 14, 2022, Judge Silverstein commenced the BSA's
Chapter 11 confirmation hearing. She conducted it like a civil
trial, without a jury. It included three weeks of evidentiary hearings, with twenty-six witnesses testifying live or by written declaration or video deposition. More than a thousand exhibits were

admitted as evidence, and Silverstein heard six days of closing arguments by lawyers.

Interspersed with testimony about legal precedents, financial calculations, and objections to the plan were some revealing glimpses of the very human considerations that had figured into the proceedings.

Methodist bishop John Schol spoke to the complexities of addressing sexual abuse that, in many cases, had occurred decades earlier. The United Methodist Church, one of the Boy Scouts' largest chartering organizations, pledged $30 million to the settlement trust fund—to be raised by passing the collection plate at services around the country—and agreed to try to drum up $100 million more. Schol, who led the Methodist effort, noted the difficulty in such fundraising, especially in congregations that bore little resemblance to when the abuse had occurred decades earlier. He cited the example of a New Jersey congregation that in the 1970s had had several hundred worshippers, all of them white.

"Today, in that urban community, that congregation has about 25 or 30 worshippers, African-American, Caribbean, Filipino," he said; "it's just a completely different congregation today."[2] In other words, a congregation of that size and composition, with limited resources and no direct connection to sexual abuse that had occurred long before, might be less than enthusiastic about paying the wages of past sins.

Other witnesses included abuse survivors who had objected to the often modified reorganization plan in its early iterations but now supported its passage. They included Doug Kennedy, a cochair of the Tort Claimants' Committee.

Kennedy's dad died when he was a year old, so he never got to know him. His mom, raising him as a single parent, nudged him into Scouting so he could have positive male role models. He joined Troop 25 in Totowa, New Jersey, and among other activities went to summer camp at Ten Mile Scout Reservation in New York State. He was sexually abused there on multiple occasions. "I can close my eyes and I can put myself back in that place," he said. "So that's why I try and keep busy, because my demon is I don't ever want to have any down time where those memories start creeping back into my head."[3]

Like so many other survivors, he had kept his abuse to himself for decades, telling no one, including his family, about what had happened. By middle age, he could no longer keep his traumatic experience bottled up and reported his abuser to the police; they told him there was nothing they could do because the statute of limitations had long since expired.[4]

Then in 2019, a ray of hope appeared. The New York State Assembly, in step with lawmakers in California and other states, passed the Child Victims Act, a "look-back" law that allowed sexual abuse victims to sue their attackers—and the institutions responsible for them—regardless of when the wrongdoing had occurred. Kennedy, a Virginia Wesleyan University professor of sport and recreation professions, remembers watching a streamed feed of the vote from his office and breaking down in tears when the bill passed. Right after it was signed into law, he sued the camp director and the Boy Scouts, and he was looking forward to his day in court when the BSA filed for bankruptcy protection in February 2020, slamming the brakes on his lawsuit and hundreds of others pending or planned at the time. "So waiting all those years and then saying, 'Great, now I'm going to be able to bring suit,' and then here we are in bankruptcy," he said.[5]

Kennedy's hope that bankruptcy would yield a swifter resolution than a civil lawsuit evaporated as weeks turned into months and months into years. In the meantime, he was tapped to serve as an unpaid volunteer on the Tort Claimants' Committee, an experience that would prove to be as dismaying as it was eye-opening and, at times, rewarding. He participated in more than three hundred meetings and spent an "unbelievable" three years plus tangling with a "multiheaded monster": the BSA and its local councils, insurance companies, mass tort lawyers, and others, all within the confines of bankruptcy laws that seemed ill equipped to deal with sexual abuse claims and appeared to favor the Boy Scouts.

"There's a real feeling of 'I was abused as part of a bad system,' and here I find myself in another system—a system that is set up to accommodate or look after the needs of the Boy Scouts, not of the survivors," Kennedy said. After the first public bankruptcy hearing, in which the judge said that the primary goal was to preserve the Boy Scouts' mission, Kennedy said his phone had exploded with calls from exasperated survivors. "'What's going on here?' they had asked. 'We are the reason the Boy Scouts went into bankruptcy. Why is the judge so concerned with them and their mission?'...So again, it's this feeling among myself and [other] survivors of just 'Here we are, getting abused by another system.'"[6]

Kennedy's dogged, grind-out-a-deal advocacy for the survivors and the backlash he and the TCC encountered, including being blasted on Twitter as sellouts by a former ally, Kosnoff, took a heavy toll on him and his family. "I haven't hidden the fact that the reason I never owned a gun was because in my darkest days, when I'd had enough of this—" he said, not finishing his thought out loud. Fortunately, he added, he "had come out on the other end, being able to just sort of look at the comedy of the whole thing."

Kennedy and the TCC had flatly rejected early versions of the BSA's confirmation plan and advised the survivor claimants to vote it down. By the time Silverstein convened the confirmation hearing in March 2022, however, he and the committee had come around to endorsing the plan, which now held $2.7 billion in the trust fund and mandated stronger child protection measures, a key element for many survivors, for whom "It's not all about the money" actually meant just that. Among other things, Scouting parents would now be able at least to find out how many complaints of sexual abuse had been filed involving their sons' troops, a big upgrade from the BSA's customary near-total lack of transparency on abuse issues.

What's more, Kennedy testified at the confirmation hearing, there was no good alternative: if the plan failed to pass, there would be no resolution at all for many survivors. Some would be time barred from ever suing their abusers or the BSA, and others would not live long enough to endure a protracted do-over of the bankruptcy. "They do not have a viable path forward," he said of the aging survivors, noting that some 12,400 claimants were over seventy and 2,200 of those were older than eighty. One of his fellow members on the Tort Claimants' Committee was pushing eighty and driving for Door Dash to make ends meet.[7]

In a 281-page opinion issued in late July 2022, Silverstein signaled her tentative approval of the reorganization plan, walking through the testimony and evidence presented during the month-long hearing that spring. She, too, said it was time. "Many survivors have been waiting for thirty, forty, or even fifty years to tell their stories and receive a meaningful recovery," she wrote. "This Plan makes that happen."[8]

The plan had drawn thirty-nine objections during the hearing, most significantly from insurance companies that declined to settle and refused to contribute to the victims' trust fund. Among other things, their lawyers argued, the procedures for distributing the funds would strip insurers of their contractual rights to defend against claims. They also contended that mass tort lawyers had ginned up thousands of bogus claims through aggressive marketing campaigns, presenting testimony from two expert witnesses that substantial numbers of them must have been fraudulent. How else to explain that an organization that had faced 275 lawsuits and 1,400 pending claims prebankruptcy was now staring up at a stack of 82,209 claims in Chapter 11? Silverstein was not persuaded.

"I reject out-of-hand the notion that this explosion of claims, alone, could be grounds for denial of confirmation," she wrote. "There is no doubt that plaintiff lawyers aggressively advertised for clients which, apparently, is nothing new. But there is no evidence from which I can conclude that plaintiff firm advertising alone created the groundswell of Direct Abuse Claims."[9] She went on to say that the huge jump in the numbers might also be attributed to the BSA's own ad campaign, which had been designed to reach 96 percent of all American men over the age of fifty and encouraged those who'd been molested in Scouting to file claims. She also noted that there now was less stigmatization and a "more welcoming environment" for abuse survivors to come forward, thanks in part to the #MeToo movement, as well as the "solace in numbers" in the company of thousands of victims. "In any event, having presided over these cases, I have no doubt that insurers would have made the same objections had there been 'only' 50,000 proofs of claim or 25,000 proofs of claim, or 10,000 proofs of claim," she wrote.[10]

The judge also swatted down other significant objections by deeming third-party releases of potentially liable parties to be lawful and appropriate, with one major exception: she refused to approve the BSA's $250 million settlement with the Church of Jesus Christ of Latter-day Saints. Silverstein said it was unclear that the evidence supported it and that it "stretches third-party releases too far" by providing the Mormon Church more protection from liability than was warranted. She sent the Boy Scouts back to the drawing board to resolve that issue and some other points. The BSA returned with yet another modified reorganization plan, which excised the Mormons' $250 million contribution, clearing the way for abuse survivors to sue the LDS Church outside the bankruptcy and shrinking the settlement fund to $2.46 billion.

On September 8, 2022, Silverstein confirmed the plan. It was one big step closer to resolution for the eighty-two thousand survivors. But they were still a long, long way from the finish line.

More than a dozen of the Boy Scouts' insurers wasted no time in trying to kill Silverstein's confirmation order in the crib. Those "nonsettling" insurers, including AIG and Liberty Mutual, petitioned the US District Court, which must sign off on bankruptcy proceedings, to reverse her order. They cited the same objections Silverstein had previously overruled, accusing mass tort lawyers of drumming up clients with flimsy or no proof of their claimed sexual abuse. Clients they said would have gone begging for legal representation, if not for the bankruptcy, were now pointing "an 82,000-claim bazooka" at insurers, creating "hydraulic pressure" on them to pay up.[11]

"This Court should not tolerate the bad faith, collusion, and outright fraud by claimants' counsel that resulted in this plan—conduct to which BSA was, at best, willfully blind," the insurers' lawyers wrote in their opening brief, alleging again that the plan would gut their contracts with the BSA, including provisions that allowed them to contest claims. "This is an abuse of the bankruptcy system and a violation of the insurers' right to due process."[12]

Plaintiffs' lawyers denied wrongdoing and said they were surprised there hadn't been even more claims filed, considering the scope of the Boy Scouts' sexual abuse problem, which spanned generations and all geographic regions and socioeconomic strata. What everyone could agree on was that the insurers' legal challenge would mean even more delay for the eighty-two thousand claimants, who had been on hold for two years already. And it left unanswered the $2.46 billion question: "Who will get how much and when?" As survivor Christopher Meidl might say, "Simple question, complicated answer."

If and when a federal judge approved the reorganization, most of the claimants would face a new gantlet of trust distribution procedures. The reorganization's main feature is something called the Claims Matrix, which assigns a range of damages values to everything from "sexual abuse—no touching" at $3,500, to "anal or vaginal penetration by adult perpetrator" at $2.7 million, with various other abusive sex acts and their assigned dollar amounts in between.[13] But those amounts would vary according to where the abuse had occurred; claims filed by survivors in states with inflexible statutes of limitation would receive far less than those in states such as California and New York that had passed look-back laws.

Some 30 percent of the eighty-two thousand claims alleged penetration, the top-of-the-scale offense. One law firm alone filed five thousand such claims, which if paid at the maximum amount would have exhausted the entire fund just for that group of survivors. So despite Silverstein's legal finding that the bankruptcy would compensate "100 percent" of the claims, it was unlikely that huge numbers of plaintiffs would receive the maximum $2.7 million.

Thousands of claimants would avoid the Matrix altogether by opting for an "expedited distribution" of $3,500, which required minimal scrutiny for approval. Also known as the "quick-pay" or "no-questions-asked" option, it was likely to be favored by those who could show little proof of their abuse or could not remember exactly when or where it had occurred or who had done it. Before the bankruptcy, legions of former Scouts now in their sixties, seventies, and eighties had never told anyone of their abuse, much less kept detailed records of it or even so much as noted their troop numbers and leaders' names. They would clearly face challenges in the vetting process to come. Nearly 7,400 selected the quick-pay option when voting on the plan in late 2021. Some of their attorneys urged them to reconsider.

"I strongly encourage you to revote and not select this option," Andrew Van Arsdale said in a video message to his Abused in Scouting clients. "Under our analysis, your claim should likely be worth more than $3,500. But because you selected that box on your ballot for the expedited, quick-pay $3,500, that is all that you would be able to receive....If you elect that option, that's it. You're stuck at that number." And so were their lawyers. There's no doubt that Van Arsdale had his clients' best interest at heart, but it's worth noting that Abused in Scouting—like other plaintiffs' attorneys working on a contingency basis in the bankruptcy—stood to take a 40 percent cut of any award, be it $3,500 or much more than that.

Claimants who did not choose the quick-pay option would have to complete a detailed questionnaire, signed under oath, and submit any records related to their abuse. They also had to agree to undergo an interview and oral or written testing, if requested by the settlement trustee. Among other information, the questionnaire requested the details of the abuse, the abuser's name or physical description, where and when the abuse had occurred, and how old the victim had been at the time.

Submissions that received initial approval would then go to settlement trust administrator Barbara Houser, a retired Texas bankruptcy judge appointed to oversee and divvy up the compensation fund.[14] She and her staff would assess the claims on the basis of several criteria, deciding among other things whether abuse had occurred and if it and the perpetrator had been directly related to Scouting activities. Houser would be required to consult with a seven-member advisory committee of claimants' attorneys and would also have access to Boy Scout records such as membership rolls, staff rosters, lists of volunteers, and the perversion files.

Claims that did not meet the vetting criteria would be rejected. Those that did would then be run through the Matrix and the award amounts adjusted up or down by scaling factors such as duration or frequency of abuse, the long-term harm it had caused, and whether the abuser was a repeat offender or a family member. Added weight would be given to claims naming abusers who showed up in the perversion files—indicating that the Boy Scouts were or should have been aware of them—and those who had had multiple victims.

Claimants who disagreed with the settlement trustee's award determination could seek reconsideration. Those who believed their cases would garner more than the Matrix maximums if pursued in civil court could request an independent review by a "neutral third party"—a retired judge—but would have to pay an up-front fee of $20,000 to cover the costs and then prove that the BSA was negligent.[15] That pay-to-play feature was disdained by many survivors, and questioned by some bankruptcy experts. "The idea that claimants have to pay $20,000 up front is a bit offensive to me," said Melissa Jacoby, a law professor at the University of North Carolina at Chapel Hill, who was closely monitoring the BSA bankruptcy. "Really, you're asking people to self-fund that process in a way that people don't do when they're in the civil justice system—you don't pay a court $20,000 to review your case."[16]

After Silverstein gave the confirmation a thumbs-up, the obviously relieved BSA said that it was "enormously grateful to the survivor community" for its part in shaping the reorganization plan. But with various legal challenges pending, how long it would take for the case to be fully resolved and closed was sheer conjecture, with estimates ranging from months to years to never.

The process took a huge step forward in late March 2023, when US District Judge Richard Andrews rejected insurers' arguments and upheld Silverstein's confirmation order.[17] The BSA emerged from bankruptcy a month later, on April 19, and the reorganization plan became effective immediately. Insurers then appealed Andrews's decision to the US Court of Appeals for the Third District, a move that probably will delay full payment to survivors but is unlikely to unravel the BSA's reorganization.

"Our hope is that our Plan of Reorganization will bring some measure of peace to survivors of past abuse in Scouting, whose bravery, patience and willingness to share their experiences has moved us beyond words," said Roger Mosby, the bespectacled, avuncular chief Scout executive, president, and chief executive officer, issuing the latest in a string of formal statements that rang hollow to many of the 82,209 claimants.[18] The BSA also put out an open letter to abuse survivors, signed by Mosby and the top two volunteer leaders, National Chair Dan Ownby and National Commissioner Scott Sorrels. "To the thousands of lives that were forever changed when individuals took advantage of Scouting programs to abuse innocent children—we have failed you and we are truly, deeply sorry," it read. "On behalf of the BSA and all who hold the future of the mission close to our hearts, please know: we will make it our lives' work to honor you. Your courage will serve as a permanent reminder of the obligations we have to all young people in our programs."

Three and a half years into the proceedings, as the Boy Scouts' fees for attorneys and other professionals marched past $300 million in billings, survivors had yet to collect a single penny. Some doubted that they ever would.

"As a 74-year-old Scout…who was abused at age 11, I have come to the conclusion that none of us who have managed to survive the ordeals these so-called leaders put us through will ever see a dime," a survivor named Mike wrote in an online conversation with other claimants.[19] He had just been diagnosed with amyotrophic lateral sclerosis, Lou Gehrig's disease, and figured that his "sell-by date" would arrive long before the check to compensate him for the abuse he had suffered six decades earlier. "There was no one to help us then, and nothing has changed," he said. "God Bless everyone. I probably won't live to see the outcome but I wish all of you the best, and try to heal if you can."

In September 2023, three years and seven months after the BSA filed its bankruptcy petition, the first payments to abuse survivors began to trickle out, with $150,000 divvied up among fifty-seven claimants who'd filed for the expedited $3,500 option.[20] Those checks would continue to be issued every two weeks until all of the "no-questions-asked" minimum payments were made. When the 75,000 survivors waiting for larger settlements would see any money was still anyone's guess. By February 2024, a full four years into the bankruptcy, the settlement trust had made 3,166 payments totaling just $7.9 million.

CHAPTER 18

AFTER THE BANKRUPTCY

A s the Boy Scouts of America emerges from bankruptcy, its future is anything but certain. Its finances have been depleted by more than half a billion dollars in legal fees and contributions to the $2.46 billion settlement fund, its membership has been decimated, and its reputation is battered, perhaps beyond repair. At this point, the question is not simply "Can the Boy Scouts survive?" but "Should it?"

For their part, BSA officials insist that the 113-year-old organization *must* survive, contending that its emergence from Chapter 11 will allow it to fulfill its commitment to fairly compensate sexual abuse survivors and preserve Scouting's character-building mission—promises it made when it filed its bankruptcy petition in February 2020. With its reorganization confirmed, the BSA said it now looks to "its bright future of delivering timeless values and meaningful experiences" that unite communities and families and help young people become the best versions of themselves. "We firmly believe that Scouting is needed now more than ever, and we are dedicated to providing character development and

values-based leadership training to youth across the country,"
said Roger Mosby, the BSA's chief Scout executive, president, and
CEO.[1] He also touted the BSA's existing "multi-layered safeguards,"
including mandatory youth protection training for all volunteers
and employees.

Mosby and other BSA leaders are eager to turn the page on an
era marked not just by bankruptcy and a sex abuse scandal but also
bloody culture war battles over whether to admit gay youth members and adult leaders, girls, and people who don't believe in God.
When the smoke cleared, the gays and girls were in; the atheists
and the agnostics were out, as always; and 425,000 Mormon Boy
Scouts had decamped, likely never to return. Factor in the competition for American kids' time and attention from organized sports,
video games, and TikTok, and the net effect of all of those things,
along with the negative impacts of the covid-19 pandemic, is that
the BSA today is a shadow of its formerly robust self.

Youth membership, which had once verged on 5 million,
plummeted to 762,000 during the pandemic.[2] It rebounded somewhat before leveling off at just over 1 million in 2023,[3] still a nearly
80 percent drop from its zenith in the early 1970s. In another sign
of flagging participation, the BSA's 2023 National Jamboree drew
only fifteen thousand Scouts, including about three thousand
girls, a stark contrast to better times for the quadrennial event
billed as "360-degrees of fun, friends and fellowship."[4] The 2023
attendance was far off the forty thousand who had showed up at
the last Jamboree, in 2017, before girls were eligible to attend, and
less than one-third of the fifty-one thousand who had converged
on the southern California hills overlooking the Pacific for the
star-studded 1953 event.

The BSA's anemic participation numbers don't tell the whole
story, of course, but they are symptomatic of looming problems
for its bottom line. "Membership is the heart of the organization,"
said Brian Whittman, a BSA restructuring adviser. "It drives the

membership revenue to the organization, it drives supply sales and indirectly impacts virtually every other line" on the BSA's profit-and-loss statement.[5] To his point, from 2019 to 2020, the BSA's gross revenues plunged from $394 million to $187 million.[6] On the upside, even after liquidating scores of valuable properties through the bankruptcy, the national organization has net assets of nearly $1 billion and its roughly 250 local councils still hold some $3.3 billion in real estate,[7] including camps and office buildings around the country. Among the most treasured of these are four High Adventure bases in New Mexico, Minnesota, West Virginia, and the Florida Keys, which offer wilderness programs and training and together can bring in as much as $50 million a year in fees.[8]

While finances are key to the viability of "the company," as some insiders refer to the BSA, its future also hinges on other, less tangible factors.

Michael Bellavia, the CEO of HelpGood, a social impact marketing and communications agency that works with nonprofits and "purpose-driven" organizations—i.e., those with a cause—predicts that the Boy Scouts of America will have a long uphill climb to recover the trust and respect it has lost in recent decades. Bellavia, who is in his midfifties and based in Los Angeles, remembers his time in Scouting in Queens, New York, in the 1980s for its camaraderie and a sense of personal achievement as he racked up merit badges, "always striving for more" en route to earning his Eagle Scout rank.

Putting aside his personal fond memories, Bellavia said it will take nothing less than "a wholesale re-envisioning" of the BSA to salvage its damaged brand. He likened the process to redesigning a home from the studs up: You look at the bones and see what's worth keeping. You figure out which of your "statement pieces" will work in the new space and you jettison the rest, with an eye toward creating a place where you, your family, and your friends will feel safe and comfortable. The same formula holds for remaking Scouting, he said: everything must be reconsidered, including its membership policies, its leadership, its communications strategy, the Scout Oath, the Scout Law, the BSA itself. The usual trappings might no longer be necessary.

"I think at its core, there always will need to be a place for young people to commune with others, to explore themselves, to explore other cultures, to explore areas that they may want to pursue later in life, to really learn some kind of strong values," Bellavia said. "Can you get that through Scouting? Yes. Can you get that through some church activity? Yes. Can you get that from just playing on the street with your close friends? Yes."

He would like to see Scouting survive, he said, but only if it is "radically changed."[9] Others have echoed that sentiment, including some who love Scouting but believe the BSA itself has become too toxic to save.[10]

Tim Miller is among them. As far back as Miller can remember, he wanted to be a Boy Scout. His maternal great-grandfather organized one of the BSA's earliest troops, in Danbury, Connecticut, and his grandmother's house was filled with Scouting memorabilia, including an old wagon in the garage that had been used to shuttle the boys on camping trips a century ago. As a boy, Miller was drawn to Scouting because it seemed like "a pathway to manhood" and because by the time he was six or seven his parents had split and he was growing up in Manchester, Connecticut, in a house without a dad. He joined Cub Scouts, moved up to Boy Scouts, and eventually became an Eagle Scout. Along the way, he was repeatedly sexually assaulted by an adult summer camp staffer. "The final incident of my abuse was a pretty violent rape," said Miller, who was a teenager in the early 1990s when it occurred.[11]

Miller told no one about it at the time, but the abuse took a toll. He failed classes, had disciplinary problems, and was smoking marijuana and drinking as he went from a 4.0 grade point average in high school to barely graduating. But he stuck with Scouting and finally reported his abuse to Scouts officials several years later when he was a member of the staff at the same camp where he had been raped and the man who had assaulted him was working there again. The alleged abuser was fired after getting drunk on the job in a sting operation conducted by some of the Scouts, Miller said, and he was booted eventually from Scouting and placed in the Ineligible Volunteer files because of the abuse allegations.

By then, Miller was doing his best to move on with his life, albeit with considerable baggage from his abuse. The most palpable harm, he said, was in the form of long-simmering anger and an unrequited desire for "justice or retribution or vengeance" that manifested itself as lashing out at authority figures. "Anybody ever told me to do anything, my answer was always 'Fuck you!'" he said.

Despite his anger issues, Miller managed to build an impressive résumé. At Dartmouth he earned a bachelor's degree in physics and a master's in engineering. He landed a dual appointment at the Harvard School of Engineering and the Boston Museum of Science, a job that involved "taking the cool things they were doing in scientific research" and presenting them to the public through speaking engagements, podcasts, and shows. He started a consulting business to teach communications and public speaking skills to scientists, attended the University of Southern California film school, with his tuition paid by the National Science Foundation, and eventually joined the faculty of the University of Connecticut as a professor of digital media.

He also had two failed marriages and struggled with alcohol abuse and a sense of shame for having been unable as a teenager to fight off his much older and stronger attacker, blaming himself for not having prevented his rape. For years he kept quiet about it, before sharing it with a girlfriend and ultimately deciding to file a claim in the BSA bankruptcy. More than three years into the Chapter 11 proceedings, he was not optimistic about the outcome, at least not about survivors' prospects of being equitably compensated. But he also was not ready to give up on Scouting.

"The experiences that I had in Scouting, the exposure to a broad swath of Americans...was absolutely the most important sort of formative thing that happened to me in my young life," he said. "And yeah, as a result of my Boy Scout experience, I have some symptoms of post-traumatic stress disorder, have a problem with authority, have some very painful memories of some very bad things that happened to me. But I also have a commitment to seeing the wrong set right. I have the courage and the confidence to stand up tall and tell my story in a loud and clear voice to everybody who's willing to hear it, and I got *that* from the Boy Scouts, too."

Miller draws a clear distinction between the Scouting movement, which he describes as a grassroots, volunteer-driven effort that is all about patriotism, community, self-reliance, and respect for the natural world, and the Boy Scouts of America, which he calls a "corrupt, inward-looking, insular, incestuous organization" that turned a blind eye to decades of child sexual abuse and has never been fully held to account. He is all for keeping the former and scrapping the latter, starting with pushing for revoking the congressional charter that grants the sole propriety of all things Scouting, including the word Scouting, to the Boy Scouts of America. That would force the BSA to compete with other youth-serving groups that could oversee Scouting, including one made up "of like-minded former Scouts and volunteers who would be better stewards" that he hopes to organize himself.

"The end of the bankruptcy proceeding is not the end of the battle," he said.

*   *   *

IF THE BSA IS to survive, Bellavia and others say, it will need new leadership and fresh ideas. Chief Scout Executive Mosby, who took the helm in December 2019, arrived just ahead of the bankruptcy and stayed long enough to see the BSA emerge from it before announcing his plans to retire. (He was replaced in November 2023 by Roger Krone, a former Boeing executive and retired CEO of the information technology firm Leidos.) Mosby, a former energy industry executive, was an unusual pick for the BSA's top job in that he was not a longtime, up-through-the-ranks professional Scouter.[12] But like his predecessors, whose keep-it-in-the-family orientation had contributed to decades of institutional insularity, he routinely chose to communicate with the outside world in sound bite–quality prepared statements.

Repeated requests to interview Mosby for this book dragged on for nearly a year and were met with a string of "We're working on it" excuses by BSA's chief spokesman, Scott Armstrong, who delayed and dissembled and never delivered on promises to make available the chief Scout executive and/or other top officials.[13] After reassurances that the BSA had "agreed to work with" the author and was lining up a list of requested interviews, Armstrong abruptly pulled the plug and said that no one from the organization would sit for an interview after all; he cited the BSA's unhappiness with two documentary films that had no connection to this book or its author, and he insisted that any questions about the BSA and its history had already been "asked and answered to death in the public discourse." In lieu of interviews, he offered to take written questions—and then he and BSA leaders answered none of them, declining to reflect on the past or share their vision for the future.[14]

On the infrequent occasions when top BSA officials have publicly addressed Scouting's sexual abuse problem, some have demonstrated a glaring lack of awareness about it. In 1990, the late Joseph Anglim, one of three national Scout officials who jointly made all of the decisions about adding suspected sexual abusers to the blacklist, said he had never read *any* of the Ineligible Volunteer files, even though he had put his personal stamp of approval on hundreds of them over the years.[15]

In November 2018, nine members of Congress, led by California Democrat Jackie Speier, wrote to Chief Scout Executive Michael Surbaugh to express their concerns about the BSA's lobbying against proposed laws in several states, including New York, Michigan, and Georgia, to ease the statutes of limitation on sexual abuse lawsuits.[16] The legislation would clear the way for victims of past sexual abuse to sue for damages in cases that otherwise would be time barred. The BSA's resistance, Speier and her fellow lawmakers wrote, had troubling implications for the safety and well-being of former, current, and future Boy Scouts:

> Historically, BSA has instilled in countless boys and young men the importance of service to others and the self-confidence to succeed in academics and the workforce. Former Boy Scouts have gone on to become leaders in their communities and beyond, thanks to the values that BSA taught them. That is why reports of coverups of child sexual abuse, and efforts to stymie the passage of state laws to allow survivors to seek justice, is so concerning from an organization that prides itself on building young people up.[17]

Surbaugh wrote back that he and other BSA officials cared deeply about victims of child sexual abuse and were outraged that some individuals had taken advantage of Scouting to harm children. But he flatly rejected Speier's allusion to the BSA's institutional cover-ups of abuse: "We want you to know that at no time in our history have we ever knowingly allowed a sexual predator to work with youth."

Anyone who had read the publicly available perversion files, which detail multiple instances of abusive leaders being put on probation or otherwise knowingly allowed back into the ranks, only to abuse again, knew that Surbaugh's assertion was not true.

It would take Surbaugh five months to do it, but in May 2019 he retracted his statement in a follow-up letter to Speier. "I have reviewed information that now makes clear to me that decades ago BSA did, in at least some instances, allow individuals to return to Scouting even after credible accusations of sexual abuse," he wrote. "I am devastated that this ever occurred. On behalf of BSA, I sincerely apologize to the individuals affected by this practice."[18]

Despite the BSA's best efforts to cast sexual abuse as a historical problem, concerns about protecting today's Scouts have continued to dog the organization. So have persistent headlines about current and former scoutmasters molesting boys, engaging in child pornography, or committing suicide when the allegations came to light. In September 2023, Michigan attorney general Dana Nessel announced a continuation of a criminal investigation into sexual abuse in Scouting that she had launched in 2021 after learning that thousands of the bankruptcy claimants were from her state. In its first two years, her investigation yielded one conviction, of a former suburban Detroit Scout leader who had molested two boys twenty years earlier.[19] "Regardless how much time has passed, or how difficult the circumstances of a case may be, I am committed to seeing abusers held accountable for their crimes," Nessel said.[20]

One prominent ex-BSA insider, ex–youth protection director Michael Johnson, has also sounded alarms. Johnson served in that post from mid-2010 to December 2020. He contends he was terminated for refusing to keep quiet about the continuing peril faced by boys and girls in the organization. "The truth is clear: No child is safe in Scouts BSA programs," he wrote in October 2021. "The institution, as it stands today, continues to be a HIGH-RISK organization for child sexual abuse, due to the accessibility and opportunity the program presents to a range of sex offenders."[21]

Johnson, who said he had refused the BSA's offer of "a large sum of money" to sign a nondisclosure/nondisparagement agreement when he left, blasted the organization's "disregard for needed safety reforms" and its "decades-long lack of transparency" in an open letter to Congress seeking a "robust congressional investigation and hearings into the past, present, and continuing high risk of child sexual abuse" in the youth group.[22] Two years later, he had not backed off those contentions, which had drawn no response from anyone in the House or Senate. "I hoped, but I did not expect one," he said. "The Boy Scouts have a lot of clout in Congress, a *lot* of clout."[23]

Marci Hamilton, the CEO of the nonpartisan academic think tank CHILD USA, which has advocated for lifting sex abuse statutes of limitation, is not surprised that Johnson's letter to lawmakers went unanswered: Congress has never been keen on investigating child sexual abuse in religious organizations, she said, and Scouting enjoys the same hands-off treatment. Not only is the BSA "a very powerful organization," she added, but "unlike any other child-serving organization, it is Congress's baby" by virtue of its charter.

"With the Boy Scouts, what you have is all of these lawmakers saying, 'Oh, well, this is the flag, American pie. This is America,'" Hamilton said. "And besides, they were all members of the Boy Scouts. So the notion that you should end the Boy Scouts and then reconfigure it? In a perfect world, that would make sense, but politically, it's absolutely impossible."

FORTY-SIX SUMMERS HAVE COME and gone since Doug Kennedy was sexually abused at a Boy Scout summer camp in New York, but he is still coming to grips with what happened. Married and the father of two sons, it took him decades to tell anyone about his abuse, but when he did, he went all in. He sued the Boy Scouts and his alleged abuser, who was the camp director. When his lawsuit was put on hold by the bankruptcy, he took up the fight for himself and 82,208 other survivors by accepting an appointment to the official Tort Claimants' Committee that represented their collective interests.

Kennedy, a Virginia college professor, thinks the BSA has faced too little scrutiny for its handling of a sexual abuse problem that has devastated so many lives. Like Johnson, he has called for a congressional investigation. Since 2018, House and Senate panels have held hearings into the sexual abuse of 250 girls and women by the predatory team doctor of the US women's national gymnastics team, Dr. Larry Nassar, along with the failure of sports governing bodies and the US Olympic Committee to protect athletes. It was only right to do that, Kennedy said, but he wonders why the abuse claims of eighty-two thousand former Boy Scouts don't warrant the same attention from legislators. "There has to be an investigation to find out who knew what, who's at fault and why didn't they do anything about it," he said. "You want to keep your congressional charter? At the least, that should be a requirement."[24]

Kennedy is often asked if he would put his own kids into Scouting. He did, and his older son became an Eagle Scout. But his boys never left his sight. When they went to camp, he went with them, serving as a volunteer Scout leader. He was able to do that because, as an educator, he had summers off, creating an opportunity to keep a close watch on his kids that most Scout parents don't have. Although pleased by the new child safety measures built into the bankruptcy settlement, Kennedy has concluded that there is no way to protect all of the boys and girls in the program all of the time. The incidence of sexual abuse has declined dramatically since he was in Scouts, he said, but some children will continue to be victimized every year.

"Let's just say it's a hundred. If we were going to form an organization and say, 'We're going to be a national organization, it's going to serve a lot of kids, but a hundred are going to get abused, are you cool with that?' The answer would probably be no," he said. "We know that we can't guarantee their safety, and I can't endorse the organization because of that. It breaks my heart."[25]

There was no joy in his voice.

POSTSCRIPT

TEN YEARS ON

APRIL 2024

A decade after the landmark trial in Portland, Kerry Lewis was living in Wellington, Colorado, an hour north of Denver on I-25, the last town before the Wyoming state line. He had moved there to start over, once again, after a year in El Paso, Texas, and a couple of posttrial, drug-related run-ins with the law in Klamath Falls, Oregon. When I caught up with him by phone, he had recently turned fifty. He and his Siberian husky, Koda, were living with his brother Heath and had found Wellington, population 8,500, much to their liking. "I don't have an extravagant life, but I have a nice full life," he says. "The people here are really friendly. The whole town knows my dog."[1]

Lewis, who testified at trial about his substance abuse, has always been candid about his struggles with booze and meth. He said he'd "used to be a big alcoholic" but no longer drinks to excess and for years has limited his intake to one or two drinks when he goes out. "The drug part is a different issue, which comes and goes," he says. "Right now, I've been clean for two years, but I've had years when I've not been clean. Sometimes I fall down and have to get up and dust myself off again. Sometimes it's the biggest triumph of my life, and sometimes it's the biggest screwup of my life. It depends on that year and what I do with myself when that happens: Am I going to keep on going and get high for another ten years? Or am I going to do something else?"

He makes no promises, except not to be a burden on anyone else. With his settlements from the Boy Scouts and the Church of Jesus Christ of Latter-day Saints, he bought an annuity and made some other investments, so that he never has to worry about being broke and dependent on anyone. These days, he spends much of his free time racing four-wheel all-terrain vehicles in motocross events in the West, sometimes competing alongside his daughter, Samara, who is in her twenties and, according to her dad, inherited his feisty personality.

Lewis doesn't dwell on his childhood molestation by Scout leader Timur Dykes but says it has affected him in several ways, all of them common among survivors of child sexual abuse. He does not trust men and has difficulty maintaining long-term relationships with women. And he has long had trouble with authority figures, not so much with the cops who arrested him in Klamath Falls—he had grown up there with many of them—as with his teachers in school and his bosses when he was younger and in the workaday world.

"I don't dig too deep into it," he says. "There is a lot of stuff I don't remember and a lot of stuff I would rather not remember. It has had an effect on my life, but I have tried to make it not my whole life. It's not who I am. It's part of who I am, not the whole me. It doesn't define me." Lewis, who as a kid thought of himself as "the best in the West" at everything, says he has carried that can-do attitude into adulthood. "I like being the underdog, and I like proving people wrong when they say I can't do something. I don't get scared. I don't back down. You can't intimidate me. I don't care how big you are. You can stand there looking down on me, I don't care. I say, 'Let's go.'"

Dykes, the former Scout leader who admitted to abusing seventeen boys before he molested the eleven-year-old Kerry Lewis, was sentenced in 1994 to eighteen years in prison after three convictions for sex crimes involving children. A public records search identified his most recent address as a community center in downtown Portland that provides showers, laundry facilities, and a mail drop for a mostly homeless clientele. I had hoped to connect with him in person on a trip there in the spring of 2022 but had to settle for a couple of phone conversations later. Dykes, then just shy of his sixty-sixth birthday, was polite but guarded and reluctant to speak at length or in detail. He has, by his own reckoning, led a rocky life since he left prison in 2005.

"It's done and over with, best not to think about it," he says of the Lewis trial and its aftermath. "Life goes on hold, and it doesn't matter how hard you try: You have trouble getting anything done. It never goes away." He says that "many lies were told" about him, in news accounts and elsewhere, but he didn't deny his culpability: "The worst thing is not being able to help the ones you hurt. I can't get anywhere near them." I asked him how he thought he might now help those he had victimized years earlier. "If nothing else, maybe sit down and apologize," he says, "and let them know it wasn't anything they did. It wasn't their fault. I hope someday they may forgive me."[2]

Dykes cut short our first call, and when I followed up a couple of weeks later, he declined to say much more. "I thought about it, and I don't see much good coming from it," he says. "It really doesn't matter what I say or do; eventually it would hurt those kids more, and I don't want to hurt them any more. I've done enough."

Lewis hasn't seen or spoken with Dykes in the nearly forty years since his abuse, and he is remarkably sanguine about the man he once trusted and idolized. People always ask him what he would do if their paths crossed. "He's gotten what he deserved: He's got no future, no family. What else could I take away from him?" he asks. "He's already broken, so I'd leave the guy alone. Let karma or God deal with him."

He is less forgiving of the Boy Scouts, which he says is "supposed to be helping kids, not throwing them to the wolves." When recalling the trial in Portland, he immediately thought of the Scouts' attempt to cut a last-minute deal before the case went to the jury. He says that BSA lawyers offered him a million dollars, but he turned it down. "Win or lose, I was not turning back and not backing down. They called me a liar, when it was them who lied about everything. Their story always changed, but mine never did. I said, 'You know what, let's see what the jury has to say about this.' I was all about getting it done and getting it done right so that this shit doesn't happen to anybody else."

The jury awarded him $1.4 million for his pain and suffering, then hit the BSA with $18.5 million more in punitive damages, much of it earmarked for a state victims' compensation fund. The amounts were later renegotiated in a confidential settlement of the claims of all six of the original plaintiffs in the lawsuit, preempting an appeal by the Boy Scouts. Twelve years later, Lewis says he still believes the BSA put protecting its image above maintaining the safety of kids in its program, kids who might have been spared long-lasting effects. "It makes me wonder how my life would be different now," he says. "Maybe I'd be happily married by now and have a great family and a great job, you know? I don't know, and I don't dwell on it. Why live in the past and the what-ifs? There's now and there's tomorrow, and that's what matters."

WHEN I SPOKE WITH Richard "Skip" Leifer, one of the fifty-one thousand Boy Scouts who had attended the 1953 Jamboree in southern

California, he was very much the walking, talking personification of what Scouting professes to be, at its best.

Like many Boy Scouts of his era, he is convinced that the organization helped make him a better man and a better father. Four generations of his family have been involved with Scouting. His dad, who was a local Scouts official in Madison, Wisconsin, helped build a 1,200-square-foot log cabin out of salvaged creosote-soaked telephone poles with a massive rock fireplace, where troops held meetings and social gatherings. Located in Firemen's Park in nearby Maple Bluff, the structure is listed on the National Register of Historic Places.[3]

Skip joined Scouting in 1946, as an eight-year-old Cub, and was still actively participating more than five decades later, as a merit badge counselor, when he stepped down in 2000. He is a Vigil Honor member of the Boy Scouts' Order of the Arrow, Scouting's national honor society. Well into his eighties, he still keeps a trove of Jamboree mementos and other Boy Scout memorabilia, including an autographed photo of Norman Rockwell painting a self-portrait, which is simply inscribed, "To Skip from Norman."

"I think Scouting molded my life, along with my Christianity and having very strong, loving, disciplining parents," he says. "The fact that my dad was involved in Scouting meant a lot to my brother and me, because we could go camping together. As my son grew up, it was the same thing: I went camping with him. It became a generational thing. We've got a tradition of Eagle Scouts and Scouting in our family, and it's been a vital part of our lives. I can still recite the Scout Law and the Scout Oath. I still have a uniform hanging in my closet."[4]

Yet even Leifer is pained by what has happened to his beloved Boy Scouts in recent years, including the damaging sex abuse scandal. He believes that the BSA made a major mistake by admitting gay leaders, a move that helped cost it more than 425,000 members, or nearly 20 percent of its total roster, when the Mormon

Church cut its long-standing ties with the organization in 2018. But he also holds the BSA responsible for not protecting boys from sexually abusive scoutmasters. He had first heard about it as a kid, when his dad had talked about the "red ball files," the confidential folders on suspected abusers, each marked with a red dot.

"It angers me and it saddens me that somebody didn't do more about it," he says. "And now it's costing the Boy Scouts the farm, for all intents and purposes. It's sad. It's like losing an old friend."

In the 114 years since its founding, The Boy Scouts of America has weathered the Great Depression, two world wars, the social and political upheaval of the 1960s, and the burgeoning culture conflicts of the 1980s. Yet the BSA now finds itself in its most precarious position ever, after a tumultuous twenty-five-year stretch exacerbated by a massive sexual abuse scandal, controversy over whether to admit gay Scouts and leaders, and a costly four-year-long bankruptcy that is still playing out.

Roy Williams, Robert Mazzuca, Wayne Brock, Michael Surbaugh, and Roger Mosby—the chief Scout executives who presided over the past two and a half decades, and the decimated membership and depleted finances that came with them—are all retired or deceased. One can only wonder what Robert Baden-Powell, William D. Boyce, Ernest Thompson Seton, Daniel Carter Beard, James West, and other founders and early leaders of the worldwide and US Scouting movements would think of their modern-day successors' stewardship of the BSA and its prospects for the future.

In November 2023, Mosby retired and was replaced as president and chief Scout executive by Roger Krone,[5] an Eagle Scout, aerospace engineer, former Boeing executive, and retired CEO of Leidos, a $15 billion defense, aviation, and information technology company. Krone has promised to move Scouting forward by enhancing its appeal to Digital Era Scouts while emphasizing the BSA's traditional offerings of camping, hiking, and adventure. "That means we need to meet the kids where they are," he said. "Get them off the couch, get them away from their small screen device, get them outdoors."[6]

He has also touted an emphasis on inclusivity, saying he hopes to diversify both youth membership and adult leadership ranks. "Everyone is welcome in scouting," he said, apparently *not* referring to atheists and agnostics, who remain personae non gratae.[7]

Krone inherited an organization whose membership has plummeted, dragging down its finances. Even so, he optimistically predicts that in five years, BSA's youth membership will double from its current level of about 1 million. But even at twice its current size, it would be less than half as large as in its heyday fifty years ago.

The new chief Scout executive has had little to say publicly about the BSA's sexual abuse scandal, beyond parroting what has become a boilerplate apology expressed by Mosby and other leaders: "BSA is really deeply sorry for the pain endured by survivors and for the lifelong impact it has on them and their loved ones." Nor has he laid out any sweeping new plans for child protection programs. But he has promised to bolster those already in place. "Scouting is safer today than it ever has been," he said. "And under my leadership, we will continue to evolve and improve our program so that we have the safest youth program that we can possibly have."[8]

He clearly has work to do to convince skeptics, including the Most Reverend Larry Silva, the bishop of the Diocese of Honolulu, which encompasses all of Hawaii. In January 2023, Silva wrote in a letter to "Pastors and Principals" that Catholic congregations in his state would cut ties to Scouting because of the sexual abuse allegations:[9]

Unfortunately, given the liability issues and our dissatisfaction with the BSA's cooperation on the issue, we will no longer allow parishes and parish schools to charter a BSA unit, nor will BSA units be allowed to meet in our facilities.…

It is important that we continue to minister to our youth in various ways, but continuing our longstanding relationship with BSA has become more of a liability than we judge it prudent to bear.

Silva left the door open to reconsidering his decision. But whether Krone has the vision and the skill to win back Silva's support and to achieve his stated goals for the BSA remains an open question.

It is one thing to get kids off the couch; it is quite another to convince millions of American parents to entrust their children's safety to the Boy Scouts.

AFTER CARL MAXWELL, JR., and four of his buddies mustered the courage to end Scoutmaster Rodger Beatty's months of abuse, he quit the troop and tried to put the ordeal behind him. By then his grades were suffering, he'd become more and more withdrawn emotionally, and on top of it all, he was dealing with being a gay teenager in the small, conservative town of Newport, Pennsylvania. But Carl and his parents and his older sister, Cindy, remained close and were determined to get back to life as they had known it before Beatty had turned it inside out.

"We basically just picked our lives back up as kids and a family and just got on with the rest of our lives," Carl told me in the summer of 2022, shortly after his sixtieth birthday and forty-six years since Beatty had sexually abused him and other members of Troop 222. It had been a long and twisting ride, by turns fun and bumpy, that had begun in Newport and taken him to Philadelphia and New York before circling back to his hometown, where he lives with his elderly, widowed mom for about half of the year. He spends the rest of the year in Rehoboth Beach, Delaware, a seaside resort town known for its boardwalk and its welcoming of gay residents and tourists.

Carl graduated from Newport High School in 1981 and then enrolled at the Art Institute of Philadelphia, intent on becoming a professional photographer after getting a 35-millimeter camera for Christmas one year and discovering the joy of making pictures. His academic pursuits were short lived. After growing up in a town of fewer than two thousand residents, Carl felt "like a kid in a candy store" in Philly, a relative metropolis that beckoned him to an active social life. He was all of eighteen, too young to be a bartender, so he got a job as a barback at a gay nightclub, where he struck up a relationship with a guy who was a year older and operated the lighting system there.

The two hit it off and headed for New York, where the 1980s club scene was thriving.[10] Disco might have been dead by then, but glitzy dance spots lived on, including Visage, the Upper West Side nightspot where Carl and his partner, Joseph, landed for a while. It featured velvet walls, American Realist sculptures, Lalique crystal masks, and hot-and-cold water features including a skating rink with a synthetic ice surface and a pool with live mermaids. Carl, who tended bar there, was quick to note that "life got a little crazy" during his nine years in Manhattan: too much alcohol, too many drugs, too little self-restraint.[11]

"I'm not bragging, but there wasn't a drug that came across me that I did not at least try," he says. "I'm thankful to God that the only one that stuck with me was weed. I have no regrets for trying all that stuff, but I always knew when enough was enough." By the time the '90s rolled around, Carl had had enough of New York and of his sometimes turbulent relationship with Joseph. When he told his friends he was heading back to Newport, they said, "'Oh, my God, you're going back to that, you know, that tiny little town after being in New York for nine years?' I said, 'It's fine. It's home.'...After all that craziness, I was ready to go home."

Carl tended bar in Harrisburg, a half-hour drive from Newport. He worked there for about eight years before being sidelined by pulmonary hypertension, a progressively debilitating form of high blood pressure that affects vessels in the lungs, decreases blood oxygen levels, and can lead to heart failure. Even walking short distances can be difficult.

When I first met him in 2012, Carl had retired on a medical disability. A couple of years later, his financial picture brightened a bit when, like a multitude of other former Scouts who had read their abusers' perversion files, he sued the Boy Scouts of America and settled for an undisclosed sum. It was sealed by a confidentiality agreement but was enough to pay for new siding and a remodeled bathroom for his mother's duplex in Newport and a Nissan Juke for himself, the only new car he's ever owned. "I'll never have a chance to do something like that again," he says.

Carl and I have stayed in touch over the years, which is pretty unusual in my experience as a reporter. I rarely keep up, long term, with people I've written about, except maybe to check once in a while if the really bad actors are still in prison or have popped up in polite society again. Time passes, fresh stories push the older ones to the back of the line, life moves on. The difference with Carl, I think, is that our first encounter, when he invited me into his kitchen, made such a deep and lasting impression on me. I was amazed that anyone could have such a vivid recollection of even the smallest details of something that had happened thirty-six years earlier, no matter how good or how bad it had been. That first interview still stands as one of the most memorable in my forty-five years as a journalist. These days, I enjoy shooting the breeze with Carl on politics and lighter topics. We're pals, albeit mostly long distance.

Rodger Beatty, the scoutmaster who abused Carl and his chums in Troop 222, did not recover from his stroke and died in November 2012. A decade later, his friends are still mystified by the allegations against a man they knew as a University of Pittsburgh assistant professor and public health researcher and educator. "It certainly didn't sound like the Rodger Beatty I knew, but of course I know that is a common response in a situation like this. It's just hard for me to fathom," says David Korman, a Pitt colleague. He recalls Beatty speaking of his affinity for Scouting but never hinting at anything in his past as nefarious as child sexual abuse. And as far as Korman knows, no new allegations have surfaced in the years since his death. "It is just one of the great mysteries, which I will go to my grave with," he says.[12]

Ten years on from our first conversation, Carl's memories remain vivid. More difficult, it seems, is trying to measure the full impact that awful experience had on his life. Did it trigger the excessive drinking and drugging of his young adulthood? Maybe. Did it make him warier of people who tried to get closer to him? Probably. It certainly took a toll on his relationships with men. "Do I think any of that changed my life? It's hard to say," he said, mulling it over for a bit. "I probably lean more toward 'no'—other than the trust issue. It is probably the reason I don't have a partner now, because of a lack of trust. The handful that did get close to me, there have always been those trust issues."

He still does not trust the Boy Scouts of America. "From what I know of everything, if I had a kid that age, I don't think I'd let him in Scouts."

ACKNOWLEDGMENTS

On My Honor is made possible thanks to the help and cooperation of many people, but especially Carl Maxwell, Kerry Lewis, Tim Miller, Doug Kennedy, and all of the abuse survivors who shared their stories. More than a thousand of them detailed their experiences in letters to bankruptcy judge Laurie Selber Silverstein. I read them all.

My colleagues Jason Felch, Julie Marquis, and the data team at the *Los Angeles Times* were critical partners during initial reporting for this book.

Attorneys from both sides who were involved in the many lawsuits described in this story were invaluable. They include Gillion Dumas, Tim Kosnoff, Paul Mones, Christopher Hurley, Andrew Van Arsdale, Michael Rothschild, Chuck Smith, and Mark Honeywell. Thanks also to Mike Johnson, who once was the Boy Scouts of America's director of youth protection, and James Dale, who sued the BSA after it banned him because of his sexuality.

Sociologist and child sex abuse expert David Finkelhor helped me understand that critical aspect of this story, and experts Lynn LoPucki and Melissa Jacoby helped me navigate the world of bankruptcy law.

I'm indebted to the researchers and writers whose work preceded mine, including historians Benjamin Rene Jordan and David

Scott, as well as authors Patrick Boyle, Tim Jeal, Bill Hillcourt, David Macleod, and Michael Rosenthal. In addition, I'm grateful for the cooperation of Margaret Malarkey and Timur Dykes, and the help of public servants in courts and local governments who aided my research, especially those in Cayuga County, New York.

Martin J. Smith offered helpful feedback in the final stages of writing *On My Honor*, which was championed by my literary agent, Becky Sweren at Aevitas Creative Management, and shepherded into print by Colin Dickerman, Amar Deol, and Ian Dorset, my editors at Grand Central Publishing. I'm grateful to them all.

Finally, I've dedicated this book to my wife Christina Christensen, for her undying love, unwavering support, and for putting up with me for more than forty years.

NOTES

CHAPTER I: FEUDING FOUNDERS AND THE BOY PROBLEM

1   Theodore Roosevelt, *African Game Trails* (New York: Charles Scribner's Sons, 2017 [1910]), 406.

2   Robert Peterson, "The Man Who Got Lost in the Fog," *Scouting*, October 2001, https://scoutingmagazine.org/issues/0110/d-wwas.html.

3   Harriet Hughes Crowley, "The Great African Safari Bust," *American Heritage*, April 1975, https://www.americanheritage.com/great -african-safari-bust.

4   David Scott, "Is the Boy Scouts of America Really Founded upon a Myth?," *International Scouting Collectors Association Journal*, September 2016, 26–29.

5   Crowley, "The Great African Safari Bust."

6   W. D. Boyce, publisher's letter to readers, *Chicago Ledger*, August 26, 1891.

7   "The Scout Law," *Washington Herald*, April 21, 1910, and other US newspapers.

8   Janice A. Petterchak, *Lone Scout: W. D. Boyce and American Boy Scouting* (Rochester, IL: Legacy Press, 2003), 49–64.

9   Crowley, "The Great African Safari Bust."

10 Petterchak, *Lone Scout*, 60.

11 Crowley, "The Great African Safari Bust."

12 Petterchak, *Lone Scout*, 6.

13 Petterchak, *Lone Scout*, 62.

14 David C. Scott and Brendan Murphy, *The Scouting Party: Pioneering*

and Preservation, Progressivism and Preparedness in the Making of the Boy Scouts of America (Red Honor Press, 2010).

15   Interview with David Scott.

16   Petterchak, *Lone Scout*, 66.

17   "Urban and Rural Population: 1900 to 1990," US Census Bureau, October 1995, https://www2.census.gov/programs-surveys /decennial/tables/1990/1990-urban-pop/urpop0090.txt.

18   "City Life in the Late 19th Century," Library of Congress, https:// www.loc.gov/classroom-materials/united-states-history-primary -source-timeline/rise-of-industrial-america-1876-1900/city-life -in-late-19th-century/, and related articles in "U.S. History Primary Source Timeline."

19   Michael Schuman, "History of Child Labor in the United States— Part 1: Little Children Working," *Monthly Labor Review*, U.S. Bureau of Labor Statistics, January 2017, https://doi.org/10.21916 /mlr.2017.1.

20   Julia Grant, "A 'Real Boy' and Not a Sissy: Gender, Childhood, and Masculinity, 1890–1940," *Journal of Social History*, Summer 2004, https://www.academia.edu/860371/A_Real_Boy_and_Not_a _Sissy_Gender_Childhood_and_Masculinity?email_work_card =thumbnail.

21   Tim Jeal, *Baden-Powell: Founder of the Boy Scouts* (London: Hutchinson, 1989), Kindle ed., 182–84.

22   Mpho Manaka (née Maripane), "'From Spoiling Natives to No Work, No Food': Food Scarcity and the Controversy of Food Rations During the South African War," *Scientia Militaria: South African Journal of Military Studies* 50, no. 3 (2022): 1–23, https://www.ajol.info /index.php/smsajms/article/view/239406/226268. Other historical accounts describe Baden-Powell's unequal rationing of food to whites and Blacks during the siege of Mafeking; some dispute that he intentionally starved Black residents.

23   Michael Rosenthal, *The Character Factory* (New York: Pantheon Books, 1984), 30.

24   Jeal, *Baden-Powell*, 218.

25   Piers Brendon, *Eminent Edwardians* (London: Martin Secker & Warburg, 1979). The author noted that "Many a 'joyous little dodge' with which he attempted to outwit the enemy smacked more of the showman's stage than the theater of war [and] were not altogether effective" (227–28).

26   Jeal, *Baden-Powell*, 252.

27 William Hillcourt with Olave, Lady Baden-Powell, *Baden-Powell: The Two Lives of a Hero* (Houston: The "Green Bar Bill" Hillcourt Foundation, 1964), 182. Olave Baden-Powell was married to Robert Baden-Powell from 1912 until his death in 1941.

28 Jeal, *Baden-Powell*, 302.

29 Rosenthal, *The Character Factory*, 30.

30 Robert Baden-Powell, *Aids to Scouting, for N.-C.O.s and Men*, rev. ed. (London: Gale & Polden, 1915 [1899]), 6.

31 Robert S. S. Baden-Powell, *Scouting for Boys* (London: Horace Cox, 1908), Kindle ed., 189.

32 Jeal, *Baden-Powell*, 384–86; Hillcourt and Baden-Powell, *Baden-Powell*, 264–71.

33 Jeal, *Baden-Powell*, 570. Jeal noted, "For many men, Baden-Powell among them, the Boy Scouts provided the blessed illusion of reclaiming their stolen childhoods."

34 Keir B. Sterling, "Seton, Ernest Thompson (1860–1946), Naturalist, Artist, Writer, and Lecturer," American National Biography, February 2000, https://www.anb.org/display/10.1093/anb/978019860 6697.001.0001/anb-9780198606697-e-1301495?rskey=LUq1rl &result=1; various other sources.

35 William Farley, "Troops and Tribes: Masculinity, Playing Indian, and the Social Politics of Ernest Thompson Seton's Expulsion from the Boy Scouts," *Connecticut History Review* 60, no. 2 (Fall 2021): 54–66.

36 Edgar M. Robinson, "Recollections of the Early Days of the Boy Scouts of America," Springfield College, 1934, Springfield College Archives and Special Collections.

37 D. C. Beard, *The Boy Pioneers: Sons of Daniel Boone* (New York: Charles Scribner's Sons, 1909), v, vi, 4.

38 "Robinson, Edgar M.," Springfield College, https://springfield.as .atlas-sys.com/agents/people/554.

39 David I. Macleod, *Building Character in the American Boy: The Boy Scouts, YMCA, and Their Forerunners, 1870–1920* (Madison: University of Wisconsin Press, 1983), 48.

40 Robinson, "Recollections of the Early Days of the Boy Scouts of America."

41 Robinson, "Recollections of the Early Days of the Boy Scouts of America."

42 Petterchak, *Lone Scout*, 69.

43 Robinson, "Recollections of the Early Days of the Boy Scouts of America."

44   Theodore Roosevelt himself had called Native Americans "reckless, revengeful, [and] fiendishly cruel" in a speech in 1886. "I don't go so far as to think that the only good Indians are the dead Indians, but I believe nine out of every ten are, and I shouldn't like to inquire too closely into the case of the tenth," he said. Hermann Hagedorn, *Roosevelt in the Bad Lands*, vol. 1 (New York: Houghton Mifflin Company, 1921), 355.

45   "Boy Scout Leaders Dine Baden-Powell," *New York Times*, September 24, 1910, https://timesmachine.nytimes.com/timesmachine /1910/09/24/105092110.html?pageNumber=8.

46   *Waldorf-Astoria Hotel Interiors: Designation Report*, NYC Landmarks Preservation Commission, March 7, 2017, http://s-media.nyc.gov /agencies/lpc/lp/2591.pdf.

47   Michael Pollak, "Answers to Questions About New York," *New York Times*, October 21, 2011, https://www.nytimes.com/2011/10/23 /nyregion/peacock-alley-in-the-waldorf-astoria-remembered.html.

48   Benjamin René Jordan, *Modern Manhood and the Boy Scouts of America: Citizenship, Race, and the Environment, 1910–1930* (Chapel Hill: University of North Carolina Press, 2016), 23.

49   "How Boy Scouts Began," *New-York Tribune*, September 24, 1910, 16.

50   "Boy Scout Leaders Dine Baden-Powell," *New York Times*, September 24, 1910, https://timesmachine.nytimes.com/timesmachine /1910/09/24/105092110.html. A slightly different version of the comment was included in William D. Murray, *The History of the Boy Scouts of America* (New York: Boy Scouts of America, 1937).

51   "Tell of Boy Scout Begging," *New York Times*, December 14, 1910, https://timesmachine.nytimes.com/timesmachine/1910/12/14 /104956314.html?pageNumber=9.

52   Ernest Thompson Seton, *Boy Scouts of America: A Handbook of Woodcraft, Scouting, and Life-Craft* (New York: Doubleday, Page & Company, 1910), xi, xii.

53   Dan Beard, *The Book of Camp-Lore and Woodcraft* (Garden City, NY: Garden City Publishing, 1920), 157, 242–43.

CHAPTER 2: AMASSING POWER

1   "James E. West Chief Scout Executive," Boy Scouts of America Order of the Arrow, https://oa-bsa.org/history/james-e-west-chief-scout -executive.

2   Edward L. Rowan, *To Do My Best: James E. West and the History of the Boy Scouts of America* (privately published, 2005), 14.

3   Michael Schuman, "History of Child Labor in the United States—
     Part 1: Little Children Working," *Monthly Labor Review*, U.S.
     Bureau of Labor Statistics, January 2017, https://doi.org/10.21916
     /mlr.2017.1.

4   Matthew A. Crenson, *Building the Invisible Orphanage: A Prehistory
     of the American Welfare System* (Cambridge, MA: Harvard University
     Press, 1998), 8; Dale Keiger, "The Rise and Demise of the American
     Orphanage," *Johns Hopkins Magazine*, April 1996, https://pages.jh
     .edu/jhumag/496web/orphange.html.

5   Rowan, *To Do My Best*, 13–22; William D. Murray, *The History of the
     Boy Scouts of America* (New York: Boy Scouts of America, 1937), 42.

6   David Macleod, *Building Character in the American Boy: The Boy
     Scouts, YMCA, and Their Forerunners, 1870–1920* (Madison: Universi-
     ty of Wisconsin Press, 1983), 131.

7   Edgar M. Robinson, "Ernest Thompson Seton: An Unforgettable
     Personality," 1941, Springfield College Archives and Special Collec-
     tions.

8   Ernest Thompson Seton, letter to Daniel Carter Beard, November
     26, 1915, in "Correspondence and Notes on the Early History of the
     Boy Scouts of America," Springfield College Archives and Special
     Collections.

9   Beard, letter to Seton, November 30, 1915, Springfield College Ar-
     chives, https://cdm16122.contentdm.oclc.org/digital/collection
     /p15370coll2/id/4361/rec/3.

10   William Farley, "Troops and Tribes: Masculinity, Playing Indian, and
     the Social Politics of Ernest Thompson Seton's Expulsion from the
     Boy Scouts," *Connecticut History Review* 60, no. 2 (Fall 2021): 54–68.

11   Edgar M. Robinson, "Recollections of the Early Days of the Boy
     Scouts of America," April 1934, Springfield College Archives and
     Special Collections.

12   "Seton Still Insists on Quitting Scouts," *New York Times*, December
     6, 1915, https://timesmachine.nytimes.com/timesmachine/1915
     /12/06/105049228.html?pageNumber=6.

13   "West Says Seton Is Not a Patriot," *New York Times*, December 7,
     1915, https://timesmachine.nytimes.com/timesmachine/1915
     /12/07/issue.html.

14   "'Resigned'—Seton; 'Was Dropped'—West," *Brooklyn Daily Eagle*,
     December 6, 1915.

15   Rowan, *To Do My Best*, 45. Beard said, "I don't know where he got
     the title, but it seems to have offended everyone, because he is not

a scout in the sense that they are and hence has not the ability to be the Chief Scout. He is essentially the secretary, and a good one."

16 Robert W. Peterson, *The Boy Scouts: An American Adventure* (New York: American Heritage, 1984), 64.

17 Rowan, *To Do My Best*, 43–44.

18 James E. West, "The Real Boy Scout," *Leslie's Illustrated Weekly*, January 4, 1912, 448.

19 BSA position statement, 1991: "We believe that homosexual conduct is inconsistent with the requirement in the Scout Oath that a Scout be morally straight and…clean in word and deed." The revised 1993 version stated, "The Boy Scouts of America has always reflected the expectations that Scouting families have had for the organization. We do not believe that homosexuals provide a role model consistent with these expectations. Accordingly, we do not allow for the registration of avowed homosexuals as members or as leaders of the BSA." Quoted in *Boy Scouts of America v. Dale*, 530 U.S. 640, June 28, 2000, https://supreme.justia.com/cases/federal /us/530/640/.

20 Murray, *The History of the Boy Scouts of America*, 54.

21 Don Rittner, "Boy Scouts, Detachable Collars, and a Troy Connection?," December 30, 2020, https://drittner.wordpress .com/2021/01/.

22 "Catholics Join Boy Scouts," *New York Times*, August 26, 1912, https://timesmachine.nytimes.com/timesmachine /1912/08/26/104905616.html?pageNumber=8.

23 "Excerpt from the Declaration of Religious Principle," BSA Youth Application, 2023: "Only persons willing to subscribe to this Declaration of Religious Principle and to the Bylaws of the Boy Scouts of America shall be entitled to certificates of membership." https:// filestore.scouting.org/filestore/pdf/524-406.pdf.

24 "The History of the MCD: The Great Flood of 1913," Miami Conservancy District, Dayton, Ohio, 2005, https://web.archive.org /web/20070311004644/http://www.miamiconservancy.org/about /1913.asp.

25 "Boy Scouts Aid the Relief Work," *Dayton Daily News*, April 13, 1919.

26 "Scouts Respond to Needs of Flood Sufferers," *Osage* [Oklahoma] *Chief*," April 25, 1913.

27 "Congressional Report in Support of Act to Incorporate Boy Scouts of America," House Report no. 130, 64th Cong., 1st Sess., February 7, 1916, quoted in "Charter and Bylaws of the Boy Scouts of Ameri-

ca, as Amended Through May 2021," https://www.scouting.org
/wp-content/uploads/2021/09/Charter_Bylaws_May2021.pdf, v.

28 Boy Scouts of America National Council Bylaws, June 15, 1916, sec.
3 states, "That the purpose of this Corporation shall be to promote,
through organization and cooperation with other agencies, the ability of boys to do things for themselves and others, to train them in
Scoutcraft, and to teach them patriotism, courage, self-reliance, and
kindred virtues, using the methods which are now in common use
by Boy Scouts." Quoted in "Charter and Bylaws of the Boy Scouts of
America, as Amended Through May 2021," https://www.scouting
.org/wp-content/uploads/2021/09/Charter_Bylaws_May2021.pdf, vi.

29 Benjamin René Jordan, *Modern Manhood and the Boy Scouts of America: Citizenship, Race and the Environment, 1910–1930* (Chapel Hill:
University of North Carolina Press, 2016), 187.

30 Jordan, *Modern Manhood and the Boy Scouts of America*, 109.

31 "$82,503 and a Camp for the Boy Scouts," *New York Times*, Decem-
ber 12, 1915, https://timesmachine.nytimes.com/timesmachine
/1915/12/12/104018144.html?pageNumber=12.

32 James West, "Scouts and the War," *Scouting*, May 1, 1917.

33 Peterson, *The Boy Scouts*, 89–91.

34 Woodrow Wilson, "Proclamation 1520—Boy Scout Week," May 1,
1919, The American Presidency Project, https://www.presidency
.ucsb.edu/documents/proclamation-1520-boy-scout-week.

35 Interview with Benjamin René Jordan.

CHAPTER 3: A WILD NIGHT IN WEEDSPORT

1 "House Stormed by Mob to Get Scout Master," Rochester, NY, *Democrat and Chronicle*, April 27, 1918, and the newspaper's subsequent
coverage of the incident and criminal case.

2 "Scout Master Fires on Mob That Threatens Him," *Auburn* [NY] *Citizen*, April 26, 1918.

3 Cayuga County grand jury records, May 1918 term. Grand jurors indicted Townsend on two counts of sodomy involving a twelve-year-
old boy and one count of attempted sodomy of another boy whose
age was not provided.

4 "Townsend Is Freed of Alleged Crime: Still Two Charges Against
Him," Rochester, NY, *Democrat and Chronicle*, June 7, 1918. Also
reported by the *Auburn* [NY] *Citizen*, June 12, 1918.

5 Records searches by the offices of Cayuga County Clerk and Cayuga
County Historian yielded no information on the final disposition

of Townsend's court case. Local newspaper articles showed that he ultimately left Weedsport and headed west, where he resumed his newspaper career and later managed a southern California chamber of commerce. He died in California in 1958, according to an obituary in the *Arizona Republic* that July 19.

6   *Iowa City Press-Citizen*, April 12, 1923. A story about BSA operations included one paragraph on the Records Department, which contained a rare public reference to the perversion files: "Through their red flag list they are able to keep an accurate check on scoutmasters who have proved to be undesirable."

7   William D. Murray, *The History of the Boy Scouts of America* (New York: Boy Scouts of America, 1937), 359.

8   "Boy Scouts' 'Red Flag List' Bars Undesirables, Col. Roosevelt Says," *New York Times*, May 18, 1935, https://timesmachine.nytimes.com /timesmachine/1935/05/18/94609796.html?pageNumber=1.

9   Janet Warren, "Boy Scouts of America Volunteer Screening Database: An Empirical Review 1946–2016," 2019, 3, filed as an exhibit to bankruptcy debtors' brief in *In re Boy Scouts of America and Delaware BSA, LLC*, https://casedocs.omniagentsolutions.com/cmsvol2 /pub_47373/799040_4.pdf, 68. Tim Jeal also referred to the Grey List in chapter notes for his biography *Baden-Powell: Founder of the Boy Scouts* (London: Hutchinson, 1989).

10   Jeal, *Baden-Powell: Founder of the Boy Scouts*, Kindle ed., 103.

11   "Blanshard Demands Scout List of Reds," *New York Times*, May 19, 1935, https://timesmachine.nytimes.com/timesmachine/1935 /05/19/94610566.html.

12   Heywood Broun, "It Seems to Me," *Indianapolis Times* and other newspapers that carried his syndicated column, May 21, 1935.

13   Heywood Broun, "It Seems to Me," May 28, 1935.

14   "Boy Scouts' Head Explains 'Red' List," *New York Times*, June 9, 1935, https://timesmachine.nytimes.com/timesmachine /1935/06/09/93688211.html.

15   Jason Felch and Kim Christensen, "Boy Scout Files Reveal Repeat Child Abuse by Sexual Predators," *Los Angeles Times*, August 4, 2012, https://www.latimes.com/local/la-me-boyscouts-20120805-m-story .html.

16   "Procedures for Ineligible Volunteer File Desk," undated BSA memorandum; various BSA Ineligible Volunteer files memos, including those dated June 17, 1994, and May 21, 1999; various Paul Ernst depositions in BSA sexual abuse lawsuits.

17   BSA Ineligible Volunteer file of Robert O'Callaghan, February 11,
       1960, https://documents.latimes.com/robert-ocallaghan/?_gl
       =1*1otm91f*_gcl_au*MTUyNjc1ODQzOS4xNjk1NjY0MzUz.

18   Deposition of Paul I. Ernst, BSA director of registration and statisti-
       cal services, in *Dale v. Monmouth Council and Boy Scouts of America*,
       March 14, 1992.

19   *Official Report of the Second Biennial Conference of Boy Scout Execu-
       tives* (New York: Boy Scouts of America, 1922), 143. This is an early
       admission by a top BSA official, George W. Ehler, that scouting had
       a sexual abuse problem even at that early date and that abusive
       scoutmasters moved from one place to another in an attempt to
       reenter scouting.

20   George W. Ehler, comments to Second Biennial Conference of Boy
       Scout Executives, from *Official Report of the Second Biennial Confer-
       ence of Boy Scout Executives*.

21   BSA Ineligible Volunteer file of Robert O'Callaghan, February 11,
       1960; Basil Starkey, letter to George Traquair, Scout Executive of
       Wachusett Council, October 6, 1960.

22   BSA Ineligible Volunteer file of Robert L. Hillard, June 19, 1961;
       Quivira Council Scout Executive A. Max Hatfield, letter to Basil Star-
       key, June 14, 1961, https://documents.latimes.com/robert-l
       -hillard/?_gl=1*15uy90k*_gcl_au*MTUyNjc1ODQzOS4xNjk1
       NjY0MzUz.

23   Harvey County attorney Richard Hrdlicka, letter to Scout Executive
       A. Max Hatfield, June 2, 1961, in BSA Ineligible Volunteer file of
       Robert L. Hillard.

24   National BSA official Basil Starkey, letter to local Scout Executive
       A. Max Hatfield, June 19, 1961, in BSA Ineligible Volunteer file of
       Robert L. Hillard.

25   "Kansas Scouts Help Czech Friend Escape from Red-Ruled Home-
       land," *Boys' Life*, March 1961.

26   "'Game Over. Life's Short': Virgin Boss Jayne Hrdlicka Clears the
       Air About Past—and Present—Turbulence," *Sydney Morning Herald*,
       March 12, 2021, https://www.smh.com.au/national/game-over-life
       -s-short-virgin-boss-jayne-hrdlicka-clears-the-air-about-past-and
       -present-turbulence-20201203-p56kge.html.

27   "Richard Franklin Hrdlicka," World Biographical Encyclopedia,
       https://prabook.com/web/richard_franklin.hrdlicka/54929.

28   Brief telephone interview with Richard Hrdlicka on February 1,
       2023. After listening to a recitation of the details of the case,

Hrdlicka said, "I have no recollection of that. It was a hundred years ago. I have no time to fool around with this thing because I don't remember anything."

29   "Paul Irvin Ernst," Lucas Funerals & Cremations, January 2022, https://www.lucasfuneralhomes.com/obituaries/Paul-Ernst/#! /Obituary. Ernst's obituary noted his eighty-year affiliation with Scouting, including his four decades on the payroll, the pride he had felt when both of his sons had become Eagle Scouts, and the many years of volunteer service he'd given to his Methodist Church and his community of Grapevine, Texas. His obituary "tribute wall" was a reflection of the conflicting sentiments about him. It had just two postings, two very different views of the same man. "Well done, good and faithful servant. May you Rest in Peace," read the first. "Thank God he is dead!!!!!!!!!!!!!!!" read the other, which was later deleted. Other biographical details were gleaned from several depositions of Ernst in sexual abuse lawsuits spanning more than thirty years.

30   Biographical information from deposition of Paul Ernst, October 10, 1986, in *William Walton Carter v. Boy Scouts of America et al.*, 13–18.

31   Paul I. Ernst, "Maintaining Standards of Leadership," memo to "All Scout Executives," December 4, 1972, marked "Personal and Confidential," https://documents.latimes.com/boy-scouts-america -1972-policy/.

32   BSA Ineligible Volunteer file of James R. Lankton, September 30, 1981, https://documents.latimes.com/james-r-lankton/?_gl=1* jv7oz0*_gcl_au*MTUyNjc1ODQzOS4xNjk1NjY0MzUz.

33   Deposition of Paul Ernst, April 17, 2013, in *Doe 1–6 v. Boy Scouts of America et al.*, Pierce County [WA] Superior Court. This is one of several depositions in which Ernst testified that his job was to exclude suspected sexual abusers from Scouting, not push for criminal prosecutions or embarrass the accused.

34   Interview of Joseph Anglim in 1990 by Patrick Boyle for his book *Scout's Honor: Sexual Abuse in America's Most Trusted Institution* (Rocklin, CA: Prima Publishing, 1994). Anglim told Boyle he did not know how many cases of abuse there had been each year because he'd never read any of the files, even though he had signed off on hundreds of them.

35   BSA Ineligible Volunteer file of Carleton T. Coffey, December 23, 1986, updated October 11, 1988, https://documents.latimes.com

/carleton-t-coffey/?_gl=1*ym6cgk*_gcl_au*MTUyNjc1ODQzOS4x
Njk1NjY0MzUz.

36   Felch and Christensen, "Boy Scout Files Reveal Repeat Child Abuse
     by Sexual Predators."

37   BSA Ineligible Volunteer file of Carleton T. Coffey.

CHAPTER 4: HALCYON DAYS

1   Fashion Island, https://www.fashionisland.com/guest-services. A
     plaque commemorating the 1953 National Jamboree is mounted
     near the top of the outdoor escalator at the shopping center.

2   *Jamboree*, also known as *Boy Scouts of America 1953—Jamboree*,
     January 1954, available at Quest for Peace, *Boy Scouts of America
     1953—Jamboree*, YouTube, October 28, 2013, https://www
     .youtube.com/watch?v=fMzcjp7dzJU. The film had been all but lost
     for decades before it was rediscovered in 2018; https://www
     .ocregister.com/2017/07/13/newport-historical-society-screens-film
     -on-1953-boy-scout-jamboree-that-put-spotlight-on-orange-county/.

3   *Jamboree*.

4   Phil Brigandi, "The 1953 Boy Scout National Jamboree," OC History-
     land, 2019, https://www.ochistoryland.com/jamboree.

5   "History," The James Irvine Foundation, https://www.irvine.org
     /about-us/history/.

6   "Donald Bren," *Forbes*, April 2024, https://www.forbes.com/profile
     /donald-bren/?list=billionaires&sh=10292d8b3bbe.

7   Dorany Pineda, "Phil Brigandi, Chronicler of Orange County's
     History, Dies at 60," *Los Angeles Times*, December 18, 2019, https://
     www.latimes.com/obituaries/story/2019-12-18/phil-brigandi
     -historian-orange-county-dead.

8   Brigandi, "The 1953 Boy Scout National Jamboree."

9   Brigandi, "The 1953 Boy Scout National Jamboree."

10   Interview with Richard "Skip" Leifer. He was among a group of
     former Boy Scouts who gathered in November 2018 at the site of
     the 1953 National Jamboree for a sixty-fifth reunion of attendees.
     OCPublicLibraries, *65th Anniversary of the 1953 Boy Scout Jamboree*,
     YouTube, November 27, 2018, https://www.youtube.com
     /watch?v=8_ii3xSdoMY.

11   King Rose Archives, *Dinah Shore 'See the U.S.A. in Your Chevrolet'—
     1953*, YouTube, March 17, 2013, https://www.youtube.com
     /watch?v=boertpylK0M.

12   "Stars Move In on Boy Scouts," Associated Press, July 21, 1953.

13 Sixty-four years later, in 2017, President Donald Trump would address the 2017 National Jamboree in person, delivering a divisive, self-serving political speech for which BSA Chief Scout Executive Michael Surbaugh would later apologize. Liam Stack, "Boy Scouts Apologize over President Trump's Remarks at Jamboree," *New York Times*, July 27, 2017, https://www.nytimes.com/2017/07/27/us/boy-scouts-trump-apology.html.

14 *Jamboree.*

15 "Jamboree (1954)," AFI Catalog of Feature Films, https://catalog.afi.com/Catalog/MovieDetails/50724.

16 "Jamboree Jigsaw Fast Taking Shape," *Los Angeles Times*, July 16, 1953.

17 "Servicemen's Readjustment Act (1944)," National Archives, https://www.archives.gov/milestone-documents/servicemens-readjustment-act (the act was also known as the G.I. Bill); Suzanne Mettler, *The Creation of the G.I. Bill of Rights of 1944: Melding Social and Participatory Citizenship Ideals* (Cambridge, UK: Cambridge University Press, 2009); Edward Humes, *Over Here: How the G.I. Bill Transformed the American Dream* (New York: Houghton Mifflin Harcourt, 2006).

18 Robert D. Putnam, *Bowling Alone: The Collapse and Revival of American Community* (New York: Simon & Schuster, 2000), Kindle ed., 54.

19 John Kenneth Galbraith, *The Affluent Society* (New York: Houghton Mifflin, 1958), 223.

20 "Social Justice Challenge," Jim Crow Museum, Ferris State University, Michigan, https://jimcrowmuseum.ferris.edu/social.htm.

21 John F. Kennedy, "Remarks to a Representative Family Selected by the Boy Scouts of America in Conjunction with Boy Scout Week, 8 February 1962," John F. Kennedy Presidential Library and Museum, https://www.jfklibrary.org/asset-viewer/archives/JFKWHA/1962/JFKWHA-072-003/JFKWHA-072-003.

22 *Boy Scout Handbook*, 7th ed. (New York: Boy Scouts of America, 1967), 94.

23 Boy Scouts of America, *Annual Report to Congress: Boy Scouts of America* (Washington, DC: U.S. Government Printing Office, 1973).

CHAPTER 5: UPHEAVAL AND BACKLASH

1 John Noble Wilford, "Neil Armstrong, First Man on the Moon, Dies at 82," *New York Times*, August 25, 2012, https://www.nytimes.com/2012/08/26/science/space/neil-armstrong-dies-first-man-on-moon.html.

2   "Apollo 11: Real-Time Mission Experience, Fri Jul 18 1969, 12:14:46
       AM +200," NASA, https://apolloinrealtime.org/11/?t=056:42:46.
       Twenty of the twenty-four men who flew to the moon on Apollo
       missions from 1968 to 1972 were former Boy Scouts, according to
       NASA's Glenn Research Center; the astronaut ranks have included
       more than forty Eagle Scouts.

3   Boy Scouts of America, *59th Annual Report to Congress* (Washington,
       DC: U.S. Government Printing Office, 1969).

4   "Is Scouting in Tune with the Times?," report by Daniel Yankovich,
       July 1968.

5   Chuck Wills, *Boy Scouts of America: A Centennial History* (New York:
       DK Publishing, 2009), 156.

6   Boy Scouts of America, *59th Annual Report to Congress*.

7   Wills, *Boy Scouts of America*, 161.

8   Janice Petterchak, *Lone Scout: W. D. Boyce and American Boy Scouting*
       (Rochester, IL: Legacy Press, 2003), 69.

9   Edward L. Rowan, *To Do My Best: James E. West and the History of the
       Boy Scouts of America* (privately published, 2005), 47.

10   Wills, *Boy Scouts of America*, 161.

11   "Scouts Adapt to Urban Needs," United Press International, January
       19, 1972.

12   Robert W. Peterson, *The Boy Scouts: An American Adventure* (New York:
       American Heritage Publishing, 1984), 197.

13   "Youth: Digging the Stoners," *Time*, November 30, 1970, https://
       content.time.com/time/subscriber/article/0,33009,904526,00.html.

14   Jay Mechling, "The Boy Scouts of America at 100," *American Interest*,
       November–December 2010.

15   Interview with Larry John O'Connor. Now eighty-one and living in
       a small town in Alaska, O'Connor was so affected by the Boy Scouts'
       membership cheating decades earlier that he flew to Portland, Ore-
       gon, at his own expense in 2010 to testify about it at the landmark
       civil trial that resulted in a nearly $20 million jury verdict against
       the BSA. Yet he still cares deeply about Scouting and plans to will
       the proceeds of a $50,000 life insurance policy to the BSA upon his
       death.

16   Interview with Larry John O'Connor.

17   David Young, "Phantoms Fill Boy Scout Rolls," *Chicago Tribune*,
       June 9, 1974.

18   David Young, "Scout Pledge Lost in Signup Drive," *Chicago Tribune*,
       June 10, 1974.

19   Interview with David Scott.

20   Mark Ray, "'Green Bar Bill,' the Scoutmaster to the World," *Scouting*,
      January–February 2018, https://scoutingmagazine.org/2017/12
      /scoutmaster-to-the-world/.

21   Ray, "'Green Bar Bill,' the Scoutmaster to the World."

22   Robert Peterson, "America's Best-known Scouter," *Scouting*, January–
      February 2001, https://scoutingmagazine.org/issues/0101/d-wwas.html.

23   Peterson, *The Boy Scouts*, 205.

24   "Ending the Vietnam War, 1969–1976," Office of the Historian, U.S.
      State Department, https://history.state.gov/milestones/1969-1976
      /ending-vietnam#:~:text=Having%20rebuilt%20their%20forces
      %20and,Saigon%2C%20effectively%20ending%20the%20war.

25   "Newport History," Newport Borough Office, https://www
      .newportboro.com/information/history/#:~:text=In%201840
      %2C%20Newport%20was%20incorporated,the%20late%201800s
      %20was%20laid.

26   "Pennsylvania—Perry County," National Register of Historic Places,
      https://nationalregisterofhistoricplaces.com/pa/perry/state.html.

27   Interview with Carl Maxwell, Jr.

28   Interview with Carl Maxwell, Jr.

29   Separate interviews with Carl Maxwell, Jr., and Mike Kunkel.

CHAPTER 6: DOWNPLAY, DENY, DEFLECT

1   "Abuse Victim Gets $4.3 Million," Associated Press, April 4, 1987.

2   BSA confidential record sheet on William Elwood Tobiassen, July
     20, 1984, https://documents.latimes.com/william-e-tobiassen
     /?_gl=1*1jsvunx*_gcl_au*MTUyNjc1ODQzOS4xNjk1NjY0MzUz.

3   Chief Scout Executive Ben Love, memo to Scout executives, July 20,
     1989: "We are pleased to report that on July 17, 1989, the Oregon
     appellate court vacated the award of punitive damages on the grounds
     that BSA and the local council had not engaged in [willful, wanton,
     or gross misconduct]." The court let stand a $540,000 compensatory
     award. From perversion file of William Tobiassen, July 20, 1984.

4   Boy Scouts of America, perversion file of Carlton L. Bittenbender,
     October 29, 1985.

5   Thomas Heath, "Ex-leader of Scouts Recalls Role," *Washington Post*,
     December 21, 1988, https://www.washingtonpost.com/archive
     /local/1988/12/22/ex-leader-of-scouts-recalls-role/09c8101c-61e2
     -465a-be30-04bb8dbcc43b/.

6   *Infant C. v. Boy Scouts of America, Inc. et al.*, Supreme Court of Virginia, 239 Va. 572 (Va. 1990), April 20, 1990, https://casetext.com/case/infant-c-v-boy-scouts-of-america.

7   Lynn Swann, testimony, hearing on HR 1237 before the House Judiciary Subcommittee on Civil and Constitutional Rights, 103rd Congress, July 16, 1993.

8   Mark C. Lear, "Just Perfect for Pedophiles? Charitable Organizations That Work with Children and Their Duty to Screen Volunteers," *Texas Law Review* 76, no. 1 (November 1997): 143–82.

9   Lawrence F. Potts, testimony, hearing on HR 1237 before the House Judiciary Subcommittee on Civil and Constitutional Rights, 103rd Congress, July 16, 1993.

10   Lawrence F. Potts, "The Youth Protection Program of the Boy Scouts of America," *Child Abuse & Neglect* 16, no. 3 (1992): 441–45.

11   Lawrence F. Potts, deposition, *Jonathan Mizrack v. Jerrold Schwartz, Boy Scouts of America, et al.*, Supreme Court of the State of New York, County of New York, December 15, 2004.

12   Boy Scouts of America, 1993 Annual Report.

13   Lawrence F. Potts, testimony, hearing on HR 1237.

14   Jason Felch and Kim Christensen, "Boy Scouts' Opposition to Background Checks Let Pedophiles In," *Los Angeles Times*, December 2, 2012, https://www.latimes.com/local/la-me-scouts-screening-20121202-story.html.

15   Felch and Christensen, "Boy Scouts' Opposition to Background Checks Let Pedophiles In."

16   Felch and Christensen, "Boy Scouts' Opposition to Background Checks Let Pedophiles In."

17   Eric Zubel, letter to Boulder Dam Council Scout Executive Dan Gasparo, in BSA Ineligible Volunteer file of William Stanley Schilling, November 28, 1989, https://documents.latimes.com/william-s-schilling/?_gl=1*14p4e5y*_gcl_au*MTUyNjc1ODQzOS4xNjk1NjY0MzUz.

18   Lawrence F. Potts, deposition, *Jonathan Mizrack v. Jerrold Schwartz, Boy Scouts of America, et al.*

19   *Kerry Lewis v. Boy Scouts of America, et al.*, Multnomah County Circuit Court, Portland, OR, March 2010, 448.

20   Donald Wolff, interviewed on *Day One*, ABC News, June 14, 1993.

21   John Phillips, "Selling America: The Boy Scouts of America in the Progressive Era, 1910–1921," MA thesis, University of Maine, 2001,

https://digitalcommons.library.umaine.edu/cgi/viewcontent.cgi
?article=1195&context=etd.

22 Interview with Benjamin René Jordan.

CHAPTER 7: THE THREE G'S: GAYS, GIRLS, AND GOD

1 Kinga Borondy, "Seminar Addresses Needs of Homosexual Teens," *Newark Star-Ledger*, July 8, 1990.

2 Michael D. Shear, "Abortion Debate: A Clash of Signs and Chants," *Los Angeles Times*, April 27, 1989, https://www.latimes.com/archives /la-xpm-1989-04-27-mn-1651-story.html.

3 Getty Images, https://www.gettyimages.com/detail/news-photo /daniel-martino-holds-a-cross-while-protesting-outside-the-news -photo/748111?utm_medium=organic&utm_source=google&utm _campaign=iptcurl l.

4 Interview with James Dale.

5 James Dale, "Why Did I Challenge the Boy Scouts' Anti-gay Policy? Because I Am a Loyal Scout," *Washington Post*, February 8, 2013, https://www.washingtonpost.com/opinions/why-did-i -challenge-the-boy-scouts-anti-gay-policy-because-i-am-a-loyal -scout/2013/02/08/346ebab2-7159-11e2-a050-b83a7b35c4b5 _story.html.

6 Borondy, "Seminar Addresses Needs of Homosexual Teens."

7 *Boy Scouts of America v. Dale*, U.S. Supreme Court, 53 U.S. 640 (2000), June 28, 2000, https://caselaw.findlaw.com/court/us -supreme-court/530/640.html.

8 Justice John Paul Stevens, in his dissent to the decision in *Boy Scouts of America v. Dale*, wrote that the 1978 BSA policy excluding homosexuals "was never publicly expressed—unlike, for example, the Scout's duty to be 'obedient.' It was an internal memorandum, never circulated beyond the few members of BSA's Executive Committee. It remained, in effect, a secret Boy Scouts policy."

9 Interview with James Dale.

10 Gregory Herek, "Facts About Homosexuality and Child Molestation," https://lgbpsychology.org/html/facts_molestation.html. Herek cited several studies, including one from 1982 by A. Nicholas Groth that stated in part, "The research to date all points to there being no significant relationship between a homosexual lifestyle and child molestation."

11 Tim Curran, "What the Boy Scouts—and I—Lost," CNN, July 21,

2015, https://www.cnn.com/2015/07/21/opinions/curran-boy
-scouts.

12 Curran, "What the Boy Scouts—and I—Lost."

13 Matt Lait, "Scout Leader Who Backed Randall Twins Loses His Post,"
    Los Angeles Times, November 11, 1991, https://www.latimes.com
    /archives/la-xpm-1991-11-14-me-2107-story.html.

14 Boy Scouts of America, "Position Statement: Homosexuality and the
    BSA," June 24, 1991, http://www.qrd.org/qrd/orgs/gay.in.scouting
    /bsa.position.statement.

15 Richard J. Ellis, *Judging the Boy Scouts of America* (Lawrence: Uni-
    versity Press of Kansas, 2014), 102; *Dale v. Boy Scouts of America*,
    Supreme Court of New Jersey, 160 N.J. 562 (N.J. 1999), August 4,
    1999, https://casetext.com/case/dale-v-boy-scouts-of-america.

16 *Dale v. Boy Scouts of America.*

17 *Dale v. Boy Scouts of America.*

18 Thomas Martello, "Boy Scout Gay Ban Overruled," Associated Press,
    Cape Cod Times, August 5, 1999, https://www.capecodtimes.com/story
    /news/1999/08/05/boy-scout-gay-ban-overruled/51029713007/.

19 *Boy Scouts of America and Monmouth Council, et al. v. James Dale*, U.S.
    Supreme Court, hearing, April 26, 2000, https://www.supremecourt
    .gov/pdfs/transcripts/1999/99-699_04-26-2000.pdf, 3.

20 BSA's 1978 position statement on homosexuality, its first public ar-
    ticulation of such a policy, read in part, "The Boy Scouts of America
    is a private, membership organization and leadership therein is a
    privilege and not a right. We do not believe that homosexuality and
    leadership in Scouting are appropriate. We will continue to select
    only those who in our judgment meet our standards and qualifica-
    tions for leadership."

21 *Boy Scouts of America and Monmouth Council, et al. v. James Dale*,
    hearing, 17.

22 *Boy Scouts of America and Monmouth Council, et al. v. James Dale*,
    hearing, 34.

23 *Boy Scouts of America v. Dale*, C-SPAN, April 26, 2000, https:
    //www.c-span.org/video/?156794-1/boy-scouts-america-v-dale.

24 *Boy Scouts of America v. Dale*, C-SPAN.

25 Interview with James Dale.

26 *Boy Scouts of America et al. v. Dale*, U.S. Supreme Court, 530 U.S.
    240, June 28, 2000, https://caselaw.findlaw.com/court/us-supreme
    -court/530/640.html.

27   Garrett Epps, "Some Animals Are More Equal than Others: The Rehnquist Court and 'Majority Religion,'" *Washington University Journal of Law & Policy* 21 (2006): 323–47, https://scholarworks .law.ubalt.edu/cgi/viewcontent.cgi?referer=&httpsredir=1&article =1241&context=all_fac.

28   *Boy Scouts of America et al. v. Dale*, June 28, 2000.

29   Interview with James Dale.

30   "Text: H.R. 4892—106th Congress (1999–2000)," https://www .congress.gov/bill/106th-congress/house-bill/4892/text.

31   "Text: H.R. 4892—106th Congress (1999–2000)," *Congressional Record* 146 (2000), part 12, https://www.govinfo.gov/content/pkg /CRECB-2000-pt12/html/CRECB-2000-pt12-Pg17737-3.htm.

32   "Text: H.R. 4892—106th Congress (1999–2000)."

33   Buyer was later convicted of securities fraud charges for insider trading and was sentenced to nearly two years in prison in 2023. See "Former Congressman Sentenced to 22 Months in Prison for Insider Trading," United States Attorney's Office, Southern District of New York, September 19, 2023, https://www.justice.gov/usao-sdny/pr /former-congressman-sentenced-22-months-prison-insider-trading.

34   "Text: H.R. 4892—106th Congress (1999–2000)."

35   "Text: H.R. 4892—106th Congress (1999–2000)."

36   Although she spoke in favor of the Boy Scouts and against the bill, Representative Lee was harshly critical of the BSA's antigay policies. See "Text: H.R. 4892—106th Congress (1999–2000)."

37   "Text: H.R. 4892—106th Congress (1999–2000)."

CHAPTER 8: FRENCH FRIES FOR BREAKFAST

1   *Multnomah County Courthouse Renovation Study, Final Report*, vol. 1, April 13, 2011, https://multco-web7-psh-files-usw2.s3-us-west-2 .amazonaws.com/s3fs-public/SERA%20MCCH%20Renovation %20Study%20Final%20Report%204.13.11.pdf; Aimee Green, "After Decades of Trying, Multnomah County Opens a $324 Million New, Spacious, Seismically Safer Courthouse," *Oregonian*, October 4, 2020, https://www.oregonlive.com/news/2020/10/after-decades-of -trying-multnomah-county-opens-a-324-million-new-spacious -seismically-safer-courthouse.html.

2   Helen Caldwell, testimony, March 23, 2010, Lewis trial transcript, 1190–350; testimony of Jimmy Lewis, March 30, 2010, Lewis trial transcript, 2084–123.

3   Kerry Lewis, testimony, March 23, 2010, Lewis trial transcript, 1374.

4   Helen Caldwell, testimony, March 23, 2010, Lewis trial transcript, 1229–30.

5   Helen Caldwell, testimony, March 23, 2010, Lewis trial transcript, 1233.

6   Interview with Kerry Lewis.

7   Retired Multnomah County Judge William Snouffer, testimony, March 29, 2010, Lewis trial transcript, 1758.

8   Interview with Helen Caldwell.

9   Helen Caldwell, testimony, March 23, 2010, Lewis trial transcript, 1252.

10   Interview with Kerry Lewis.

11   Kerry Lewis, testimony, March 24, 2010, Lewis trial transcript, 1498.

12   Helen Caldwell and Jimmy Lewis, testimony; interview with Helen Caldwell.

13   Kerry Lewis, testimony, March 23–24, 2010, Lewis trial transcript.

14   Interview with Helen Caldwell; testimony of Helen Caldwell, testimony, March 23, 2010, Lewis trial transcript, 1286.

15   Interview with Gilion Dumas.

16   Interview with Gilion Dumas.

17   Interview with Kerry Lewis.

18   Testimony of one of the John Doe plaintiffs, March 17, 2010, Lewis trial transcript, 555.

19   Videotaped deposition of Bishop Gordon McEwen, recorded on May 5, 2008, and shown to jurors at Lewis trial on March 17, 2010.

20   McEwen deposition played at Lewis trial.

21   Retired Multnomah County Sheriff's detective Chuck Shipley, testimony, March 19, 2010, Lewis trial transcript, 733.

22   Report filed by Shipley in case 83-2631, quoted by Lewis's attorney during deposition of Bishop Gordon McEwen, May 5, 2008.

23   The exchange was from Mones's deposition of Nathaniel Marshall on January 28–29, 2010, for the Lewis lawsuit. Video of it was played for jurors during opening statements by Lewis's attorneys; see Lewis trial transcript, 455–57.

24   Nathaniel Marshall, testimony, March 19 and March 22, 2010, Lewis trial transcript.

25   BSA Ineligible Volunteer file of Michael D. Nonclerg, August 21, 1971, https://documents.latimes.com/michael-d-nonclerg/?_gl=1 *1ihuht7*_gcl_au*MTYxOTY0NjYzNi4xNjg3ODg4MTQ4.

26   BSA Ineligible Volunteer file of Kenneth A. Burns, Jr., September 28, 1983, https://documents.latimes.com/kenneth-a-burns/?_gl

=1*1mc38uf*_gcl_au*MTYxOTY0NjYzNi4xNjg3ODg4
MTQ4.

27 Michelle Theriault Boots, "Files Detail Allegations of Abuse by Seven Alaska Boy Scout Leaders," *Anchorage Daily News*, October 18, 2012, updated September 29, 2016, https://www.adn.com/alaska-news /article/files-detail-allegations-abuse-alaska-seven-boy-scout-leaders /2012/10/19/.

28 Nathaniel Marshall, March 22, 2010, Lewis trial transcript, 1047–48.

29 Kerry Lewis, testimony, Lewis trial transcript, 1400.

30 Kerry Lewis, testimony, Lewis trial transcript, 1416.

31 Kerry Lewis, testimony, Lewis trial transcript, 1477.

32 Kerry Lewis, testimony, Lewis trial transcript, 1530.

33 Gary Schoener, testimony, March 24, 2010, Lewis trial transcript, 1612.

34 Janet Warren, testimony, April 2, 2010, Lewis trial transcript, vol. 16, 28.

35 Jon Conte, testimony, April 6, 2010, Lewis trial transcript, 1903.

36 Lorah Sebastian, testimony, March 31, 2010, Lewis trial transcript, 2315.

37 Eugene Grant, testimony, March 31 and April 1, 2010, Lewis trial transcript, 2705.

38 Interview with Helen Caldwell.

39 Kelly Clark, plaintiff's closing statement, April 8, 2010, Lewis trial transcript, 816.

40 Chuck Smith, defendants' closing statement, April 8, 2010, Lewis trial transcript, 880.

41 Paul Xochihua, defendants' closing statement, April 8, 2010, Lewis trial transcript, 947.

42 Interview with Chuck Smith.

43 Kelly Clark, plaintiff's opening statement in damages phase, April 20, 2010, Lewis trial transcript, vol. 22, 23.

44 James Terry, testimony in damages phase, April 21, 2010, Lewis trial transcript, vol. 22, 57. Terry died in 2016; see "James Johnston Terry Jr.," Legacy, https://www.legacy.com/us/obituaries/dfw/name /james-terry-obituary?id=10937576.

45 In interviews wih the *Los Angeles Times* in 2012 and with the author in 2023, Finkelhor disputed that his researchers had found nothing of value in the Ineligible Volunteer files. He said that he had submitted a written proposal to the BSA to conduct further analysis of them and the BSA had rejected his recommendations.

46   Interview with Margaret Malarkey, whose name at the time of trial was Margaret Ormsbee.

47   Interview with Margaret Malarkey.

48   Interview with Margaret Malarkey.

49   Kerry Lewis, remarks at press conference after damages award, the *Oregonian*, "Kerry Lewis Awarded $18.5 Million for Abuse by Boy Scouts," YouTube, April 24, 2010, https://www.youtube.com /watch?v=EmluPT_rp2o.

CHAPTER 9: THE LID COMES OFF

1   Lewis trial transcript, 663.

2   Jason Felch and Kim Christensen, "Boy Scouts Failed to Report Abuser," *Los Angeles Times*, October 29, 2011, https://www.latimes .com/local/la-me-scouts-molest-story-htmlstory.html.

3   BSA perversion file of Richard John Turley, September 27, 1979, https://documents.latimes.com/boy-scout-americas-perversion -file-turley/.

4   Interview with Richard Turley by *Los Angeles Times* reporter Jason Felch and Canadian Broadcasting Corporation team.

5   Interview with Ed Iris.

6   Interview with Ed Iris.

7   BSA perversion file of Richard Turley.

8   Felch and Christensen, "Boy Scouts Failed to Report Abuser."

9   *Infant C. v. Boy Scouts of America, Inc.*, Supreme Court of Virginia, 239 Va. 572 (Va. 1990), April 20, 1990, https://casetext.com/case /infant-c-v-boy-scouts-of-america.

10   Patrick Boyle, "Scouting's Sex Abuse Trail Leads to 50 States," *Washington Times*, May 20, 1991.

11   "The State: Citizen of the Year Molested Boys," *Los Angeles Times*, March 8, 1989, https://www.latimes.com/archives/la-xpm-1989-03 -08-mn-66-story.html.

12   Interview with Michael Rothschild.

13   Jason Felch and Kim Christensen, "In Scouting Reports, a Pattern of Molestation," *Los Angeles Times*, October 17, 2012, https:// www.latimes.com/local/la-me-scouts-patterns-20121017-story .html.

14   Kim Christensen and Jason Felch, "Boy Scouts Helped Alleged Molesters Cover Tracks, Files Show," *Los Angeles Times*, September 16, 2012, https://www.latimes.com/local/la-me-boy-scouts-files -20120916-story.html.

15   Christensen and Felch, "Boy Scouts Helped Alleged Molesters Cover Tracks, Files Show."

16   Jason Felch and Kim Christensen, "Boy Scout Files Reveal Repeat Child Abuse by Sexual Predators," *Los Angeles Times*, August 4, 2012, https://www.latimes.com/local/la-me-boyscouts-20120805-m-story .html.

17   BSA perversion file of Arthur W. Humphries, June 6, 1984, https:// documents.latimes.com/arthur-w-humphries/.

18   Chesapeake Mayor Marian P. Whitehurst, letter to Arthur Humphries, April 24, 1978: "It was a special privilege for me to have the opportunity of presenting the Mayor's Outstanding Service Award for the considerable amount of volunteer service you give to the handicapped boys in the city."

19   BSA perversion file of Arthur W. Humphries, June 6, 1984, 8.

20   BSA perversion file of Arthur W. Humphries, June 6, 1984, 21.

21   Jack B. Terwilliger, letter to BSA official Jack Richmond, April 24, 1980, in BSA perversion file of Arthur W. Humphries, June 6, 1984, 17. Terwilliger is deceased.

22   BSA perversion file of Keith M. Gardner, June 6, 1984, https:// documents.latimes.com/keith-m-gardner/.

23   Eve Markowitz, "Man Gets 16-Year Term for Assaulting Scouts," *Virginian-Pilot*, March 6, 1985.

24   Kim Christensen and Jason Felch, "Court Orders Boy Scouts to Release Sexual Abuse Files," *Los Angeles Times*, June 14, 2012, https:// www.latimes.com/archives/la-xpm-2012-jun-14-la-na-scouts -20120615-story.html.

25   Interview with Paul Mones.

26   "Inside the Perversion Files," *Los Angeles Times*, https://documents .latimes.com/boy-scouts-paper-trail-of-abuse-documents/

CHAPTER 10: A FINE LITTLE TOWN

1   BSA perversion file of Roger Lee Beatty, August 18, 1976, https:// documents.latimes.com/rodger-l-beatty/?_gl=1*13t3h6u*_gcl _au*MTUyNjc1ODQzOS4xNjk1NjY0MzUz.

2   "Obituary: Rodger L. Beatty," *University Times*, University of Pittsburgh, November 21, 2012, https://www.utimes.pitt.edu /archives/?p=23541.

3   Kim Christensen, "Men Tell of Sexual Abuse by Scoutmaster Decades Ago," *Los Angeles Times*, October 20, 2012, https://www

.latimes.com/local/la-xpm-2012-oct-20-la-me-10-21-scouts-beatty
-20121022-story.html.

4   The author's personal experience.

5   Brief interview with man at Rodger Beatty's home in Pittsburgh.

6   I had experienced that uneasy feeling before. In 1993, while working for the *Orange County Register*, I went to the home of a man who'd lost his foster care license for sexually abusing five teenage girls, the lurid allegations detailed in the search warrant affidavit in my back pocket. The man, a fifty-three-year-old delivery driver for my newspaper, could not have been more polite as I stood on his porch and we spoke through a steel-grate security door. "Thank you for coming here and asking me about that, but I just can't comment right now—maybe some other time," he said in the congenial way a coworker might decline a lunch invitation. Overnight, as he was picking up bundles of newspapers that carried my story about him, he suffered a massive heart attack, collapsed on the loading dock, and died.

7   Interview with Carl Maxwell, Jr.

8   Interview with Carl Maxwell, Jr.

9   Christensen, "Men Tell of Sexual Abuse by Scoutmaster Decades Ago."

10   Excerpts of Scouts' statements from BSA perversion file of Rodger Lee Beatty, August 18, 1976.

11   Interview with Carl Maxwell, Jr.

12   Christensen, "Men Tell of Sexual Abuse by Scoutmaster Decades Ago."

13   Rodger Beatty, letter to Arthur Lesh, July 1, 1976, in BSA perversion file of Rodger Lee Beatty, August 18, 1976.

14   Arthur Lesh, letter to Rodger L. Beatty, July 8, 1976, in BSA perversion file of Rodger Lee Beatty, August 18, 1976.

15   Interview with Arthur A. Lesh; "Arthur A. Lesh, 1935–2019," Penn Live, https://obits.pennlive.com/us/obituaries/pennlive/name/arthur-lesh-obituary?id=12403963.

16   Kim Christensen, "Man Named in Scouting Abuse Dies at 66," *Los Angeles Times*, November 15, 2012, https://www.latimes.com/archives/la-xpm-2012-nov-15-la-me-scouts-beatty-20121115-story.html.

17   "Obituary: Rodger L. Beatty," *University Times*.

18   Interview with Carl Maxwell, Jr.

CHAPTER II: THE FLOODGATES OPEN

1   Detective Mike website, https://detectivemike.com/.
2   Interview with Michael Johnson.
3   Interview with Michael Johnson.
4   Interview with Michael Johnson.
5   "Inside the Perversion Files," *Los Angeles Times*, August 4, 2012, https://documents.latimes.com/boy-scouts-paper-trail-of-abuse -documents/.
6   Michael Johnson, letter to The Honorable Members of Congress, October 6, 2021, https://www.andersonadvocates.com/wp-content /uploads/2021/10/Michael-Johnson-Letter-to-Congress.pdf.
7   Interview with Michael Johnson.
8   Interview with Michael Johnson; Michael Johnson, letter to The Honorable Members of Congress, October 6, 2021.
9   Timothy Kosnoff, deposition, *In Re: Boy Scouts of America and Delaware BSA, LLC, et al.*, United States Bankruptcy Court, District of Delaware, November 22, 2021, 7–9.
10 Timothy Kosnoff, deposition, *In Re: Boy Scouts of America and Delaware BSA, LLC, et al.*, November 22, 2021, 10–11.
11 Timothy Kosnoff, deposition, *In Re: Boy Scouts and Delaware BSA, LLC, et al.*, U.S Bankruptcy Court, November 22, 2021, 193.
12 "100 Years for Ex–Scout Aide," *Chicago Tribune*, December 14, 1989.
13 *John Doe 2, et al. v. Thomas Hacker and Boy Scouts of America, et al.*, Cook County [IL] Circuit Court, 2012.
14 John Doe 2, affidavit attached as an exhibit to a plaintiff's motion for summary judgment, *John Doe 2, et al. v. Thomas Hacker and Boy Scouts of America, et al.*
15 Affidavit of Dr. Jon Conte, October 16, 2014, quoted in Illinois Appellate Court Decision, *John Doe No. 2 et al. v. Boy Scouts of America et al.*, 2016 IL App. (1st) 152406, https://www.illinoiscourts.gov /Resources/7d8c2ebb-a90c-42d4-ad81-39392719f1aa/1152406 .pdf, 17.
16 Affidavit of Dr. Jon Conte, *John Doe No. 2 et al. v. Boy Scouts of America et al.*, 17, 18.
17 *John Doe No. 2 et al. v. Boy Scouts of America et al.*, 26.
18 BSA perversion file of Thomas E. Hacker, June 8, 1970, with updates through 1989, https://documents.latimes.com/redacted-thomas -e-redacted-hacker/?_gl=1*18ayl1i*_gcl_au*MTYxOTY0NjYzNi4 xNjg3ODg4MTQ4.
19 Letter from Indiana Scouts official whose name was redacted to Earl

Krall, BSA director of registration, February 26, 1970, from Hacker perversion file.

20   Affidavit of John Doe No. 2, *John Doe 2, et al. v. Thomas Hacker and Boy Scouts of America, et al.*

21   Appellate court opinion, summarizing a former Scout's sworn deposition testimony in *John Doe No. 2 et al. v. Boy Scouts of America et al.*, September 30, 2016, 11.

22   "Ex–Boy Scout Leader Faces Abuse Charges," *Chicago Tribune*, February 11, 1988.

23   Appellate court opinion, *John Doe No. 2 et al. v. Boy Scouts of America et al.*, September 30, 2016, 12.

24   Interview with Christopher Hurley.

25   Thomas E. Hacker, deposition, July 30, 2013, *In Re: John Doe v. Thomas E. Hacker and Boy Scouts of America, et al.*

26   Thomas E. Hacker, deposition, *In Re: John Doe v. Thomas E. Hacker and Boy Scouts of America, et al.*

27   Thomas E. Hacker, deposition, *In Re: John Doe v. Thomas E. Hacker and Boy Scouts of America, et al.*

28   Thomas E. Hacker, deposition, *In Re: John Doe v. Thomas E. Hacker and Boy Scouts of America, et al.*

29   Thomas E. Hacker, deposition, *In Re: John Doe v. Thomas E. Hacker and Boy Scouts of America, et al.*

30   Separate interviews with Christopher Hurley and Paul Mones.

31   Bruce Griggs, BSA outside counsel, testified that the Hacker lawsuits posed "a variety of unfavorable facts that made them difficult to defend." Deposition, *In Re Boy Scouts and Delaware BSA, LLC, et al.*, 133.

32   Interview with Christopher Hurley.

CHAPTER 12: THE LONG SLIDE

1   In a 5–4 decision, the high court ruled in *Dale* that the Boy Scouts, as a private organization with a First Amendment right of expressive association, could legally exclude homosexuals. The ruling reversed a New Jersey state court decision that James Dale, an Eagle Scout and assistant scoutmaster who had been expelled after coming out as gay, should be reinstated under a state law banning discrimination based on sexual orientation.

2   Bryan Wendell, "Boy Scouts of America Clarifies Its Membership Policy," *Scouting*, June 7, 2012, https://blog.scoutingmagazine.org /2012/06/07/boy-scouts-of-america-clarifies-its-membership-policy/.

3   Wendell, "Boy Scouts of America Clarifies Its Membership Policy."
4   Kim Christensen and Jason Felch, "Boy Scouts Proposal Would Lift
       Ban on Gay Youths," *Los Angeles Times*, April 19, 2013, https://www
       .latimes.com/nation/la-xpm-2013-apr-19-la-na-nn-boy-scouts
       -ban-gays-20130419-story.html.
5   Boy Scouts of America National Council, "The Boy Scouts of Ameri-
       ca Media Statement," April 19, 2013, https://www.motherjones
       .com/wp-content/uploads/media_statement.pdf.
6   Kirk Johnson, "Compromise on Gays Pleases No One, Scouts Are
       Learning," *New York Times*, May 8, 2014, https://www.nytimes.com
       /2014/05/09/us/compromise-on-gays-pleases-no-one-scouts-are
       -learning.html.
7   "Dr. Robert M. Gates, Former Secretary of Defense," U.S. Depart-
       ment of Defense, https://www.defense.gov/About/Biographies
       /Biography/article/602797/.
8   Robert M. Gates, "National Annual Business Meeting Remarks," Boy
       Scouts of America, May 21, 2015, http://www.scoutingnewsroom.org
       /wp-content/uploads/2015/05/DR-GATES-REMARKS.pdf, 13–14.
9   Interview with Michael Johnson.
10   "Adult Leadership Standards Update and Resources," Boy Scouts of
       America, July 2015, https://www.scoutsforequality.org/wp-content
       /uploads/2015/07/Adult-Leadership-Standards-Update-and
       -Resources-for-Key-3.pdf.
11   Zach Wahls, "Scouts for Equality Hails Historic Vote by Boy Scouts
       of America," July 27, 2015, https://www.scoutsforequality.org
       /scouting/breaking-bsa-executive-board-votes-to-end-national-ban
       -on-gay-adults/.
12   Interview with Michael Johnson.
13   Boy Scouts of America, "Statement from the Boy Scouts of America
       Regarding Adult Leadership Standards," July 27, 2015, https://www
       .prnewswire.com/news-releases/statement-from-the-boy-scouts-of
       -america-regarding-adult-leadership-standards-300119387.html.
14   Email to the author from a managing director at Mercury LLC, a
       global strategic communications firm retained by Girl Scouts of the
       USA, September 2017.
15   Kathy Hopinkah Hannan, National President, Girl Scouts of the
       USA, letter to Randall Stephenson, National President, Boy Scouts of
       America, August 21, 2017, first reported by BuzzFeed News, https://
       s3.documentcloud.org/documents/3940009/Mr-Randall
       -Stephenson-BSA-August-21-2017.pdf.

16   Julie Bosman and Niraj Chokshi, "Boy Scouts Will Accept Girls,
      in Bid to 'Shape the Next Generation of Leaders,'" *New York Times*,
      October 11, 2017, https://www.nytimes.com/2017/10/11/us/boy
      -scouts-girls.html. Girls Scouts of the USA later sued the Boy Scouts
      for trademark infringement; a federal judge dismissed the lawsuit
      in April 2022, and the two sides agreed to settle their dispute two
      months later, releasing a joint statement that they were "looking
      forward to focusing on their respective missions to serve youth."

17   Associated Presss, *Mormon Leader: We Didn't Leave Boy Scouts, They
      Left Us*, YouTube, November 15, 2019, https://www.youtube.com
      /watch?v=qOpQ6W4s4UM; Gary Fields and Brady McCombs, "Mor-
      mon Leader: We Didn't Leave Boy Scouts, They Left Us," Associated
      Press, November 15, 2019, https://apnews.com/article/us-news
      -ap-top-news-ut-state-wire-medical-marijuana-reinventing-faith
      -bd0129a803df40f08e0240d75dd66f2b.

18   Boy Scouts of America annual reports; "Boy Scouts and Girl
      Scouts—Membership and Units, 1960–1969," U.S. Census Bureau,
      https://allcountries.org/uscensus/443_boy_scouts_and_girl_scouts
      _membership.html; Matthew Finn Hubbard, "A Cartographic
      Depiction and Exploration of the Boy Scouts of America's Historical
      Membership Patterns," master's thesis, University of Kansas, 2016,
      https://kuscholarworks.ku.edu/bitstream/handle/1808/24173
      /Hubbard_ku_0099M_15024_DATA_1.pdf?sequence=1.

19   "States Consider Easing Statute of Limitations on Child Sex-Abuse
      Cases," *PBS NewsHour*, January 23, 2019, https://www.pbs.org
      /newshour/nation/states-consider-easing-statute-of-limitations-on-
      child-sex-abuse-cases.

20   Interview with Paul Mones.

21   Katy Stech Ferek, "Boy Scouts of America Considers Bankruptcy
      Filing amid Sex-Abuse Lawsuits," *Wall Street Journal*, December 12,
      2018, https://www.wsj.com/articles/boy-scouts-of-america
      -considers-bankruptcy-filing-amid-sex-abuse-lawsuits-11544649657.

22   Interview with Marci Hamilton.

23   Bethan Moorcraft, "Boy Scouts of America Battle Insurers over
      Coverage for Sex Abuse Scandal," Insurance Business, December 19,
      2018, https://www.insurancebusinessmag.com/us/news/breaking
      -news/boy-scouts-of-america-battle-insurers-over-coverage-for-sex
      -abuse-scandal-119599.aspx.

24   Kim Christensen, "Boy Scout Sex Abuse Scandal's Stunning Toll:
      Over 12,200 Reported Victims," *Los Angeles Times*, May 15, 2019,

https://www.latimes.com/local/california/la-na-boy-scouts-child
-sex-abuse-20190515-story.html.

25 "Delayed Disclosure: A Factsheet Based on Cutting-Edge Research on
Child Abuse," CHILD USA, March 2020, https://childusa.org
/wp-content/uploads/2020/04/Delayed-Disclosure-Factsheet-2020
.pdf.

26 Christensen, "Boy Scout Sex Abuse Scandal's Stunning Toll."

27 Interview with Tim Kosnoff.

28 "Debtors' Informational Brief," *In Re: Boy Scouts of America and
Delaware BSA, LLC*, U.S. Bankruptcy Court for the District of
Delaware, February 18, 2020, https://casedocs.omniagentsolutions
.com/cmsvol2/pub_47373/799040_4.pdf, 6.

29 Kim Christensen, "Boy Scouts Seek Bankruptcy Under Wave of New
Sex Abuse Lawsuits," *Los Angeles Times*, February 17, 2020, https://
www.latimes.com/california/story/2020-02-17/boy-scouts
-bankruptcy.

30 Peg Brickley and Andrew Scurria, "The Strategy Behind the Boy
Scouts Bankruptcy," *Wall Street Journal*, February 18, 2020, https://
www.wsj.com/articles/the-strategy-behind-the-boy-scouts
-bankruptcy-11582071435?mod=article_inline.

31 "Boy Scouts of America McKenzie Statue," Scout Shop, https://www
.scoutshop.org/the-boy-scout-statuette-17513.html.

32 BSA financial expert Nancy Gutzler, declaration, *In Re: Boy Scouts
of America and Delaware BSA, LLC*, U.S. Bankruptcy Court for the
District of Delaware, March 19, 2022, https://casedocs.omniagent
solutions.com/cmsvol2/pub_47373/f33f0249-9312-4009-93b6
-05cef69212c5_9398.pdf.

33 "Debtors' Informational Brief," *In Re: Boy Scouts of America and
Delaware BSA, LLC*, February 18, 2020, 3.

34 "Debtors' Informational Brief," *In Re: Boy Scouts of America and
Delaware BSA, LLC*, February 18, 2020, 38.

CHAPTER 13: THE NEW MESOTHELIOMA

1 Exhibits F-1 and F-2, BSA motion on supplementing the bar date
order, *In Re: Boy Scouts of America and Delaware BSA, LLC*, U.S.
Bankruptcy Court for the District of Delaware, August 25, 2020,
https://casedocs.omniagentsolutions.com/cmsvol2
/pub_47373/842040_1145.pdf, 70, 72.

2 BSA motion on supplementing the bar date order, *In Re: Boy Scouts
of America and Delaware BSA, LLC*, 12.

3   Biography of Andrew Van Arsdale, "Meet AVA Law Group's Legal
      Team," AVA Law Group, https://avalaw.com/our-legal-team/; biog-
      raphy of Andrew Van Arsdale, "Who We Are," Reciprocity Industries,
      https://reciprocityind.com/about-us/.
4   Public records for 3667 Voltaire Street, San Diego, CA 92106.
5   Biography of Andrew Van Arsdale, "Who We Are," Reciprocity Indus-
      tries, https://reciprocityind.com/about-us/.
6   "Who We Are," Abused in Scouting, https://abusedinscouting.com
      /about-us/.
7   Interview with Tim Kosnoff.
8   Veronica Stenulson, declaration, April 14, 2021, attached as an
      exhibit to Century Indemnity Co.'s objections, *In Re: Boy Scouts of
      America and Delaware BSA, LLC*, U.S. Bankruptcy Court for the Dis-
      trict of Delaware, May 12, 2021.
9   Interview with Veronica Stenulson.
10   Veronica Stenulson, declaration, *In Re: Boy Scouts of America and
      Delaware BSA, LLC*, U.S. Bankruptcy Court for the District of Dela-
      ware, April 14, 2021.
11   Interview with Veronica Stenulson.
12   Veronica Stenulson, declaration, *In Re: Boy Scouts of America and
      Delaware BSA, LLC*, U.S. Bankruptcy Court for the District of Dela-
      ware, April 14, 2021.
13   Veronica Stenulson, declaration, *In Re: Boy Scouts of America and
      Delaware BSA, LLC*, U.S. Bankruptcy Court for the District of Dela-
      ware, April 14, 2021.
14   Evan Roberts, FTI Consulting, supplemental declaration, *In Re: Boy
      Scouts of America and Delaware BSA LLC*, U.S. Bankruptcy Court for
      the District of Delaware, August 30, 2020, https://casedocs
      .omniagentsolutions.com/cmsvol2/pub_47373/843636_1192
      .pdf.
15   Ashley Cullins, "Bill O'Reilly Harassment Claims Detailed by Wendy
      Walsh, Independent Investigation Called For," *Hollywood Reporter*,
      April 3, 2017, https://www.hollywoodreporter.com/news/general
      -news/wendy-walsh-talks-bill-oreilly-calls-fox-news-investigation
      -990746/.
16   Exhibit B-1, BSA motion on supplementing the bar date order, *In
      Re: Boy Scouts of America and Delaware BSA, LLC*, U.S. Bankruptcy
      Court for the District of Delaware, August 25, 2020, https://
      casedocs.omniagentsolutions.com/cmsvol2/pub_47373/842040
      _1145.pdf, 23.

17　"Sex Abuse," Consumer Attorney Marketing Group, https://www
　　.camginc.com/legal-areas/legal-areas-sex-abuse/.

18　"US Boy Scouts Launch Ads on How Abuse Victims Can Seek Money," Associated Press, Voice of America, September 1, 2020, https://
　　www.voanews.com/a/usa_us-boy-scouts-launch-ads-how-abuse
　　-victims-can-seek-money/6195301.html.

19　BSA motion on supplementing the bar date order, *In Re: Boy Scouts
　　of America and Delaware BSA, LLC*, U.S. Bankruptcy Court for the
　　District of Delaware, August 25, 2020, 17, 18.

20　Jessica Boelter, cease-and-desist letter to Tort Claimants' Committee,
　　August 10, 2020.

21　Judge Laurie Selber Silverstein, order *In Re: Boy Scouts of America
　　and Delaware BSA, LLC*, U.S. Bankruptcy Court for the District of
　　Delaware, September 16, 2020, https://casedocs.omniagent
　　solutions.com/cmsvol2/pub_47373/849049_1331.pdf.

22　Interview with Andrew Van Arsdale.

23　Janet I. Warren, "Boy Scouts of America Volunteer Screening Database: An Empirical Review 1946–2016," 2019, attached as Exhibit 2
　　to "Debtor's Informational Brief," *In Re: Boy Scouts of America and
　　Delaware BSA, LLC*, U.S. Bankruptcy Court for the District of Delaware, February 18, 2020, https://casedocs.omniagentsolutions.com
　　/cmsvol2/pub_47373/799040_4.pdf, 52–62.

24　*The Nature and Scope of Sexual Abuse of Minors by Catholic Priests
　　and Deacons in the United States 1950–2002*, John Jay College of
　　Criminal Justice, City University of New York, February 2004,
　　https://tile.loc.gov/storage-services/master/gdc/gdcebookspublic
　　/20/19/66/72/66/2019667266/2019667266.pdf.

25　"Summary of Sexual Abuse Claims in Chapter 11 Cases of Boy
　　Scouts of America," compiled by attorneys for the official Tort
　　Claimants' Committee from BSA proof of claim forms. https://www
　　.pszjlaw.com/assets/htmldocuments/BSA%20Summary%20of%20
　　Sexual%20Abuse%20Claims.pdf.

26　Kim Christensen, "Boy Scouts Deluged with 92,700 Sexual Abuse
　　Claims, Dwarfing U.S. Catholic Church's Numbers," *Los Angeles
　　Times*, November 16, 2020, https://news.yahoo.com/boy-scouts
　　-deluged-88-500-222415848.html.

27　Omni Agent Solutions' docket notifications posted daily to Boy
　　Scouts of America Restructuring Website, https://cases.omni
　　agentsolutions.com/home?clientId=3552.

CHAPTER 14: LETTERS FROM HELL

1   Letter to Justice Laurie Selber Silverstein regarding abuse, July 12,
     2021, https://casedocs.omniagentsolutions.com/cmsvol2
     /pub_47373/e8b60022-d121-4e9c-bea8-b440093281ce_5548
     _Redacted.pdf.

2   Letter to Justice Laurie Selber Silverstein regarding abuse, May 18,
     2021, https://casedocs.omniagentsolutions.com/cmsvol2
     /pub_47373/8e5cf7c6-0b38-4863-8616-11bac84f5e74_4629.pdf.

3   Letter to U.S. Bankruptcy Court regarding abuse, May 10, 2021,
     https://casedocs.omniagentsolutions.com/cmsvol2/pub_47373
     /a590d070-c45e-4144-9baa-ebaefb613795_4366_Redacted.pdf.

4   Letter to Justice Laurie Selber Silverstein regarding abuse, April 28,
     2021, https://casedocs.omniagentsolutions.com/cmsvol2
     /pub_47373/dfd7b132-987c-4977-b62c-515b75e6a349_2761.pdf.

5   Letter to Justice Laurie Selber Silverstein regarding abuse, May 11,
     2021, https://casedocs.omniagentsolutions.com/cmsvol2
     /pub_47373/0072490a-29b9-4859-8f84-360060e6cdcf_4445.pdf.

6   Letter to Justice Laurie Selber Silverstein regarding abuse, May 21,
     2021, https://casedocs.omniagentsolutions.com/cmsvol2/pub_47373
     /e6789c38-4373-412e-b4ed-1193aa9aee0c_4768_Redacted.pdf.

7   Letter to Justice Laurie Selber Silverstein regarding abuse, May
     21, 2021, https://casedocs.omniagentsolutions.com/cmsvol2
     /pub_47373/d13461b0-f27f-462e-bcc6-6f30591d642d_4730.pdf.

8   Letter to U.S. Bankruptcy Court regarding abuse, May 18, 2021,
     https://casedocs.omniagentsolutions.com/cmsvol2/pub_47373
     /e1ff98c2-1458-495d-8ada-82fa2a345c2a_4443_Redacted.pdf.

9   Letter to Justice Laurie Selber Silverstein regarding abuse, May
     18, 2021, https://casedocs.omniagentsolutions.com/cmsvol2
     /pub_47373/24b9960a-6152-4dce-8562-7e8c76fdb54f_4425.pdf.

10   Letter to Justice Laurie Selber Silverstein regarding abuse, April 27,
     2021, https://casedocs.omniagentsolutions.com/cmsvol2
     /pub_47373/a19b0463-c153-4201-b162-b220feebbda9_3087.pdf.

11   Letter to Justice Laurie Selber Silverstein regarding abuse, May
     18, 2021, https://casedocs.omniagentsolutions.com/cmsvol2
     /pub_47373/886ffad7-8b05-4a4a-82dd-07751fc1c21d_4512
     _Redacted.pdf.

12   Letter to Justice Laurie Selber Silverstein regarding abuse, July 12,
     2021, https://casedocs.omniagentsolutions.com/cmsvol2/pub
     _47373/e8b60022-d121-4e9c-bea8-b440093281ce_5548
     _Redacted.pdf.

13   Letter to U.S. Bankruptcy Court regarding abuse, May 25, 2021, https://casedocs.omniagentsolutions.com/cmsvol2 /pub_47373/8e55b31d-ea21-472b-a861-45f56b36ee92_4929.pdf.

14   Letter to Justice Laurie Selber Silverstein regarding abuse, May 17, 2021, https://casedocs.omniagentsolutions.com/cmsvol2 /pub_47373/43932e74-c9b0-45e1-9aef-8765fa28281b_4374.pdf.

15   Letter to Justice Laurie Selber Silverstein regarding abuse, May 13, 2021, https://casedocs.omniagentsolutions.com/cmsvol2 /pub_47373/c9f0314a-b141-4ca2-b15f-a3ffd163ece7_4867.pdf.

16   Letter to U.S. Bankruptcy Court regarding abuse, May 25, 2021.

17   Letter to Justice Laurie Selber Silverstein regarding abuse, May 12, 2021, https://casedocs.omniagentsolutions.com/cmsvol2 /pub_47373/c5d4e389-1951-4702-8150-8b1d0c744320_4441 _Redacted.pdf.

18   Letter to Justice Laurie Selber Silverstein regarding abuse, May 13, 2021, https://casedocs.omniagentsolutions.com/cmsvol2 /pub_47373/48febce7-278e-42e8-a4ad-7f9995308ff3_4736 _Redacted.pdf.

19   Letter to Justice Laurie Selber Silverstein regarding abuse, May 25, 2021, https://casedocs.omniagentsolutions.com/cmsvol2 /pub_47373/369229dc-d93a-4729-8fdb-441035e65fd8_4986.pdf.

20   BSA perversion file of David MacDonald Rankin, May 15, 1987, https://documents.latimes.com/david-macdonald-rankin/?_gl=1* 11j8id8*_gcl_au*MTYxOTY0NjYzNi4xNjg3ODg4MTQ4.

21   Keith Harriston, "Ex–Md. Scoutmaster Gets 15 Years for Child Abuse," *Washington Post*, February 8, 1988, https://www.washington post.com/archive/local/1988/02/09/ex-md-scoutmaster-gets-15 -years-for-child-abuse/cf01f128-7b1b-410a-a6d2-0eb3a0d573eb/.

22   Letter to U.S. Bankruptcy Court regarding abuse, May 18, 2021.

23   "David M. Rankin," Legacy, https://www.legacy.com/us/obituaries /washingtonpost/name/david-rankin-obituary?id=6036424.

CHAPTER 15: A MELTING ICE CUBE

1   Status conference, U.S. Bankruptcy Court in Delaware, February 11, 2022, 65.

2   Seventh interim application for compensation by White & Case, for February 1, 2022, to April 30, 2022, August 23, 2022, https://case docs.omniagentsolutions.com/cmsvol2/pub_47373/c5b55a6e -a8a8-4485-9d32-52f24212b5bb_10233.pdf.

3   Patrick Smith, "White & Case Revenue Climbs 20%, Propelled by

More Cross-Border Work," *American Lawyer*, February 17, 2022, https://www.law.com/americanlawyer/2022/02/17/white-case -revenue-climbs-20-propelled-by-more-cross-border-work/.

4 Postconfirmation report, *In Re: Boy Scouts of America*, U.S. Bankruptcy Court for the District of Delaware, for quarter ending June 30, 2023. BSA's approved cumulative fees for White & Case totaled $74,674,000.

5 Postconfirmation report, *In Re: Boy Scouts of America*, U.S. Bankruptcy Court for the District of Delaware, for quarter ending June 30, 2023. BSA's approved cumulative fees and expenses totaled $297.6 million.

6 Postconfirmation report *In Re: Boy Scouts of America*, U.S. Bankruptcy Court for the District of Delaware, for quarter ending June 30, 2023. BSA's approved cumulative fees for Justin Rucki totaled $1.14 million.

7 Maria Chutchian, "Boy Scouts Bankruptcy Judge Bemoans 'Staggering' Legal Fees," Reuters, March 17, 2021, https://www.reuters.com /article/bankruptcy-boy-scouts-idUSL1N2LF3S4/; Randall Chase, "Frustrated Judge Tells BSA Bankruptcy Lawyers to Work Harder," Associated Press, March 18, 2021, https://apnews.com/article /delaware-dover-b54cb7d9a53f394fe78ec33941e9c348.

8 The minimum payment to BSA abuse claimants is $3,500, or less than two hours' billings for the top attorneys in the bankruptcy, not counting the 30 to 40 percent of settlements survivors agree to pay their own lawyers in contingency fees.

9 Interview with Lynn LoPucki.

10 Amy Sullivan and National Journal, "How Citibank Made South Dakota the Top State in the U.S. for Business," *Atlantic*, July 10, 2013, https://www.theatlantic.com/business/archive/2013/07/how -citibank-made-south-dakota-the-top-state-in-the-us-for-business /425661/.

11 Interview with Lynn LoPucki.

12 State of Delaware, Division of Corporations, https://icis.corp .delaware.gov/ecorp/entitysearch/NameSearch.aspx.

13 Delaware BSA, LLC, monthly operating report, May 19, 2023, https://casedocs.omniagentsolutions.com/cmsvol2 /pub_47373/4b3439e0-f079-445f-a7cf-86308c6c4cba_11231.pdf.

14 Adam Levitin, "Boy Scouts of America: Venue Demerit Badge," Credit Slips, February 21, 2020, https://www.creditslips.org/credit slips/2020/02/boy-scouts-of-america-venue-demerit-badge.html.

15   Interview with Lynn LoPucki.

16   Elizabeth Warren, "Warren, Cornyn Introduce Bill to Prevent Large
       Corporations from 'Forum-Shopping' in Bankruptcy Cases," Sep-
       tember 23, 2021, https://www.warren.senate.gov/newsroom
       /press-releases/warren-cornyn-introduce-bill-to-prevent-large
       -corporations-from-forum-shopping-in-bankruptcy-cases.

17   Interview with Lynn LoPucki.

18   Peg Brickley and Andrew Scurria, "The Strategy Behind the Boy
       Scouts Bankruptcy," *Wall Street Journal*, February 18, 2020, https://
       www.wsj.com/articles/the-strategy-behind-the-boy-scouts
       -bankruptcy-11582071435?mod=article_inline.

19   Kim Christensen, "Boy Scouts Propose More than $300 Million,
       Norman Rockwell Paintings to Settle Sex Abuse Claims," *Los Angeles
       Times*, March 2, 2021, https://www.latimes.com/california/story
       /2021-03-01/boy-scouts-reorganization-plan-sex-abuse-claims.

20   "Norman Rockwell: A Brief Biography," Norman Rockwell Museum,
       https://www.nrm.org/about/about-2/about-norman-rockwell/.

21   Eliana Dockterman, "The Most Expensive American Painting Ever:
       Norman Rockwell's 'Saying Grace,'" *Time*, December 5, 2013,
       https://entertainment.time.com/2013/12/05/the-most-expensive
       -american-painting-ever-norman-rockwells-saying-grace/.

22   *Norman Rockwell: American Scouting Collection*, exhibition, Medici
       Museum of Art, https://www.medicimuseum.art/rockwell.

23   Christensen, "Boy Scouts Propose More than $300 Million, Norman
       Rockwell Paintings to Settle Sex Abuse Claims."
            For a list of creditors with the thirty largest unsecured claims,
       see *In Re: Boy Scouts of America and Delaware BSA, LLC*, U.S. Bank-
       ruptcy Court for the District of Delaware, February 18, 2020.

24   Joe Mozingo and John Spano, "$660-Million Settlement in Priest
       Abuses," *Los Angeles Times*, July 15, 2007, https://www.latimes.com
       /archives/la-xpm-2007-jul-15-me-priests15-story.html.

CHAPTER 16: LET'S MAKE A DEAL

1   Timothy Kosnoff, deposition, *In Re: Boy Scouts of America and Dela-
      ware BSA, LLC*, U.S. Bankruptcy Court for the District of Delaware,
      November 22, 2021, 13, https://casedocs.omniagentsolutions
      .com/cmsvol2/pub_47373/5b06e048-7939-43c1-ab19
      -42bfc59b2526_18.pdf.

2   Interview with Patrick Boyle.

3   Bruce Phelps was not in the perversion files at the time but was add-
      ed later as a result of the Stewart brothers' lawsuit.
4   *T.S. v. Boy Scouts of America*, Supreme Court of Washington, 157
      Wn. 2d 416 (Wash. 2006), July 27, 2006, https://casetext.com/case
      /ts-v-boy-scouts-of-am#e4273f65-9279-499c-9bef-4c2fd6232e5b
      -fn1; Jonathan Martin, "Brothers Force Scouts to Reveal Scope of
      Abuse," *Seattle Times*, August 23, 2007, updated August 23, 2010,
      https://www.seattletimes.com/seattle-news/brothers-force-scouts-to
      -reveal-scope-of-abuse/.
5   Mark Honeywell, letter to three BSA attorneys, February 20, 2008.
6   Interview with Mark Honeywell.
7   Kosnoff Law PLLC, verified statement, *In Re: Boy Scouts of America
      and Delaware BSA, LLC*, U.S. Bankruptcy Court for the District of
      Delaware, August 9, 2021.
8   Timothy Kosnoff, deposition, *In Re: Boy Scouts of America and Dela-
      ware BSA, LLC*, U.S. Bankruptcy Court for the District of Delaware,
      November 22, 2021, 116, https://casedocs.omniagentsolutions.com
      /cmsvol2/pub_47373/5b06e048-7939-43c1-ab19
      -42bfc59b2526_18.pdf.
9   Timothy Kosnoff, deposition, *In Re: Boy Scouts of America and Dela-
      ware BSA, LLC*, U.S. Bankruptcy Court for the District of Delaware,
      November 22, 2021, 22–24.
10   Kim Christensen, "Boy Scouts Propose More than $300 Million,
      Norman Rockwell Paintings to Settle Sex Abuse Claims," *Los Angeles
      Times*, March 2, 2021, https://www.latimes.com/california/story
      /2021-03-01/boy-scouts-reorganization-plan-sex-abuse-claims.
11   "The Boy Scouts of America Files for Chapter 11 Bankruptcy," Boy
      Scouts of America, February 18, 2020, https://www.bsarestructuring
      .org/press_release/boy-scouts-america-files-chapter-11-bankruptcy/.
12   Kosnoff Law PLLC, verified statement, *In Re: Boy Scouts of America
      and Delaware BSA, LLC*, U.S. Bankruptcy Court for the District of
      Delaware, August 9, 2021.
13   Kosnoff email, "Re: BSA-Claims data and insurance analysis," to
      Evan E. Smola, cc James Stang et al., June 28, 2020.
14   Objection of the Tort Claimants' Committee, *In Re: Boy Scouts of
      America and Delaware BSA, LLC*, U.S. Bankruptcy Court for the Dis-
      trict of Delaware, September 2, 2020, https://casedocs.omniagent
      solutions.com/cmsvol2/pub_47373/844583_1228.pdf.
15   Verified Statement of Kosnoff Law PLLC, verified statement, *In Re:*

Boy Scouts of America and Delaware BSA, LLC, U.S. Bankruptcy Court for the District of Delaware, August 9, 2021.

16   "Eisenberg Rothweiler Leads the Charge in Billion-Dollar Boy Scouts Sex Abuse Settlement," Eisenberg Rothweiler, September 22, 2021, https://www.erlegalteam.com/blog/boy-scouts-sex-abuse/.

17   Kim Christensen, "Boy Scouts Sex Abuse Victims Vote on $1.9-Billion Settlement Plan," *Los Angeles Times*, October 15, 2021, https://www.latimes.com/world-nation/story/2021-10-15/boy-scouts-sex-abuse-victims-vote-on-1-9-billion-settlement-plan.

18   Official Tort Claimants' Committee town hall meeting, October 7, 2021.

19   Christensen, "Boy Scouts Sex Abuse Victims Vote on $1.9-Billion Settlement Plan."

20   Interview with Timothy Kosnoff.

21   Timothy Kosnoff, letter to Abused in Scouting clients, October 18, 2021.

22   James Stang, letter to "To Whom It May Concern," November 11, 2021.

23   "Supplemental Disclosure Regarding Plan Modifications," *In Re: Boy Scouts of America and Delaware BSA, LLC*, U.S. Bankruptcy Court for the District of Delaware, February 18, 2022, https://casedocs.omni agentsolutions.com/cmsvol2/pub_47373/6e38726e-02c5-480b -9c4a-cc28884c573f_8894.pdf.

24   "Tort Claimants' Committee for Boy Scouts of America Bankruptcy Rejects Proposed Settlements," December 15, 2021, https://www .prnewswire.com/news-releases/tort-claimants-committee -for-boy-scouts-of-america-bankruptcy-rejects-proposed -settlements-301445790.html.

25   Kim Christensen, "Boy Scouts of America Falls Short in Bid to Emerge from Sex-Abuse Bankruptcy," *Los Angeles Times*, January 4, 2022, https://www.latimes.com/world-nation/story/2022-01-04 /boy-scouts-of-america-falls-short-in-bid-to-emerge-from-sex -abbankruptcy.

26   Kim Christensen, "Boy Scouts Reach Bankruptcy Deal with Attorneys for Sexual Abuse Survivors," *Los Angeles Times*, February 10, 2022, https://www.latimes.com/world-nation/story/2022-02-10 /boy-scouts-reach-bankruptcy-deal-with-attorneys-for-sexual-abuse -survivors.

27   Christensen, "Boy Scouts Reach Bankruptcy Deal with Attorneys for Sexual Abuse Survivors."

28   Lujan claimants' supplemental objection, *In Re: Boy Scouts of America and Delaware BSA, LLC*, U.S. Bankruptcy Court for the District of Delaware, August 16, 2021, https://casedocs.omniagentsolutions .com/cmsvol2/pub_47373/e8763bc0-98bb-4763-b239-4df79b9d7 ec_6039.pdf. https://www.supremecourt.gov/DocketPDF/23/23A 741/300734/20240215165222556_BSA%20Opp%20to%20Stay %20Application%20-%20final%20with%20appendix.pdf.

29   Maria Chutchian, "Boy Scouts Secure More Survivor Support Ahead of Final Battle over Sex Abuse Deal," Reuters, March 11, 2022, https://www.reuters.com/legal/transactional/boy-scouts -secure-more-survivor-support-ahead-final-battle-over-sex-abuse -deal-2022-03-11/.

CHAPTER 17: INTO THE MATRIX

1   Judge Laurie Selber Silverstein, opinion, *In Re: Boy Scouts of America and Delaware BSA, LLC*, U.S. Bankruptcy Court for the District of Delaware, July 29, 2022, https://casedocs.omniagentsolutions .com/cmsvol2/pub_47373/9ba8739e-283b-4ce4-b328-5a1eda289 f30_10136.pdf, 1.

2   Bishop John Schol, testimony, *In Re: Boy Scouts of America and Delaware BSA, LLC*, U.S. Bankruptcy Court for the District of Delaware, March 18, 2022, https://casedocs.omniagentsolutions.com/cmsvol2 /pub_47373/67d103d9-e390-413b-b0ed-1dbd7320403b_10808 .pdf, 388.

3   Tort Claimants' Committee town hall, January 14, 2021.

4   Interview with Doug Kennedy.

5   Interview with Doug Kennedy.

6   Interview with Doug Kennedy.

7   Doug Kennedy, testimony, *In Re: Boy Scouts of America and Delaware BSA, LLC*, U.S. Bankruptcy Court for the District of Delaware, bankruptcy confirmation hearing transcript, cited by Judge Laurie Selber Silverstein in her opinion issued July 29, 2022, https://case docs.omniagentsolutions.com/cmsvol2/pub_47373/9ba8739e -283b-4ce4-b328-5a1eda289f30_10136.pdf.

8   Judge Laurie Selber Silverstein, opinion, *In Re: Boy Scouts of America and Delaware BSA, LLC*, U.S. Bankruptcy Court for the District of Delaware, July 29, 2022, https://casedocs.omniagentsolutions .com/cmsvol2/pub_47373/9ba8739e-283b-4ce4-b328-5a1eda289 f30_10136.pdf.

9   Silverstein, opinion, July 29, 2022.

10   Silverstein, opinion, July 29, 2022.

11   Opening Brief of Certain Insurers, *In Re: Boy Scouts of America and Delaware BSA, LLC*, U.S. District Court for the District of Delaware, November 7, 2022.

12   Opening Brief of Certain Insurers, *In Re: Boy Scouts of America and Delaware BSA, LLC*, November 7, 2022.

13   Boy Scouts of America, "Trust Distribution Procedures for Abuse Claims," https://scoutingsettlementtrust.my.salesforce.com /sfc/p/#Dp0000016pkB/a/Dp000000sbbg/vS2dKul.uR5w5q UYwJCKVyoASd2H91pUQUVyVD_xNhs.

        AVA Law Group, *BSA $3,500 Settlement*, YouTube, December 17, 2021, https://www.youtube.com/watch?v=YxhyK-yZIoc.

14   "Who Is The Trustee of the Trust?," Scouting Settlement Trust, November 30, 2023, www.scoutingsettlementtrust.com/s/.

15   Boy Scouts of America, "Trust Distribution Procedures for Abuse Claims."

16   "About Me," Melissa B. Jacoby, https://www.mbjacoby.org/about-me.

17   Randall Chase, "Boy Scouts' $2.4 Billion Bankruptcy Plan Upheld by Judge," Associated Press, March 29, 2023, https://apnews.com /article/boy-scouts-bankruptcy-child-sexual-abuse-f6359f826b98 d471c290598573ebc5da.

18   BSA statement, April 19, 2023, https://www.bsarestructuring.org/.

19   Lyle Adriano, "Revealed—Likely Next Steps for Boy Scouts of America Insurers," Insurance Business, August 23, 2022, comments, https://www.insurancebusinessmag.com/us/news/breaking-news /revealed--likely-next-steps-for-boy-scouts-of-america-insurers -417794.aspx.

20   "Scouting Settlement Trust Begins Payments to Compensate Survivors of Sexual Abuse in Boy Scouts of America," Scouting Settlement Trust, September 19, 2023, https://www.prnewswire.com/news -releases/scouting-settlement-trust-begins-payments-to-compensate -survivors-of-sexual-abuse-in-boy-scouts-of-america-301932494 .html.

CHAPTER 18: AFTER THE BANKRUPTCY

1   Boy Scouts of America, "The Boy Scouts of America (BSA) Announces Confirmation of Plan of Reorganization and Emergence from Chapter 11 Bankruptcy to Equitably Compensate Survivors While Ensuring Scouting Continues Across the Country," April 19, 2023, https://www.bsarestructuring.org/.

2   "Amended Disclosure Statement," *In Re: Boy Scouts of America and Delaware BSA, LLC*, U.S. Bankruptcy Court for the District of Delaware, September 29, 2021, https://casedocs.omniagentsolutions .com/cmsvol2/pub_47373/2e1a8c44-7812-46a0-8a93-5aa5621 dc7b2_6431.pdf, 8.

3   Boy Scouts of America, "Report to the Nation 2023," stated that there were 580,194 boys and girls in Cub Scouts, 415,564 in Scouts BSA, and 15,400 in Venturing and Sea Scouting, for a total of 1,011,158; https://blog.scoutingmagazine.org/wp-content/uploads /sites/2/2023/04/2023-Report.pdf.

4   "Welcome to the 2023 National Jamboree!," Three Harbors Council, Boy Scouts of America, https://www.threeharborsscouting.org /program/2023-national-jamboree/75166.

5   Brian Whittman, testimony, *In Re: Boy Scouts of America and Delaware BSA, LLC*, U.S. Bankruptcy Court for the District of Delaware, March 18, 2022, https://casedocs.omniagentsolutions.com/cmsvol2 /pub_47373/67d103d9-e390-413b-b0ed-1dbd7320403b_10808 .pdf, 1746.

6   Amended Disclosure Statement, *In Re: Boy Scouts of America and Delaware BSA, LLC*, September 29, 2021, 42, 51.

7   Peg Brickley and Andrew Scurria, "The Strategy Behind the Boy Scouts Bankruptcy," *Wall Street Journal*, February 18, 2020, https://www.wsj.com/articles/the-strategy-behind-the-boy-scouts -bankruptcy-11582071435?mod=article_inline.

8   BSA annual tax returns (IRS form 990) for years 2018–2021, https://www.scouting.org/about/annual-report/.

9   Interview with Michael Bellavia.

10   Clay Risen, "Save Scouting. End the Boy Scouts," *New York Times*, February 18, 2020, https://www.nytimes.com/2020/02/18/opinion /sunday/boy-scouts-lawsuit.html.

11   Interview with Tim Miller.

12   "President and Chief Executive Officer," Boy Scouts of America, https://www.scoutingnewsroom.org/about-the-bsa/national -leadership/chief-scout-executive/.

13   Email, text, and telephone exchanges between Armstrong and the author from October 2022 through September 2023.

14   Public silence from the executive suite of the Boy Scouts of America is nothing new. Larry John O'Connor, a former BSA district executive from Kansas now living in Alaska, said that one of the first things he and other professional Scouters had been taught at a

training seminar in New Jersey in 1967 was "No PR is better than bad PR, so just keep quiet." More recent former BSA employees, including Michael Johnson, the director of the Youth Protection program from 2010 to 2020, said that that unofficial policy has persisted.

15   Patrick Boyle, *Scout's Honor: Sexual Abuse in America's Most Trusted Institution* (Rocklin, CA: Prima Publishing, 1994). In an interview in 2023, Boyle recalled Anglim's assertion that he'd never read the perversion files as "a pretty stunning comment" by a then-high-ranking BSA official. Boyle said it was impossible to know what had been in Anglim's mind, but his impression at the time was that his answer had reflected a "designed benign neglect" on the BSA leader's part. "Having never read a file doesn't mean you don't know what was in the file," Boyle said.

16   Elise Viebeck, "Boy Scouts Lobby in States to Stem the Flow of Child Abuse Lawsuits," *Washington Post*, May 9, 2018, https://www .washingtonpost.com/powerpost/boy-scouts-lobby-in-states-to -stem-the-flow-of-child-abuse-lawsuits/2018/05/08/0eee0a44-47d8 -11e8-827e-190efaf1f1ee_story.html.

17   Representative Jackie Speier et al., letter to BSA Scout Executive Michael Surbaugh et al., November 20, 2018.

18   Michael Surbaugh, letter to The Honorable Jackie Speier, May 28, 2019, https://www.scribd.com/document/412383206/Letter -Representative-Jackie-Speier-5-28-19.

19   Anna Liz Nichols, "First Person Sentenced in Michigan's Boy Scouts of America Investigation," *Detroit News*, December 14, 2022, https:// www.detroitnews.com/story/news/local/macomb-county /2022/12/14/first-person-convicted-in-boy-scouts-sex-abuse -sentenced/69728791007/.

20   Michigan Department of Attorney General, "AG Nessel Reissues PSA to Remind Michigan Residents That Her Department Is Still Accepting Boy Scouts of America Abuse Complaints," September 21, 2023, https://www.michigan.gov/ag/news/press-releases/2023/09/21 /ag-nessel-reissues-psa-to-remind-michigan-residents.

21   Michael Johnson, letter to The Honorable Members of Congress, October 6, 2021, https://www.andersonadvocates.com/wp-content /uploads/2021/10/Michael-Johnson-Letter-to-Congress.pdf.

22   Michael Johnson, letter to The Honorable Members of Congress, October 6, 2021.

23   Interview with Michael Johnson.

24 Interview with Doug Kennedy.

25 Interview with Doug Kennedy.

POSTSCRIPT: TEN YEARS ON

1 Interview with Kerry Lewis.

2 Interview with Timur Dykes.

3 "Maple Bluff Boy Scout Cabin," Wisconsin Historical Society, https://www.wisconsinhistory.org/Records/NationalRegister/NR2534.

4 Interview with Richard "Skip" Leifer.

5 Boy Scouts of America, "Boy Scouts of America Selects Roger Krone as New President and Chief Executive Officer," November 3, 2023, https://www.prnewswire.com/news-releases/boy-scouts-of-america -selects-roger-krone-as-new-president-and-chief-executive-officer -301977231.html.

6 Mark Thiessen, "Retired Businessman Will Lead Boy Scouts of America as It Emerges from Scandal-Driven Bankruptcy," Associated Press, November 3, 2023, https://apnews.com/article/boys-scouts -new-president-bankruptcy-516869e181513c073ac7edc139ad48d3.

7 Alexander Fabino, "'Scouting Is Safer Today': BSA Head Steers Scouting's Rebirth," Newsweek, November 12, 2023, https://www .newsweek.com/bsa-rejuvenation-roger-krone-vision-safety -technology-inclusivity-scandal-1842891.

8 Thiessen, "Retired Businessman Will Lead Boy Scouts of America as It Emerges from Scandal-Driven Bankruptcy."

9 Bishop Larry Silva, letter to Pastors and Principals, January 31, 2023, https://www.catholichawaii.org/media/651233/boy-scouts-of -america-ltr-to-pastors-and-principals-january-31-2023-1.pdf.

10 Lisa Wolfe, "Dancing Up a Storm in the Clubs," New York Times, April 5, 1985, https://timesmachine.nytimes.com/timesmachine /1985/04/05/145024.html?pageNumber=43.

11 Interview with Carl Maxwell, Jr.

12 Interview with David Korman.

INDEX

ABOUT THE AUTHOR

Kim Christensen spent more than forty years writing for news-papers, starting with the *Dayton Daily News* in his hometown in Ohio and capping his career as an investigative reporter at the *Los Angeles Times*. He shared two Pulitzer Prizes, at the *Orange County Register* in 1996 for fertility fraud at the University of California, Irvine, and in 2001 at *The Oregonian* for investigations of the US Immigration and Naturalization Service. He lived in Long Beach, California, with his wife, Christina, a former newspaper and mag-azine editor.